Fundamentals of

Intellectual Property Valuation

A Primer for Identifying and Determining Value

AMERICAN BAR ASSOCIATION
Defending Liberty
Pursuing Justice

THE ABA SECTION OF
Intellectual
Property Law

INTELLECTUAL PROPERTY VALUATION

A PRIMER FOR IDENTIFYING AND DETERMINING VALUE

Weston Anson
Author and Editor

Donna Suchy
Co-editor and Contributor

Contributors:

Chaitali Ahya

A. Scott Davidson

David C. Drews

Carmen R. Eggleston

R. Mark Halligan, Esq.

Richard F. Weyand

THE ABA SECTION OF
Intellectual
Property Law

AMERICAN BAR ASSOCIATION
Defending Liberty
Pursuing Justice

To Susan, my partner and wife.

The American Bar Association, Chicago 60610
© 2005 by the American Bar Association
All rights reserved

10 09 08 07 06 05   2 3 4 5

ISBN: 1-59031-430-1

Cataloging-in-Publication Data is on file at the Library of Congress

This book neither provides, nor is intended to provide, legal advice, which should be obtained only from a lawyer who is competent in the practice of intellectual property law and the patent system. Information on how to locate such a lawyer can be obtained from your state or local bar association.

Additional copies of this book are available from:
American Bar Association
Section of Intellectual Property Law
321 N. Clark Street, 19th Floor
Chicago, IL 60610

Or by calling the ABA Service Center at 1.800.285.2221

CONTENTS

PART I

Introduction to Intellectual Property Valuation

Primer

An elementary textbook used in teaching children or others to read. A small introductory book on any subject, e.g., something introducing initial instruction in a particular subject, practice, etc. Also: A person or thing who primes something and/or first in order of time or occurrence.

In writing this book, I have attempted to strike a balance between complexity and simplicity, trying to avoid being too technical and obscure as well as pedantic. This is a tricky balance, and I hope the reader finds I have been able to maintain it.

I owe much to the American Bar Association in the writing of this primer, specifically to its Intellectual Property law section, and to Donna Suchy and her Intellectual Property Valuation Committee. Inspiration and guidance over the years has come from Gordon Smith, Russel Parr, and Greg Battersby, to whom I owe deep appreciation. Early and continuing mentoring has come from Gary Caplan, as well as continuing advice from Daryl Martin and the staff at CONSOR. I thank all of you.

INTRODUCTION

Our business and legal world has changed substantially in the last two generations, from a society and an industrial focus based on hard assets, hard work, and machinery and equipment to one that owes its strength, growth, and future to a much less visible group of attributes—our country's collective intellectual property. Compounding this change in our industrial and business base is an increasingly complex environment in which we all must live and operate. The Sarbanes–Oxley Act, Section 482 of the IRS Code, FASB 141/142/147—these are just a few of the regulations that increasingly affect corporate life and find their genesis either in, or in connection with, intellectual property. Thus, we start at the base of today's new wealth and our country's current prosperity: intellectual property.

But what is intellectual property? In many ways, a piece of intellectual property is an intangible asset, which is classified as part of a company's goodwill. However, an intangible asset is not necessarily a piece of intellectual property, and the general category of goodwill is certainly not intellectual property; although in most cases intellectual property and intangible assets can be part of the pool of goodwill. With this confusion swirling around, the questions we must answer here are: So what is a piece of intellectual property? What is an intangible asset? When are they the same and when are they different? And, most importantly, what are the different groups of intellectual property and how do we describe and value them?

Another key set of questions revolves around value: Do pieces of intellectual property have value? Do they all have value? If not, why not? Is it true that sometimes a given piece of Intellectual Property can have great value and at other times no value at all, and if so, how can this be? Of greater importance to everyday and practical business decisions is whether a piece of Intellectual Property or an intangible asset always has the same value at the same point in time; if not, why not? We must deal with the questions of what influences value of Intellectual Property and whether those influences are different from those found for tangible assets, such as buildings, equipment, automobiles, inventory, etc. The short answer is that the influences on Intellectual Property are, by their very nature, less tangible and include the two most important influences: context and time. Other influences include environment, the specific strategy driving the valuation, and ownership of the Intellectual Property. Even when all of these criteria or influences remain the same, the value of the Intellectual Property may or may not be the same at all times, so that valuation is a confusing subject at best.

In this book, we attempt to cover some frequently asked questions on Intellectual Property and intangible assets and to engage in brief discussions on the subject of identifying value. We identify many of the main types of Intellectual Property and intangible assets. We also look at the primary, traditional, and not-so-traditional methods of valuing these assets and include case studies and various situations in which the valuation of these assets is required.

Why a Primer?

As the definition at the beginning of Part I implies, a primer is a first step or an initial treatise on a subject or topic. But why do we need a primer on intellectual property valuation when we have so many existing books? The answer is that there are many good in-depth books, most notably those by Gordon Smith and Russell Parr, as well as others by Robert Schweihs and Robert Reilly, Patrick Sullivan, and others. However, all these books tend to be written at a level of detail and with a degree of sophistication greater than the average businessperson or attorney requires. Although the books often deal in great and accurate detail with many aspects of Intellectual Property valuation, no single text seems to provide that simple overview sought by practicing and nonpracticing members of professional groups like the American Bar Association and the International Licensing Executives Society.

Intellectual Property valuation is a very complex subject, and to think that any given book can offer all the answers in simple terms is presumptuous. Nonetheless, that is exactly what we will attempt to do in this book. This book offers simple, straightforward, focused discussions of a complex topic, without too much detailed specialization in any one area or in any one class of intellectual property, and is written in plain English.

Why an Intellectual Property primer? As intellectual property and intangible assets become more and more important to all businesses and in virtually all areas of legal practice, a greater and more general level of knowledge should be held by businesspeople, legal practitioners, and their advisors. More and more questions are arising on intellectual property, and more and more uncertainty is arising as to classification and valuation. Yet, in our increasingly complex world, there are fewer and fewer simple explanations and solutions. In this particular case, sometimes too much detail really is too much.

What Is a Primer?

In the broadest possible terms, a primer is a "first book." It is a foundation on which to build and should be viewed as a cornerstone for the building of knowledge, not a capstone or a keystone. Another definition of primer, as found in the Oxford unabridged dictionary is "a small introductory book on a subject." We will attempt to live up to that definition. This intellectual property valuation primer is designed to be a basic document for use as a desk reference. It is hoped that this primer will provide the basic background, simple descriptions, and answers to the core questions and the core concerns that affect virtually everyone in modern industry or legal practice today. A primer is designed to offer its information in the simplest possible terms, with short, brief, but to-the-point explanations, providing a quick reference on a single topic in an easy-to-use format.

We hope this primer performs that function. It is most of all intended to be instructional, informative, and functional. With this primer, we provide a broad-brush approach to the topics of intellectual property, its valuation, and the contexts in which those valuations are done—readers will need more detailed information as they go on to explore these topics, and we encourage them to use the bibliography at the end of this primer and the other resources that we provide. Above all, this primer should serve as a resource document.

How to Use this Primer

First, use this book as a resource, second as a reference source, third as a guide to other sources, and fourth as a referral vehicle to other publications. The primer focuses on the basics: the how, what, and when.

- First, we deal with how to value intellectual property. In this section, we look at the traditional methodologies of valuation, including cost, market, and income, as well as permutations such as replacement value, substitution value, relief from royalty, etc. We also look at nontraditional and proprietary methodologies, ranging from technology factor analysis to the VALMATRIX® approach used by CONSOR.
- Second, the primer deals with what we are valuing. We specifically look at groups of Intellectual Property, including corporate identity, trademarks and brands, trade secrets and technology, patents, Internet assets, copyrights, software, Information Technology, and other intangible assets. However, we have not attempted, in the space allotted, to deal with every permutation and type of intellectual property and every class of intangible assets.
- Third, we deal with the critical part of the valuation equation: When do we value and under what circumstances? We look at valuation in a licensing scenario, in a sale or merger, in a bankruptcy or reorganization, and under various tax requirements, SEC requirements, and litigation. Each of these contexts is examined briefly for its effect on value.
- Fourth, we combine this how, what, and when of Intellectual Property valuation into a series of short case studies. These case studies are scattered throughout the primer and work to illustrate both the various types of intellectual property and various methodologies to value them.
- Fifth, and finally, the primer provides checklists, due diligence suggestions, and how-to guidelines, to help the reader proceed from the information contained in this primer to an active Intellectual Property valuation project.

Part II of the primer introduces the concept of bundling similar assets together. This section also contains a brief discussion of some basic financial conditions, constraints, and terms that one needs to be aware of in the valuation process: terms like discount rate, net present value, remaining useful life, WACC, and orderly disposal.

Part III reviews basic and traditional valuation methods. This section of the book also deals with what value is and how value is defined. Do we define value as fair market value? In-place value? Tax value? Liquidation value? Part III covers the current accepted valuation methodologies described, as well as new and proprietary methodologies.

Part IV examines the value and valuation of different and discrete types of intellectual property, from trademarks to patents, from domain names to databases. In the valuation process in Part IV, we make the basic assumption that in all cases (in that part of the primer), valuation of the assets takes place under the same basic conditions of an arm's length transaction, seeking a fair market value, with neither party compelled to buy or negotiate, and in a nonlitigation, nontax environment. As we move to the final two parts of the primer, we begin to deal with more subjective concepts.

In Part V the very important concept of context of value is discussed and illustrated. This is perhaps the single most important concept to take away from this primer. Why? Because unlike any other asset class, intellectual property and intangible assets can change in value very quickly and very substantially, depending on the context in which they are being valued. For example, a well maintained factory building has essentially the same value whether it is being sold because of a bankruptcy, being sold in an acquisition by another company, or being disposed of for litigation or for tax reasons—in all these cases, the building essentially holds its value within a range of plus or minus 8 to 10%. This is not so with intellectual property. Therefore, the context is critical in our valuation world, and so are the time and place of valuation.

The only absolute in intellectual property valuation is relativity! This primer addresses valuing Intellectual Property assets in different contexts, as mentioned previously, ranging from tax and transfer pricing to litigation and SEC reporting. For each of these, we offer a valuation case study. Because by necessity these case studies must be brief and in summary form, no single case study can hope to cover all circumstances that could be found in a specific context, such as litigation. Therefore, the reader must reach out beyond this book for his or her own research and expert advice in any particular case.

Part V also briefly deals with the single most important influence on the increase and maximization of Intellectual Property value—the licensing, leveraging, and commercialization of intellectual property. We include a short section on licensing and licensing valuation because of the continually increasing role and importance of licensing in virtually every corporation's management of its intellectual property portfolio. Two decades ago, fewer than a dozen major American corporations concentrated on licensing any of their intellectual property. Today, we estimate that more than half of the Fortune 500 have active and proactive, aggressive and strategic plans to license, leverage, or commercialize their intellectual property. As a consequence, these activities are the greatest drivers of increased value of intellectual property today.

Part VI offers conclusions and an overview process of due diligence. These chapters provide the reader with some guidelines about where intellectual property valuation is heading and also some sense of the general trends that affect intellectual property in general. Importantly, we also address the due diligence process, from the concept of engaging in the valuation of one of these important assets through the actual process itself. In the Appendices, we also include research resources and professional organizations that can be used as additional references and knowledge generators.

PART II

Definitions and Glossary

Intellectual Property

Pertaining to the intellect or understanding and/or that which appeals to, engages or requires exercise of the intellect. Nonmaterial, spiritual, and characterized as possessing a high degree of intelligence or pertaining to a characteristic or intellectual activity. See also specific definition...intellectual property is the product of creativity and does not exist in tangible form, such as patents, copyrights, etc.

CHAPTER 1

NOMENCLATURE AND DEFINITIONS: MAKING SENSE OF CONFLICTING TERMS AND DESCRIPTIONS

In the Introduction we discussed goodwill, intangible assets, and intellectual property. We pointed out that although similarities and an interlinkage exist among them, they all deserve separate treatment. One often hears the terms *goodwill, intellectual property,* and *intangible assets;* many times we are asked what are the differences among these three terms.

Other terms, such as *business enterprise value* or *going concern value,* are also used on a regular basis. We will define these terms in Chapter 5 and also provide definitions and descriptions of some other commonly used phrases and terms of intellectual property valuation. It is important to note that the terminology, descriptions, definitions, and explanations are intended for the layperson—these definitions of key terms are not intended as legal definitions under the Tax Code or the Bankruptcy Code, nor are they legal definitions under the GAAP (Generally Accepted Accounting Principles). Rather, we are attempting to lay out for the reader simple explanations of phrases, terms, and terminology that too often are used in business and legal environments today without all parties clearly understanding what they mean.

The best way to start is to describe briefly three overlapping concepts: goodwill, intangible assets, and intellectual property.

Goodwill

The concept of goodwill has been around probably as long as accounting systems have been in place. Certainly the Phoenicians, who had an early but effective method of accounting and keeping track of goods and stores in various ports, must have had some system to describe the extra value that their outpost in the city of Cadiz had. Today, this excess value, which the Phoenicians attempted to measure and treasure, would be called *goodwill.*

Many definitions of goodwill have evolved over the last two centuries; however, there have been few attempts to define goodwill once and for all. Since different groups use the word for different meanings or concepts, there is no universal agreement on a definition. Let us examine some of the definitions and descriptions of goodwill:

- Goodwill can be described as the value of an entity's image or reputation. This image or reputation can also be called the *corporate identity umbrella brand, flagship brand,* or *marketplace advantage.*
- In its simplest terms, as defined by the British in the last century, goodwill equates to the certainty or probability that a company's customers or pa-

trons will continue to do business with it, valuing its products, services, etc., above a purely monetary value.

- Another simple definition of goodwill, used on many occasions, is to equate it with the value of the corporate identity or corporate brand. Although a company's identity or brand is a valuable asset, it is certainly not the only definition of goodwill; it is simply a marketplace definition that expresses one facet of goodwill. So, goodwill is often equated with reputation or a company image.
- On the legal side, however, it is important to make the distinction that goodwill specifically attaches to a piece of intellectual property (e.g., trademark). The Courts in our land have ruled that a trademark cannot continue to maintain its value or uniqueness apart from its goodwill and that the goodwill of a particular trademark or a particular brand is inextricably linked to the trademark that describes that brand. The Courts have ruled that if you separate the goodwill of the brand from the trademark itself, the trademark no longer has value. The argument is rather spurious, however, because in the real world it is virtually impossible to separate a brand's goodwill from its underlying trademark. A purchaser would neither acquire one in the absence of the other nor be interested in acquiring a brand without a trademark or a trademark without other brand assets. We will discuss the bundle of brand assets in Chapter 2.
- Even the accounting profession has had a difficult time agreeing on a clear definition of goodwill. In various documents, the American Institute of Certified Public Accountants (AICPA) has described goodwill as all those intangibles and supporting assets that contribute to the advantage that an established business has over a comparable business that is about to be started—in other words, image, customer base, reputation, perceptions, etc.

The important thing to take away from this brief discussion of goodwill is that goodwill itself is not specifically identified as a separate, intangible asset or a piece of intellectual property, except as called for by FASB regulations. In simplest terms, goodwill in a company's balance sheet is that amount of value or assets in excess of the other assets that can be measured—both tangible assets and intangible assets. We use the brief example below to illustrate:

Company A:

Total value	$100M
Less tangible assets (plant and equipment)	$ 50M
Less trademark values	$ 25M
Less patent, copyright and software values	$ 10M
Balance left to goodwill	$ 15M

In sum, there is no absolute or universally accepted definition of goodwill. The closest, perhaps, is that value described in the preceding example. In other words, if one has valued each of the company's identifiable pieces of intellectual property and intangible assets (such as trademarks, patents, copyrights, registered software, etc.) and has also valued the company's tangible assets (such as plant and equipment), the amount that is left from a company's total value can be thought of as its goodwill. An accountant may disagree with that definition, however, because from a purely accounting perspective, goodwill can be viewed as the value of all of the intangible assets in excess of a company's tangible asset value.

Intangible Assets

Now that we have covered goodwill, it is time to look at the next broadly used term—*intangible assets*. The family of intangible assets is somewhat less elusive than goodwill: more easily described and classified and more easily valued

Table 1.1 A Partial Listing of Independent Intangible Assets

Administrative manual volumes I and II	Customer lists
Advertising campaigns and programs	Customer contracts
Agreements	Department policy manual
Airport gates and landing slots	Development rights
Appraisal plans (files and records)	Designs patterns
Blueprints and drawings	Diagnostic testing guidelines
Book and other publication libraries	Distribution networks
Bank customers—deposit, loan, trust, credit card, etc.	Distribution rights
	Drilling rights
Brand names and logos	Easements
Broadcast licenses (radio, television, etc.)	Education manual
Buy–sell agreements	Engineering drawings and related documentation
Bylaws	
Case cart/physician profiles	Environmental rights (and exemptions)
Certificates of need for healthcare institutions	Equipment manual
	Favorable financing
Chemical formulations	Favorable leases
Claims (against insurers, etc.)	FCC licenses related to radio bands (cellular telephone, paging, etc.)
Community management handbooks	
Computer software (both internally developed and externally purchased)	Film libraries
	Food flavorings and recipes
Computerized databases	Franchise agreements (commercial)
Contracts	Franchise ordinances (governmental)
Cooperative agreements	Going-concern value (and immediate use value)
Copyrights	
Credit information files	Goodwill—institutional
Critical care policies/manual	Goodwill—personal

Continued

Table 1.1 An Independent Listing of Intangible Assets—cont'd

Goodwill—professional	Patents—both product and process
Government contracts	Patient management and accounting systems
Government programs	Patient education manual
Governmental registrations (and exemptions)	Permits
Hazardous waste manual	Personality contracts
Historical documents	Personnel policy and managerial manuals
HMO enrollment lists	Possessory interest
Hospital formulary	Prescription drug files
Infection control manual	Prizes and awards (related to professional recognition)
Insurance expirations	Procedural manuals and related documentation
Insurance in force	Product designs
Job descriptions manual	Production backlogs
Joint ventures	Property use rights
Know-how and associated procedural documentation	Proposals outstanding, related to contracts, customers, etc.
Laboratory notebooks	Proprietary processes—and related technical documentation
Landing rights (for airlines)	Proprietary products—and related technical documentation
Leasehold estates	Proprietary technology—and related technical documentation
Leasehold interests	Quality assurance manual
Licenses—professional business	Royalty agreements
Literary works	Safety manual
Litigation awards and damage claims	Seldom-used forms notebook
Loan portfolios	Shareholder agreements
Location value	Solicitation rights
Management contracts	Subscription lists (for magazines, services, etc.)
Manual (vs. automated) databases	Supplier contracts
Manuscripts	Supply catalog
Marketing and promotional materials	Technical documentation
Masks and masters (for integrated circuits)	Technical and specialty libraries (books, records, drawings, etc.)
Medical staff records	Technology sharing agreements
Medical (and other professional) charts and records	Title plans
Mineral rights	Trademark and trade names
Musical compositions	Trade secrets
Noncompete covenants	Trained and assembled workforce
Nondiversion agreements	Use rights—air, water, land
Nursing policies and procedures	
Open to ship customer orders	
Operating room course/critical care course	
Options warrants	
Ore deposits	
Patent applications	

and defended. When engaging in the practice of valuing these intangible assets, an interesting footnote to remember is that once all of the intangible assets have been valued, any excess value that is left (value above the total of intangible assets) could be described as goodwill. With that in mind, intangible assets can be defined in the terms that follow and should share most of the following characteristics:

- The asset should be identifiable both within the specific company or context and in a general sense.
- The intangible asset can be legally owned.
- The birth and development of the intangible asset should be able to be traced.
- The intangible asset can be protected legally (this would include, of course, all intellectual property).
- Although the asset is intangible, there should be some proof of its existence in the form of a contract, registration, database, etc.
- The intangible asset should have a specific life span or a lifespan that can be determined, and/or a specific lifespan that can be renewed (e.g., the renewal of trademarks every 10 years is a good example).
- The intangible asset should have similar or referable assets to be found elsewhere in the marketplace.
- Finally, the value of the intangible asset can be quantified.

What is included in this group of intangible assets? The listing is extensive, and by no means has every intangible asset been identified in this primer. However, if one starts with the basic ideas that an intangible asset must have value and that value must be quantifiable, then the list of intangible assets can be substantially narrowed. In Table 1.1, we have identified multiple intangible assets. The list is not intended to be exhaustive, but it certainly is a useful starting point. In Chapter 2, we will discuss how these assets may be grouped together. For now, however, let us review an independent listing of all of these assets.

The preceding list is not meant to be exhaustive—nor can it be, because meaningful intangible assets are continuously being created. For example, little more than a decade ago, website design might not have been classified as an intangible asset with value. Today, it is clearly an important element of many companies' marketing, production, and financial operations. Similarly, so-called retail relationship assets might not have been classified as a specific intangible. Today, however, exclusive contracts between manufacturers and suppliers with particular retailers have become increasingly important. For example, an exclusive contract from Footstar Corporation to supply Thom McAn shoes to K-Mart is a classic example of a very valuable intangible asset—but not one that would not have existed a decade or two ago. On a more mundane level, an exclusive contract for a manufacturer-importer of basic unbranded garden tools, to be supplied to Target Stores, is a very valuable intangible asset. If that contract has definable life and some sort of exclusivity, it can be valued with relative accuracy.

Other specific examples of intangible assets serve to illustrate the unique nature of this group of assets. The following examples illustrate that, in all business and legal environments, one must look below the surface to identify intangible assets that are specific to the company or situation:

- A company like Halliburton, which holds a contract to cook and distribute meals and feed the soldiers in Iraq, has a unique intangible asset in the form of that contract.
- In a similar vein, Schlumberger Corporation has exclusive rights to drill and explore for oil and gas in several global oil field operations. These exclusive contracts with various governments are clearly unique intangible assets.
- The Sands Hotel in Las Vegas has an ongoing contract with Neil Diamond to perform there on a periodic, regular, and predictable basis. That particular contract is an intangible asset that clearly has substantial value.
- Pfizer Pharmaceuticals has a great amount of proprietary test data on its popular pain-killing drug Vioxx. This data and research represent an identifiable and valuable intangible asset.

Intellectual Property

In many ways, intellectual property is a subset of the family of intangible assets, and a company's family of intangible assets is a subset of its overall goodwill. The key difference between an intangible asset and a piece of intellectual property, from both a business point of view and a legal point of view, is that an intellectual property is, in fact, an intangible asset—but one with an important difference: It has been granted legal protection and recognition. Intellectual property falls into a very small group of definable assets:

- Trademarks, trade names, and service marks
- Patents
- Trade secrets and proprietary technology
- Copyrights
- Domain names and Internet assets
- Software

However, it is very important to understand that pieces of intellectual property are often supported by other intangible assets. In Chapter 2, we will discuss the concept of *bundling*. In simplest terms, bundling means that two or more pieces of intellectual property and/or intangible assets travel together.

Because this primer does not address legal issues, we will not cover in detail how specific pieces of intellectual property come into existence (e.g., trademarks or patent registrations). Instead, we will continue to focus on the value and valuation of these assets. As we conclude this chapter on definitions, a critical point must be understood by the reader, which will carry all the way through this primer.

Although this is an intellectual property valuation primer, we will focus on the value and valuation of all intangible assets—particularly those that work with, support, and travel in tandem with (or in a group with) a piece of intellectual property. For example, intangible assets, such as customer lists, logo designs, corporate colors, etc., travel with and are part of the intellectual property known as a trademark and/or brand. Therefore, the balance of this primer will use the terms *intangible assets* and *intellectual property* interchangeably, and the term *intangible asset* should be understood within the primer to encompass traditional intellectual property.

CHAPTER 2

BUNDLING AND GROUPING OF INTANGIBLE ASSETS

Traditionally, pieces of intellectual property and individual intangible assets were managed, viewed, and valued individually. After two decades, however, it became apparent to us that intangible assets were increasingly intertwined with pieces of intellectual property, both between and among themselves (e.g., patents and know-how or trademarks and domain names). In other words, a trademark does not travel in a vacuum; it has accompanying elements and assets. Nor does a patent travel alone. It is accompanied by intangible assets, such as drawings, designs, trade secrets, proprietary technology, etc. In fact, we conducted a study in the late 1990s that showed that virtually no meaningful intangible asset or intellectual property traveled alone.

Even though these assets travel together, it does not mean that they cannot be valued separately. Rather, our point is that to establish true market value, whether for business, legal, tax, accounting or financial reasons, similar intangible assets that work and support each other should be valued together. This concept—the so-called bundling of assets—is one that we pioneered and have refined over the years. At the beginning of this primer, we made it clear that this book is intended neither as a detailed explanation of all forms of intangible assets nor as a numerical or financial analysis book, except in summary form. Instead, this primer introduces and explains core concepts. It is a reflection of the concerns and realities of today's marketplace. It is not an analysis of changing market conditions, nor is it a book that attempts to deal with discrete and obscure financial and legal issues.

This is a primer of simple concepts and simple explanations. One of the simplest but most important concepts is the bundling of assets for valuation purposes. The same bundling approaches, techniques, and philosophy can be applied when dealing with intangible assets in a legal, financial, or accounting environment. Whether one is working to value assets in a bankruptcy, for a merger, or in a licensing environment, careful emphasis should be placed on identifying and grouping similar assets.

In Chapter 1, we presented a table of intangible assets as a general overview. Here, we will concentrate on specific bundles. Because every company is different and every situation unique, the bundles of assets will vary from company to company and from situation to situation. In order to illustrate the bundling process, we have chosen to focus on three of the most important bundles: the marketing bundle, the IT bundle (or information technology bundle), and the technical bundle.

Marketing Bundle

As can be seen in the list that follows, the *marketing bundle* includes and revolves around trademark and brand assets. As an example, McDonald's Corporation has an extensive bundle of marketing-oriented intangible assets that is led or anchored by the primary McDonald's trademark registration in the United States. In addition to that, however, the McDonald's logo device, its corporate colors, its graphics and marketing layouts, its internal design and store appearance, as well as other brand-related assets, are part of this marketing bundle.

Often, this marketing bundle is referred to as the *brand bundle of rights.* As the phrase implies, in many companies the marketing bundle of intangible assets revolves around one or a few core brands. Within PepsiCo, for example, the core brand bundle would be the Pepsi-Cola brand, and that bundle would include graphics, designs, logo devices, etc. A secondary brand bundle of assets within PepsiCo would include the trademark Mountain Dew, along with all of its marketing assets, such as graphics, logo devices, colors, etc. The classic and unambiguous example of a core brand bundle of assets is Coca-Cola. Its corporate identity and umbrella brand are a group of assets that, without question, has the greatest single component of value for that company. We examine the Coca-Cola brand and the valuation of its marketing bundle in Chapter 6.

Marketing Bundle of Intangible Assets
Primary trademark
Corporate name and logo
Marketing umbrella
Subbrand names
Core brand
Worldwide trademark registration
Copyrights
Secondary trademarks
Packaging design and copyrights
Trade dress
Characters

IT or Information Technology Bundle

Today, every company depends to some extent on a family or bundle of information technology, operating systems, and software installations to manage its business. In many companies, at least part of that asset bundle is proprietary specifically to that company, whereas in smaller enterprises the company or entity will depend on a bundle of IT assets from a larger supplier, such as Microsoft, Oracle, or EDS. (See Chapters 12 and 13.) Even in small enterprises, however, these IT or information assets are often overlooked in the Intellectual Property valuation process. Even the smallest of companies can have very valuable databases or customer lists, and many have important Internet assets, such as domain names and websites. Review the following examples:

- Even troubled companies like Spiegel and Eddie Bauer can find substantial market value in their databases and customer lists. Eddie Bauer also has meaningful value tied up in its website and other Internet assets.
- Companies like Budget Rent A Car or American Airlines will have IT or information assets that revolve around their proprietary reservation and processing systems, as exemplified by the global reservation networks, such as Sabre, owned by major airlines.
- A payment facilitator or credit card company, such as Visa, has enormous value locked up in its ability to manage and manipulate the information on its issuing banks, tens of thousands of merchants, and millions of credit card holders.

Following is a short list of these intangible assets. It is not intended to be exhaustive.

IT Bundle of Intangible Assets
Enterprise solutions
Custom applications
Data warehouses
Master licenses
Source code
Databases
Data mining
Domain names/URLs
e-Commerce sites
Third-party software tools
Credit/payment systems

Technical Bundle

As with the previous two bundles, the technical bundle typically has an interplay between intellectual property and intangible assets. For example, a patent that is a legally protected property right can be combined with trade secrets, proprietary processes, blending and/or product formulation systems, etc. Taken individually, many of these assets would have at least some value. Taken together as a bundle, the sum is often greater than the individual parts. The technical bundle typically has greater value than the individual parts. However, in some companies where a key patent drives all technology, that patent may have a greater value as an individual asset being sold or licensed to other companies, than does the overall bundle of technical assets. Examples of technical bundles of assets surround us, ranging from large chemical manufacturers, such as Dow or DuPont, to much smaller biotechnology start-up companies, where a single gene-splicing patent and supporting technology may be the sole asset of real value within the company.

Technical Bundle of Intangible Assets
Key patents
Trade secrets
Formulas
Packaging technology and sources
Shapes and sizes
Process technology
Design technology
Proprietary test results
Plant and production design
Product specifications
Operating platforms

Other Bundles of Value

Each company is different, so the intangible elements of value in each reorganization will be different. Some companies have substantial value in their trademark assets, others in their information technologies. Others may have real estate–related intellectual assets or broad groupings of patents and proprietary software. Some groups or bundles will have primary value in most situations; others will be less important. In this section, we identify 15 different intellectual asset bundles and briefly discuss the most important ones.

Over the last two decades, we have learned through hands-on experience that six to eight groups of Intellectual Property assets typically fall into the primary area of value for a company. Often, these groups have an interrelationship. In fact, the first three groups that we discuss in this section are closely interrelated. This is particularly true in a consumer-driven business. We identify a handful of specific assets within some of the groups that follow. This listing is not intended to be exhaustive. Instead, it is offered as an overview checklist or guide to Intellectual Property value.

Having looked at three of the major asset bundles, we will now take a moment to examine a broader range of asset bundles. We have included 15 bundles in our review. They vary from real estate–related to personnel-related asset bundles. Although no one company or situation will contain all of these bundles of assets, many will appear together in any given company. In addition, other bundles of assets will appear that are not listed in this section.

1. Trademarks

- Primary classes of registration
- Secondary classes of registration
- Logo device
- Primary country

- Secondary countries
- Pending applications
  - Foreign
  - Domestic

2. Other Brand-Related Assets

- Logo design
- Character devices
- Jingles, music
- Advertising concepts
- Copyrights
- Subbrands
- Trade dress

3. Internet-Related Assets

- Domain names
- Website design
- 1-800 numbers
- Linkages
- Retail systems
- Embedded customer base

These first three groups, mixed and melded together, form what we sometimes refer to as the *bundle of umbrella brand assets*. Perhaps the easiest way to think about this is to think of the Coca-Cola example. The core trademark assets include the Coca-Cola name itself, the Coca-Cola logo, and the word *Coke*. Related to, but separate from that primary group are the other brand assets controlled by the company, including secondary brands such as Diet Coke, marketing techniques, logo devices, corporate colors, etc. The third group of assets within that brand bundle are the so-called new economy brand assets, which include website design, Internet-based consumer promotions, domain names, etc.

As we move to identify the balance of the bundles of intellectual assets, it is well to remember that two or three bundles—such as patent-related and other technology assets—will often be grouped together for later sale or monetization.

4. Patent-Related Bundle of Value

- Bench research
- Processes
- Assembly
- Manufacturing databases

5. Other Technology Assets

- Product shapes
- Food or chemical formulas
- Plant construction

6. Product-Related Assets

- Graphics
- Packaging
- Colors
- Designs
- Warranties

7. Corporate Identity Assets

- Corporate name, logo, etc.
- Marketing campaigns, slogans

8. Intellectual Property Contracts

- In-licenses and out-licenses
- Franchises
- Cobranding agreements
- Endorsement deals
- Spokesperson contacts
- Venue naming rights

9. Software

- Source code
- Enterprise solutions
- Custom applications
- Products
- Mask works

10. Data/Information-Related Assets

- Databases
- Mailing lists
- Operating systems

11. Research-Related Assets

- Research studies
- Focus group results
- Psychographic research

The bundles briefly discussed here typically provide the core elements of value within most companies. Of course, there are important and ongoing exceptions. In the case of technology-rich companies, research-related assets or communications-related assets can be much more important. In the case of companies like Cingular or Orange, transmission, communication, and IT assets—not the trademark and brand assets—are the more important bundles of value.

12. Real Estate–Related Assets

- Zoning rights
- Permits
- Rights of way
- Easements
- Development rights
- Air rights

13. Communications-Related Assets

- Cable rights
- Transmission rights
- FCC licenses
- Bandwidth
- Certifications

14. People-Related Assets

- Embedded work force
- Work-for-hire contracts
- Prepaid temporary help contracts
- Specialty business skills
- Customer relations
- Noncompete clauses

15. Miscellaneous

- Shelving allowances
- Gambling permits

- Liquor licenses
- Retail systems
- Coating technology

This review of primary and secondary bundles is not intended to be complete, nor are the listings of individual elements within each bundle intended to be complete. Most companies will have at least a few components of value in each of their most important five or six bundles. However, it is unusual for a company to have more than five or six meaningful bundles of intellectual assets.

PART III

Valuation Methodologies

Valuation

The action of estimating or fixing the monetary or other value of something, especially by a professional evaluator. An instance of this is a real estate valuation. Also, estimated monetary value, worth or price, especially by a professional evaluator, and/or the value of worth, especially of a material nature and expressed as a current value in an appraisal or estimation of some type.

Methodology

That branch of knowledge that deals with method and its application in a particular field (e.g., the value of things, objects, or entities). Also, the study of empirical research, the techniques employed in it, and/or a body of methods used in a particular branch of study or activity—such as valuation methodology.

INTRODUCTION

In Part III of the primer, we have three general goals:

- To identify various valuation methodologies
- To discuss financial and valuation constraints encountered when engaged in valuing an Intellectual Property asset
- To introduce the reader to the basic language and terms of reference used in Intellectual Property valuation and business transactions

Chapter 3 identifies and explains the different approaches to valuation: traditional valuation methodologies, new methodologies, proprietary alternatives, and, finally, variations on all of these. The goal is to lay out these alternatives and explain them in everyday language. This chapter is not intended as a review of the mechanics of using these methodologies, nor is it intended as an explanation of the detailed financial calculations.

Intellectual Property valuation has many of the same characteristics that are used when valuing tangible assets, such as buildings or equipment. For example, the three traditional and most accepted methodologies are very similar to those used when valuing tangible and real assets. However, there are many important differences in how the methodologies are used for Intellectual Property and intangible assets versus tangible assets. The most important include the following:

- The constraints and conditions when valuing Intellectual Property can be quite different from those in a tangible-asset valuation situation.
- Intellectual Property and intangible asset valuations are more subject to outside environmental issues and pressures.

- Context is critical in valuing Intellectual Property and intangibles—Part V of this primer is devoted to dealing with the single most important differentiation in valuing Intellectual Property: the context of the valuation.
- Often, the intangible assets are difficult to categorize, identify, and separate from each other.
- Finally, intangible asset and Intellectual Property valuations are much more susceptible to the subjective judgment and relative experience of the valuation professional.

We deal with these issues in two chapters. The traditional and most accepted methodologies are explained in Chapter 3. Chapter 4 is devoted to more than 20 variations, permutations, and alternatives to the three primary methods.

The second goal of Part III is to review the financial conditions, constraints, and considerations that are unique to Intellectual Property and intangible assets (although many of the conditions and other topics discussed also have some impact on tangible asset values). In Chapter 5 we deal, first, with the overall context and conditions that are being applied to the valuation project. Second, we look at the specific considerations of what, why, and how: what is being valued, why is it being valued, and how should it be done. Third, Chapter 5 briefly addresses the environmental conditions that affect the valuation—competitive, financial, economic, and market conditions.

Chapter 5 concludes this section of the book with a glossary of basic and common terms used in intellectual property valuation. We briefly explain each term, but neither the list of terms nor the explanations are intended to be exhaustive. Rather, they offer the reader a basic grounding in terminology; we encourage that same reader to look at other sources of information, both in the appendices of this book and in financial textbooks and materials. The goal of this brief glossary is to explain the technical language of intellectual property and intangible asset valuation. We conclude with an explanation and demystification of the net present value/discount rate calculation that appears in every Intellectual Property valuation report—and that is often a source of confusion or misunderstanding when reviewed by nonprofessionals in the valuation arena.

A final comment on the valuation of intellectual property is one that we strongly believe and that we train our staff to understand and use in the analysis phase of a valuation project: When valuing intellectual property, the "devil is in the concepts, not in the details." In other words, with Intellectual Property value it is necessary to understand fully the conceptual issues of these very ephemeral and difficult-to-capture objects of the valuation process. For tangible asset valuation, the devil is in the details; for intangible asset valuation, the devil is in the concepts—the details will follow the conceptual breakthrough needed to ensure an accurate valuation.

CHAPTER 3

TRADITIONAL VALUATION METHODOLOGIES

Introduction

Valuation methodologies can be compared to Grandmother's chicken soup—everyone's grandmother has a recipe for chicken soup. However, no two individuals can agree on precisely what should be included in that chicken soup. They can agree on two or three traditional ingredients, such as the chicken itself, carrots, noodles, celery, etc. Beyond that, each grandmother will have her proprietary or specialized method of preparation, such as adding beans, peas, or rice. Each will also have a proprietary method of simmering, stewing, boiling, or otherwise cooking.

Just like Grandmother's chicken soup, the valuation of intellectual property involves individual approaches. And, as with chicken soup, there are some basic, traditional methods of valuation: the three most popular are the market approach, the income approach, and the cost approach. There are also many proprietary and specialized approaches to valuation. These range from the subtraction theory of value, to a profit-split approach, to the VALMATRIX® and Brand Value Equation ($BVE_Q^{™}$) proprietary methodologies. Thus, although some standardization exists in intellectual property valuation, in the form of the three accepted and traditional methodologies, there is a broad range of modifications, alterations, personalizations, and adaptations that can be applied to modify these three.

In this section, the discussion of methodologies is divided into three broad areas:

- The traditional methods of valuation
- Proprietary and specialized methods and definitions of valuation
- Some of the financial concerns and constraints that control or support any given methodology

The Time- and Context-Based Influences on Valuation

Before one can decide which valuation method is most appropriate, one must first decide in what context assets or bundles of assets are being valued. In Chapters 1 and 2, we attempted to cover briefly but broadly the various bundles of value. Now comes the difficult choice—how to value?

Typically, before one can begin the valuation process, one must ask, "When are we valuing the asset, and why are we valuing the asset?" The first parameter is time. Is the asset or assets in question being valued as of today? As of two and one-half years ago at the time of purchase? When litigation commenced? Five years in the future when the transfer of ownership under a master license agreement will take place? Each of these time-based scenarios will influence value.

Next, one must ask, "Why are we valuing this bundle or bundles of intangible assets and intellectual property?" Is it because of a sale or bankruptcy? Because of litigation, arbitration, or settlement? In anticipation of a license, merger, or other deal? Typically, there are a dozen or more common reasons why one enters into a valuation:

- Merger and acquisition
- Property replacement
- Tax-based transfer
- Donation
- Outright sale
- Bankruptcy and reorganization
- Corporate liquidation
- Intercompany royalty rates
- SEC: Section 141,142
- Litigation or arbitration
- Loan securitization or collateralization
- IRS Section 482
- Settlement of an estate or gift or damage claim

Each of these environments or contexts helps to determine how to value the intellectual property.

Value Definition and Its Impact on Methodology

Just as there are a number of bundles of assets, and just as there are several approaches or methodologies to valuing these assets, so are there different definitions of value. These definitions of value come into play based on whether the valuation is for legal reasons, accounting reasons, business reasons, tax reasons, etc. Some of the definitions of value are as follows:

- Fair value
- Fair market value
- In-place value
- Tax value
- Liquidation value
- Deal value
- Licensing value
- Transaction value
- Securitization value
- Disposition or dispersal value
- Replacement or reproduction value

As we move to a brief discussion of methodologies, remember some basic questions to be asked before selecting a methodology:

- What asset or bundle of assets is being valued?
- Why is this bundle of assets being valued?
- What definition of *value* is being used?
- Are there legal, tax, financial or other business implications that will affect methodology?
- When are we valuing?

Traditional Intangible Asset Valuation Techniques

The need to value intangible assets is increasing. Several different factors contribute to this growing need, including the increasing activity in mergers and acquisitions, initial public offerings, and venture capital funding. In addition, inter-company operations, such as transfer pricing, intellectual property donations, and other asset movements, have led to the need for this type of service.

When valuing intellectual property and other intangible assets, consider all the different methodologies available for intangible asset valuation in light of the information at hand and the current situation. This allows you to determine the best method or methods to use in each situation. Traditionally, the methods used to value intangibles have some elements in common with those used to value tangible assets, such as real estate. An important difference in most cases is that there is relatively less availability of the necessary data, such as finding comparable transactions or relevant financial information when valuing intangibles. Comparable transactions or benchmark information is needed to establish a logical and intellectually sound basis for valuation.

In the last two decades, the field of intangible asset valuation has grown dramatically. In our view, four different methodologies have now become the most important, whether for transaction, tax, or litigation purposes, or whether in a going concern valuation or liquidation:

1. Cost approach
2. Market approach
3. Income approach
4. Relief-from-royalty approach

The Cost Approach

Two different styles are often applied when valuing assets using the cost method:

1. Historical cost basis
2. Replacement or reproduction cost

Using the cost basis values an asset at its historical cost and depreciates it appropriately based on a reasonable useful life estimate. Replacement cost, on the other hand, uses current prices to calculate the costs of duplicating the asset today. The differences between historical cost and calculated replacement cost, therefore, include adjustments reflecting inflation (or in some cases deflation) due to market efficiencies, competition, or technological improvements.

The cost method assesses the value of assets by measuring the expenditures necessary to replace the assets in question. The historical cost to develop the intellectual property, or *cost basis,* is sometimes used to determine value. The other approach, based on replacement value, determines the level of current dollar expenditures necessary to duplicate the asset in question in terms of consumer awareness, market share, and other factors.

Costs that can be quantified include the following:

- Legal fees
- Application/registration and other fees
- Personnel costs
- Development costs
- Production costs
- Marketing and advertising costs

This method does not give an indication of the economic benefit derived from ownership and utilization of the assets; rather, it provides an absolute minimum value for the assets. A purchaser of the asset often only pays an amount that reflects the cost a company could avoid by purchasing, rather than duplicating, a similar effort.

The cost approach is based on the economic principle of *substitution.* Essentially, the premise is that potential buyers will pay no more for an asset than it would cost them to develop or obtain another asset of similar utility. Examples of the relevant costs that should be included when valuing intellectual property are legal fees, registration costs, advertising expenditures, the time and cost needed to re-create research, the number of employees needed, the probability of success, the remaining life of current patents, and equipment specific to the development of a technology. Not every cost incurred should be included in the cost approach to valuation, however. Many factors relevant to the asset's development may once have been proprietary but now are in the public domain. Also, the costs that are included when calculating value with this approach must be considered within the current economic environment. It is also important to include opportunity cost that arises from delayed market entry.

Because this approach does not reflect the earning potential of the assets, it is often used for embryonic technology or other assets where no specific market application or benefit can be identified. In any event, the cost approach can often (but not always) provide a floor or minimum value for the intangible assets in question.

The Market Approach

Here, intangible assets are valued by comparing recent sales or other transactions involving similar assets in similar markets. This approach is best if an active market exists that has several examples of recent arm's-length transactions and adequate information on their terms and conditions. However, most intangible assets are not traded frequently enough to enable one to establish a value based on market-based comparables. Moreover, it is very difficult to get enough detail on the similar transactions to be certain that all the elements of value that make goods comparable have been considered.

The market approach utilizes actual transaction values derived from the sale or license of similar assets. It has increasingly become the preferred approach in the valuation of intangible assets, if the necessary data can be found. In contrast to the other methodologies, the strength of the market approach is its reliance on market sales, rents, and royalties. In practice, when the data are available, the market approach is practical, logical, and applicable to all types of intangible assets. As with the income and relief-from-royalty approaches, the value conclusion can be reviewed at any time to see whether any adjustments are necessary. When reliable transaction data are available, the market approach is considered the most direct and systematic approach to value.

The Income Approach

The income approach is based on determining the future income streams expected from the asset under valuation. The income approach is one of the most widely used approaches, because the information necessary to determine value using this approach is usually relatively accurate and often readily available. The parameters used include the following:

- Future income stream
- Duration of the income stream
- Risk associated with the generation of the income stream

The most common error in applying this approach is the lack of differentiation between the business enterprise value and the value of the intellectual property that supports the business. When valuing intellectual property, it is critical to separate the Intellectual Property income stream and value from the value of the business as a whole.

With the income approach, an asset is worth the present value of the future economic benefits (income) that will accrue to its owner. It requires a projection of future income attributable to the Intellectual Property, an estimate of the likely duration of the income stream, and an estimate of the risk associated with generating the projected income stream. Although the income approach may seem less precise than the cost approach, due to the inclusion of multiple estimates, the information needed to make these estimates can be accurately developed and verified. An additional benefit of the income approach is that it provides the ability to perform sensitivity analyses by adjusting the parameters, which allows management to understand better the importance of the various factors driving value in their particular situation.

The Relief-from-Royalty Approach

This is a particular style of the income approach. With this method, the value of the intangible assets is calculated as the present value of the royalties that the company is relieved from paying as a result of owning the assets. It is often used to establish damages in litigation cases. In other words, this approach provides a measure of value by determining the avoided cost. It is calculated by assuming that the business does not own the trademark or technology, and thus must pay a royalty for its use. The relief-from-royalty method uses royalty rates based on marketplace transactions, and uses a forecast of revenue, as in the income approach. Thus, it combines the income approach and the market approach. The value is calculated in the form of an avoided cost or royalty payment. Specifically, it consists of the present value of the royalty payments avoided as a result of ownership of the assets. The assumption is essentially that the assets must be licensed in order to be used. This method determines what the cost would be of that hypothetical license. It incorporates a projection of future revenue, as in the income approach, and relies on comparables (usually data from real-world license agreements) as the source for the royalty rates used, as in the market approach. The inclusion of this market information adds credibility to the analysis. With both the income approach and the relief-from-royalty approach, the results can be revisited periodically for updates, if desired.

This has been a brief overview of the primary and commonly used methods to value intellectual property, but care should be taken not to oversimplify the process. In any valuation, the context often determines which methodology is used.

A note of caution: Although the relief-from-royalty method has been in use for many years, in the last decade it has become misused and abused to a great extent. Too many valuations are based on these theoretical "marketplace royalty rates" to calculate value. Although it is true that some intellectual property—particularly trademarks, brands, and copyrights—do have comparable market royalty rates that can be established, for many intellectual property valuations comparable royalty rates are speculative at best. Also, please remember that there is no such thing as an exact comparable royalty rate, and any valuation project that claims to present exact comparables is flawed in its basic logic. Nonetheless, when properly used and when appropriate royalty rate comparables or calculations are available, the relief-from-royalty rate method is a very effective valuation methodology.

This brief review of traditional valuation methodologies has been intended strictly as an overview. In later chapters, we will use the three primary methodologies (the relief-from-royalty approach is a particular style of the income approach) in at least two different case studies each to illustrate how they can be utilized on different bundles of intangible assets. For now, here are the primary lessons to take away from this chapter:

- The market approach is used when comparable sales or other transactions can be identified that are very similar to the intangible asset being valued.
- The cost approach, either historical cost or replacement or reproduction cost, is often used as a primary or secondary method to measure the economic impact of having to replace or reproduce an asset.
- The income approach, the relief-from-royalty approach, or both are used where specific income levels or streams of real or imputed royalties can be identified for a given asset bundle.

All of these methods are good, and they can be used in many situations—and, in all situations, at least two methods should be employed.

CHAPTER 4

OTHER VALUATION METHODOLOGIES

Because this book is a primer on the subject and process of Intellectual Property valuation, we want to cover as many different valuation methodologies as possible. Naturally, no one can cover all of them in detail in the space available in this short chapter. However, we do offer a brief overview of several methodologies. The methodologies are divided roughly into two types:

- Variations and specialized methodologies based on the three traditional approaches: the income, cost, and market approaches (as discussed in Chapter 3)
- Semiproprietary and other methodologies used by various practitioners

As in footwear, clothing, or diamond rings, one size does *not* fit all. The three traditional methodologies do not and cannot fit every valuation situation. Not every piece of intellectual property or intangible asset in every context can be adequately measured or valued using just one of the three traditional methodologies.

Some of the methodologies described in this chapter are tax driven. For example, the CPM method, or the profit-sharing method, is often used in transfer pricing. Some of these methodologies are specific to a type of Intellectual Property. For example, the technology factor matrix approach is used primarily with patents. Other methodologies are context driven. For example, the liquidation and orderly disposal valuation processes are used almost exclusively in a bankruptcy or reorganization environment.

As with any discipline that is relatively new and robust—the valuation of intellectual property, as a professional practice area, is only two decades old—change is constant, and methodologies are constantly changing. In the next few pages, we review a score of methodologies. Some are new and some are well established. Some are controversial and some garner great respect—we review and define all of them without judgment.

Finally, we remind the reader that in any valuation environment, tangible or intangible, more than one valuation methodology should always be used if possible. In particular, we caution that a valuation based on only one methodology, particularly when it is one of the so-called specialized or proprietary methodologies, is a situation fraught with danger and uncertainty about the validity of the valuation conclusions.

Variations and Specialized Methodologies

This chapter presents a summary. The following paragraphs are not exhaustive, and there are enough variations in these to equal or surpass the number discussed here.

Liquidation Value

Liquidation value is the lowest price at which an asset will be pegged to ensure that there will be an acquisition. Liquidation value arises most often in Chapter 7 bankruptcy proceedings, and these values are affected by other assets that may be available in the marketplace. In its simplest form, liquidation value is that price below which we can, with some certainty, guarantee that the price will not fall. With each passing month in a liquidation scenario, the value of the intellectual property can decrease by 2 to 10%.

Orderly Disposal Value

Orderly disposal value is derived from the expectation that a company has chosen to wind down its operations over a period of time, and it can be used in either Chapter 7 or merger and acquisition situations. The decision to shutter the doors leads to a sharp decline in value in the short term but allows the company the opportunity to market the assets actively to a broader group of investors, which ultimately leads to higher intellectual property values than those realized in a last-ditch "fire-sale" or liquidation scenario.

Replacement Value

Replacement value is loosely defined as the cost to re-create the intellectual property or intangible asset being valued. Replacement value, however, is different from reproduction value in that it envisions substituting or replacing the asset under study with one of equivalent value or utility.

Reproduction Value

Reproduction value is virtually self-descriptive. It is the quantification, costs, time, and effort to reproduce or replicate the asset being valued. For example, reproduction cost is a useful tool when calculating the value of a specific database or customer list, many of which can be reproduced (but not replaced) but often at substantial cost.

Subtraction Value

The premise of value here is that a given business will be worth less if it does not have a specific intangible asset. The value of the intangible asset, therefore, becomes the difference in value between the company owning the intangible asset and the company theoretically not owning the intangible asset (See later section, Snapshots-of-Value Method).

Income Differential Method of Value

In simplest terms, this is a variation on one of the three traditional methods, the income method. *Comparative income differential* simply means that a company operating and selling product A will receive less income than company B producing the same product but with the addition of a specific intangible asset. A quick example is the income differential between what Coca-Cola receives for a bottle of its soft drink versus the income received by a second-tier company such as Nehi or Dad's Old Fashioned Root Beer. (See later section, Premium Pricing Technique.)

Income Capitalization or Direct Capitalization Method of Value

This is another alternative or (alternative description) of the income approach. It measures value as the product of a stream of income expressed in today's dollars.

Profit Split Method of Value

Often used in tax-based valuation environments, the profit split method attempts to assign a share or portion of a company's profitability to an intangible asset. This method implies the ability to split or separate expressly the intangible asset from other considerations in order to allocate some portion of gross revenues, operating income, or net income to the specific intangible asset. That share of annual income over a number of years is expressed in today's terms.

Return on Assets Employed Method of Value

Often used by economists and accountants to "back into" the value of the intangible asset, this method at first appears complex. Every company has three or four or more classes of assets. These can include real estate, equipment, factories, intangible assets, etc. From a company's total income, a market rate of return is allocated to each class of tangible asset. For example, real estate might expect an annual return of 7% on its value; therefore, that amount of income would be calculated as attributable to the real estate and removed from the company's total income. This process would be repeated for each of the other tangible asset groups (factories, plant and equipment, working capital, etc.). The balance left after these allocations to the tangible asset groups represents the return to be allocated to the intangible assets as a whole. This amount can then be capitalized and expressed in today's dollars. Although technically inspired, the method is best used when a company or entity has only a single, key piece of intellectual property or a single type of intangible asset— best used, for example, in an Oracle environment. (See later section, The VALCALC® Method.)

Cost Savings Method of Value

Here, one attempts to establish the amount of money (expressed as time, materials, effort, resources, etc.) that a company does or will save by owning the intellectual property or intangible asset. For example, company A may have a very superior production process that enables them to reduce the number of people and the amount of raw materials needed to manufacture products. These costs savings would be calculated on an annual basis, and then the stream of income over a number of years would be expressed in today's dollars, or what is commonly known as the *net present value*.

Subtraction Method of Value

This approach establishes the value of a given asset by valuing a company against another company without the asset—so-called *benchmark value*. For example, one might value a producer of unbranded toothpaste or personal care products against a branded manufacturer. In this instance, if the value of the company without a brand or trademark is $2M and the value of the company with an established brand or trademark is $3M, then the subtraction theory says that the value of the trademark is the difference between the two, or $1M.

Semiproprietary and Other Methodologies of Value

This brief section outlines a number of other methodologies used by one or more well known individuals or firms in Intellectual Property valuation. These methodologies are typically used in specialized environments or by specialists in a given area of intellectual property.

Rules of Thumb

The first and most important rule of thumb is that all rules of thumb are faulty. With that in mind, one should be aware that there are rules of thumb used by sometime practitioners in Intellectual Property valuation. These include the so-called *25% rule of thumb*, which allocates one-quarter of a company's operating profit as an imputed royalty for the Intellectual Property.

Technology Factor Matrix Technique

This analysis looks at a number of factors along two scales: competitive advantage and utility. The technology is scored or ranked along both of these axes, and a numerical score is produced along a scale from -2 to $+2$. The numerical score then indicates the relative value position for the technology, which can then be applied to a range of market comparables, royalty rates, and other benchmarks of economic value.

The VALCALC® Method

Essentially a variation of the return on assets employed, VALCALC® attempts to establish the rate of return or income that a given intangible asset should be earning. This calculation of adequate return is applied to all classes of assets within a company, and then the return for each intangible asset is calculated as a result.

The Brand Value Equation Method (BVE$_Q$™)

This technique works on the principle that a brand is composed of multiple brand-based assets and intellectual property elements, including trademark, logo, trade dress, etc. A core value for the trademark is calculated, and then values for the additional, individual intangible assets are calculated. The sum of that core brand value plus the incremental asset values becomes the total brand value.

Snapshots-of-Value Method

Similar in nature to the subtraction value method outlined previously, snapshots of value attempts to establish two different values for a company's intangibles:

- One for the company having full access to the ownership of the intellectual property or intangible asset
- One for the company without that intangible asset

The difference between the two snapshots, therefore, becomes the value of the intangible asset.

Premium Pricing Technique

This is a relatively straightforward variation of the income approach. Value for an asset (typically a trademark) is established by looking at the difference between the prices paid for an average product with a trademark and an average product without the trademark. The difference between those two prices, the *price premium,* is then calculated on an annual income basis, to which is applied the net present value calculation.

VALMATRIX® Analysis Technique

This system employs a matrix of the 20 most important predictors and contributors to value for a trademark. A given trademark is ranked or measured against these value parameters, and value is established relative to similar brands or trademarks. For example, one would not compare the Ford trademark to the Marlboro trademark or the McDonald's trademark to the IBM trademark. Instead, the McDonald's trademark would be compared and assessed relative to Burger King, Wendy's, or KFC trademarks. The numerical score generated by the analysis is then used to establish a percentile ranking relative to other brands. This ranking or relative value is applied to the appropriate range of market comparables or streams of income.

The Imputed Income Technique

Most often used in a domain name valuation, value is established by looking at the activity generated by the domain name and website relative to overall activity, and imputed income is applied to this percentage of total activity generated by the domain name/website. For example, a company's website and domain name might be receiving 5,000 inquiries a day out of a total of 20,000. Assuming that these inquiries have a market value to the company, and based on projected annual levels of income, the present value calculation is made for the Internet assets.

The Concept of Relative Value

This approach is based on the premise that a domain name will represent some percentage of value of the underlying trademark. For example, if the underlying trademark or brand has a market value of $10M given a specific level of activity for that brand's website, one could allocate a relative value of 5% of the total, or $500K.

The Competitive Advantage Technique

This is a judgmental approach to valuation that is based on the supposition that company A has an advantage over its competitors because of the technology, patent, trademark, or software that it owns. This competitive advantage can be measured or expressed based on share of market, market growth, competitive pricing, etc. Although highly subjective, it can be useful when a company's portfolio of intellectual property is diverse but obviously important; although individual pieces of intellectual property within that portfolio may be difficult to measure, this competitive advantage technique allows one to estimate a value for that company's entire portfolio.

■ Case Study: Traditional plus Specialized Techniques

This case study shows an example of the melding of a traditional valuation methodology with a proprietary specialized methodology; we show how the relief-from-royalty method or the market comparable approach can be combined with the VALMATRIX® technique. In either case, the VALMATRIX® approach is used to assess the relative strengths of a patent or trademark, and this assessment is applied to a range of royalty rates and/or a range of comparable market transactions to establish a specific royalty.

First, a brief explanation of the VALMATRIX® technique: Over the past 20 years, this analytical technique has been an integral part of the royalty rate, competitive environment, and comparable transaction analyses used by the author in many valuation projects. Essentially a relative strength analysis, this technique objectively measures 20 different attributes associated with the intellectual property being valued and the past, intended, and potential usage of the assets. The attributes cover factors such as financial performance, legal strength, marketing activities, and competition, among others.

Based on two decades of research, individual VALMATRIX® analyses have been designed for patents, trademarks, copyrights, and Internet assets, and software and scoring systems have been developed for each type of asset. The assets are scored along 20 dimensions using a five-point scale. A score of zero indicates complete lack of value, or even negative value, whereas a five indicates superior strength over comparable assets, or a premier position. The cumulative score resulting from the individual factors is then compared to an index that correlates

VALMATRIX® cumulative scores with a quartile ranking of comparable market royalty rates. The attributes included in each analysis are specific to the type of intellectual property being analyzed (e.g., patent, trademark). Analyses for trademarks, patents, and copyrights reflect key differences in these various asset types. Similarly, an analysis that measures factors related to litigation matters, such as confusion and damages, varies somewhat from those performed in other valuation settings.

The VALMATRIX® analysis is useful as a predictor of current value and future commercialization or extension potential. There is a direct correlation between the relative score for a trademark or brand and its future expansion and success. As a trademark or brand moves into the second or first quartile, its value and projected royalty rates grow substantially. This is illustrated in Table 4.1. Use of this analysis is an effective predictor of specific royalty rate levels. Over the last decade, a correlation between VALMATRIX® scores and quartiles and specific royalty rates has been obtained for various pieces of intellectual property. For example, in trademark/brand licensing, more than 80% of brands with scores in the top two quartiles have also received royalty rates in the top two quartiles. We have seen similar correlative results for technology and patents. ■

An Alternative Approach for Inexact Comparables

This section illustrates an alternative approach combining relief-from-royalty with the VALMATRIX® technique. It starts with an assessment of the relative

Table 4.1 The VALMATRIX® Strength Assessment Tracks the Range of Comparable Transactions Distributed by Specific Quartiles of the Guideline Set

Range: 0.5–6.0% Comparable Rate	Frequency	Cumulative %*	Quartile
6.0%	1	100.00%	1st
5.5%	0	87.50%	1st
5.0%	0	87.50%	1st
4.5%	1	87.50%	1st
4.0%	1	75.00%	2nd
3.5%	0	62.50%	2nd
3.0%	2	62.50%	2nd
2.5%	0	37.50%	3rd
2.0%	1	37.50%	3rd
1.5%	1	25.00%	4th
1.0%	0	12.50%	4th
0.5%	1	12.50%	4th

*Rounded.

strengths of the intangible assets owned by a company, then uses this assessment to determine where the asset fits within a range of potential comparables.

Table 4.2 shows the results of a search for potential comparables for an international bank with a unique bundle of intangibles to be licensed. This company wanted to set royalty rates for its marketing intangibles, including trademarks and trade names.

Note the relatively broad range of comparables of 0.5 to 5%. Where did the international bank fit in this range? To determine this, we went through an analysis of the 20 factors associated with trademarks and marketing assets—such as consumer recognition, industry cyclicity, industry/product maturity, and breadth of distribution—and gave the bank's intangibles a score for each item based on a scale of zero to five. When the scores are summed, this particular client had a strength rating of 64, in the middle of the second quartile.

Therefore, with the range of royalty rates between 0.5 and 5%, this particular client falls slightly above the middle of the range. How do we get an exact royalty rate? The bank's particular bundle of intangibles had a score of 64, suggesting a 2.5 to 3.0% royalty.

In this example, a remaining life of 12–15 years, an annual growth rate of 2%, and a discount rate of 15% were assumed. The client had a revenue base of $400M a year. Using these facts and assumptions, we concluded that a current value of $44M to $52M was the market value for those intangibles. See Table 4.3.

Table 4.2 Comparable Marketplace Royalty Rates: Licensing of Financial/ Business Services

Licensor	Royalty Rate % (based on net revenues)
Financial services company	3.0
Financial services group	1.5–2.5
High-tech business services	4.0
Discount brokerage	0.5
Marketing consultants	5.0
Engineering/environmental	3.5
Financial services group	1.0–2.5
Overall range	1.0–5.0
Average	2.7
VALMATRIX® SCORE: 64 or second quartile	
Most comparable range	2.5–3.0

Table 4.3 Facts and Assumptions Underlying Market-Based Valuation

Range of comparable royalty rate	0.5–5.0%
Intangibles' strength rating	64
Most likely royalty rate	2.5–3.0%
Remaining life span	12–15 years
Annual growth	2.0%
Discount rate	15%
Revenue base	$406M
NPV, range of value	$44.3–$52.1M

Adapting Royalty Values and Rates to Changing Conditions

Intangibles must be adjusted over time. As they change in strength, their royalty rates and values will change, just as tangible assets change over time. If you own a building that you take good care of in a neighborhood that is improving, rents go up and the value of the building goes up. The same is true for a trademark, patent, or copyright.

It is useful to adjust value and royalty rates every two or three years, based on a new strengths analysis and current conditions. Remember when Schlitz beer was the second-best-known trademark in the business? Ten years ago, one of the best-known trademarks in the computer business was Commodore. They also had one of the best-known technical bundles of intangibles. Today, they are bankrupt. How much are their intangibles worth today? Section V of the primer examines the subject of changing values.

CHAPTER 5

FINANCIAL CONDITIONS, CONSTRAINTS, AND CONSIDERATIONS: A GLOSSARY OF TERMS

The purpose of this short chapter is to help the general practitioner or businessperson better understand the general financial conditions that affect the valuation process and to define some basic terms that are often used in the valuation process and the resultant reports. Although this chapter is aimed at the non–finance professional, it provides some detail that may expand the reader's understanding of financial calculations.

The second half of the chapter provides a list of basic terms, along with short explanations of each. This glossary is by no means complete. In fact, it contains only those terms that are useful to a non–Intellectual Property professional and non–finance professional when he or she participates in the valuation of intangible assets or intellectual property.

Before a valuation can commence, the valuation team needs to consider three general areas: constraints, considerations, and conditions. This means that there are outside influences that affect the approach to the project, as well as the results.

Constraints

First is the overall context of the valuation. Why is a valuation being done? Who has asked for the valuation? Who currently owns the intellectual property? When are we valuing it and for what purpose? And, most importantly, what are we valuing?

Other constraints are related to context. Some of the most important are tax constraints, as represented by Section 197 or Section 482 of the Internal Revenue Service Code. Other tax constraints regard donations of intellectual property. Accounting constraints include reporting for SEC purposes. Using FASB 141 and 142 rules for valuation affects the context of the value. A company in bankruptcy or reorganization is going to be affected by the bankruptcy code, such as Section 363, Sale of Assets.

In addition to those contextual constraints, there is another major constraint issue—the availability and quality of the data being used in the valuation. For example, if the valuation takes place in a litigation environment and data must be grudgingly extracted from the opposing client/attorney team, then almost invariably the quality of those data, as well as the quantity and availability of the data, will be far less than if one is valuing assets in a nonlitigation environment. All of these constraints can affect the valuation and should be at least briefly reviewed by all parties involved before valuation begins.

Considerations

Now we move to the more practical and specific questions, issues, and considerations in approaching the valuation of an intangible asset or intellectual property. These considerations are fairly straightforward: Which assets can be valued? (Some simply do not have a context in which to value.) Why are we valuing these assets—in other words, what is driving value? What is the definition of value? (See Chapter 3.) Who owns the assets, and what will they be doing with them as a result of the valuation?

Beyond that, other considerations exist. Most important are legal issues, which can range from clear title for the intellectual property to pending litigation. For example, there may be questions about trademark infringement, the pending application of a patent, the ownership of source code, etc. Other considerations are financial resources and can include very personal considerations, such as valuation as a result of a divorce proceeding. Finally, one must consider whether the valuation is for a particular transaction or circumstance and what the payment terms or other transaction elements may be important considerations.

Conditions

As an overall comment, the two most important conditions are

- How good are the assets?
- How much life do they have left?

The conditions referred to in this section are the various *environments*. For example, the competitive environment affects the financial calculations and value of the assets. The financial environment (e.g., high interest rates) also affects value. The economic environment, both on a nationwide basis and on a global basis, can be a conditional influence on value. Legal conditions, such as pending litigation, will, of course, affect value. Finally, the market environment (e.g., cyclicity) will have an impact on value.

Before we move to the glossary of terms, some quick conclusions are appropriate:

- Valuing intangible assets is a more complex process than valuing tangible assets.
- Outside considerations and conditions can have a substantial impact on the value of an asset. For example, an intangible asset valued in a liquidation environment will have its value much reduced, relative to going-concern value. To illustrate this, a real estate asset of a company that is in bankruptcy maintains a far greater proportion of its market value during that bankruptcy than any of the intangible assets owned by the company in bankruptcy.

Glossary of Terms

- **Arm's length:** A transaction in which the two parties are unrelated and dealing with each other in a market environment.
- **Amortization:** The process of reducing the value of the asset by a predetermined amount each year over a period of time.
- **BATNA (best alternative to a negotiated agreement):** Any negotiator should determine his or her BATNA before agreeing to any negotiated settlement. If the alternative is better, it should be pursued instead of the negotiated settlement.
- **Beta:** Describes and measures the relative volatility of a company or a group of assets.
- **Business enterprise value:** The total value of a business measured as a combination of a company's cash or financial assets, plus its other tangible assets, plus the intangible assets, which in total is the business enterprise value.
- **Bankruptcy code:** The set of rules and laws covering a troubled company's reorganization, restructuring, or liquidation.
- **Book value:** The value at which an asset, whether tangible or intangible, is carried on a company's balance sheet. Book value may or may not reflect any connection with true market value.
- **Buy-in:** An initial payment either in an arm's length transaction or as a term of art when dealing with transfer pricing of intangible assets.
- **CPM (comparable profits method):** A method described by the Internal Revenue Service in its Section 482 Regulations.
- **Cost sharing:** The process by which two companies develop intangible assets and share their costs in proportion to the benefits they receive from those assets—a term used most often in conjunction with IRS-based valuations.
- **CUT (comparable uncontrolled transaction):** Another IRS methodology for valuation that depends on identifying other market sales, licenses, etc.
- **Definition of value:** The process by which a specific term of value (e.g., fair market value) is used as a basis for the valuation project.
- **Delaware Holding Company (DHC):** As the term implies, a company specifically set up in Delaware that owns the intellectual property of a corporation, licenses the use of that intellectual property back to the various operating units within a company, and receives royalties in exchange.
- **Discount rate:** That percentage by which the value of money declines each year. Critical in valuations and used to arrive at a net present value of a future stream of income.
- **Discounted cash flow (DCF):** Results from using the discount rate and applying it to a future stream of income. To illustrate this very important

concept that affects all intangible asset valuations, we have included a detailed explanation and illustration at the end of this glossary.

- **Fair market value:** This description of value is the most commonly used but is often misunderstood. Other terms include *market value, true value,* and *fair value*. The following is the most appropriate definition of fair market value: The value of an asset when two unrelated persons come together for the purpose of exchanging or buying an asset—also known as that value at which an asset changes hands between a willing buyer and a willing seller, with neither of them being under compulsion to act and both having full knowledge of the facts.
- **FASB 141/142:** The new accounting rules under which a company must account for the value of its intangible assets for SEC reporting purposes.
- **GAAP:** Generally accepted accounting principles.
- **Intangible assessts:** Those assessts that cannot be fixed, touched, measured, seen, or otherwise physically quantified.
- **Intellectual capital:** A new term that is best described in books by Patrick Sullivan and Thomas Stewart as follows: "Intellectual capital is the measure of the true value of a company like Microsoft. It is more than the tangible assets, the company's value is in its intangible intellectual assets as well as in its ability to convert those assets into revenues." Alternatively used to describe the total of all of a company's intangible asset values and intellectual property values.
- **Internal rate of return (IRR):** The rate of profitability or return on a company's investments that it uses as a standard.
- **Net present value (NPV):** Related to discounted cash flow and the discounting of a stream of income, the net present value of a stream of income is that amount of dollars received today in lieu of a stream of income over a period of, for example, ten years.
- **Profit split method:** A valuation methodology that is based on allocating or splitting the profit among different asset classes. Also see the introduction to Part III.
- **Risk premium:** That amount of implied interest that needs to be added to a company's discount rate to reflect the fact that intangible assets typically have higher risk and more volatility than most classes of tangible assets.
- **Return on Assets, Return on Income, Return on Assets Employed:** These three terms (ROA, ROI, and ROAE, respectively) describe a process that calculates the amount of money that is received each year in return for the use of the assets. In other words, if an asset is worth $1,000 and each year $100 (or 10%) is received for use of that asset, then in simplest terms its return on investment or return on assets is 10%.
- **Tangible assets:** Those assets that are fixed and can be touched, measured, seen, or otherwise quantified.

- **Trade secrets:** Include formulas, patents, programs, techniques, etc., that have independent economic value and have been protected and kept secret. Trade secrets cannot be registered or protected under any government regulations; instead, they are protected and gain their value through the owner's diligence.
- **Transfer pricing:** The process of sending an asset or the income from an asset from one related company to another. Transfer pricing can occur between a parent company and a subsidiary or between two other separate but related companies.
- **Useful remaining life:** In simplest terms, this describes how much longer as asset will be functionally useful in its particular market or competitive environment.
- **WACC (weighted average cost capital):** Used in developing the discounted cash flow calculations in connection with arriving at a discount rate. It is a measure of the cost of a company's total capitalization (cost of equity funds and cost of borrowed funds), which in turn becomes its discount rate for valuing future income.

A cornerstone of a company's WACC is its discount rate calculation. This important calculation is included in *every* valuation of assets, both tangible and intangible, and must be understood in principle by anyone connected with the process of valuation. Although most readers of this primer will not be asked to engage in such a calculation, it is important, nonetheless, that they understand how the calculation takes place.

When one is projecting financial information into the future, it is appropriate to apply a discount factor that calculates the present value of the projected cash flows. The determination of the discount factor depends on the selection of a discount rate that accurately reflects the risk associated with utilizing intellectual property and captures the uncertainty inherent in the generation of the forecasted cash flow. To determine the appropriate discount rate to use in this analysis, we relied on the capital asset pricing model (CAPM).

This calculation shows the appropriate discount rate to use when applying a discount factor to the company as a whole. Because we are examining specific intangible assets within the company's financial structure, it is appropriate to include a premium to reflect the additional uncertainty incorporated in this context. In Table 5.1 we applied a 3.66% risk-free rate as a starting basis to arrive at the appropriate discount rate for Company X of 16.8%. We utilized this discount rate to calculate the core trademark value resulting from royalty savings occurring in the first 10 years. In addition, we applied a 5.0% risk premium to our calculation to reflect the greater risk or uncertainty of intangible assets. We applied this additional risk premium to account for the increased uncertainty relating to cash flows occurring more than 10 years in the future.

Table 5.1 COMPANY X Discount Rate Analysis (CAPM)

Capital Asset Pricing Model:

CAPM = Rf + B (RM − Rf) + S, where:
Rf = Risk free rate
B = Industry Beta
Rm = Expected market return
S = Size premium

Risk Free Rate, Rf	3.66% (a)
Expected Market Return, Rm	12.00% (b)
Industry Beta, B	0.68% (c)
Size Premium, S	2.50% (d)
Total Ke, Pre-Tax Basis	11.83%
Premium for Asset Class (Intangibles)	5.00% (e)
Rounded to:	16.80%

(a) 10-year yield on U.S. Treasury bonds as of 07/03/03
(b) Historical expected market return (volatility)
(c) Subjective judgment as determined by appraiser
(d) Traditional (or subjective judgment as determined by appraiser)
(e) Traditional (or subjective judgment as determined by appraiser)

PART IV

Valuation of Different Types of Intellectual Property and Intangible Assets

Goodwill

1. The amount above the fair net book value (adjusted for assumed debt) paid for an acquisition. Goodwill appears as an asset on the balance sheet of the acquiring firm and must be reduced in the event the value is impaired.
2. An intangible asset that is made up of the favor or prestige which a business has acquired beyond the mere value of what it sells, due to the personality or experience of those conducting it, their reputation for skill or dependability, the business's location, or any other circumstance incidental to the business that tends to draw and retain customers.
3. (accounting) An intangible asset valued according to the advantage or reputation a business has acquired (over and above its tangible assets).

INTRODUCTION

The next nine chapters look at different types of intellectual property and intangible assets. This section ranges across the large and broad assets, such as corporate identity or umbrella brands, to individual assets, ranging from trademarks and patents to operating software, and down to individual IT assets, such as databases or customer lists.

Each chapter describes a type of intangible asset and one or more valuation approaches. As in any intellectual property valuation, there will always be multiple approaches available. A good valuation professional will always apply at least two methodologies.

These short chapters are intended to show the differences in both the type of asset valued and the type of valuation methodology. In each chapter, the text and descriptions are backed up by one or more case studies. Chapter 6 begins with a very broad-based intangible asset: a company's corporate identity or corporate umbrella brand. From there, we move down through the other classes of assets, ending with a quick review of the all-encompassing "other intangible assets" that do not comfortably fit into one of the standard categories.

CHAPTER 6

GOODWILL: CORPORATE IDENTITY*

Over the last two decades, the definition of corporate goodwill has been much debated and analyzed, metamorphosing into today's morass of conflicting definitions. The underlying problem in defining the word *goodwill* is to answer the questions: Whose definition of goodwill is it? Why are we defining the goodwill—for tax, financial, or litigation reasons?

There are at least four distinct viewpoints on goodwill from four different groups of professionals:

- CPAs and other financial analysts
- Lawyers and contract issue reviewers
- Licensing and market transaction professionals
- The Courts

Perhaps the two most important ways of looking at the definition of goodwill are from a financial reporting viewpoint and from a market-based transaction viewpoint. In the first instance, goodwill is that amount of capitalized company value in excess of the value of *all* of its assets. In other words, once one adds up the value of all of the tangible assets (property, plant, equipment), the financial assets (cash, receivables, etc.), and intangible assets and Intellectual Property (patents, trademarks, copyrights, etc.), the amount left is termed *goodwill* for financial purposes.

An alternative definition of goodwill is that value imbedded in a company's corporate identity or umbrella brand. In simplest terms, goodwill in this definition is the value that accrues to, for example, Coca-Cola because of the halo effect of the brand or all of its other assets. By this definition, the corporate identity or corporate umbrella brand becomes synonymous with a company's goodwill.

There are many discussions of the financial parameters of goodwill and several outstanding books on the subject, most notably *Valuation of Intellectual Property and Intangible Assets* by Gordon Smith and Russell Parr, books by Robert Reilly and Robert Schweihs and by Patrick Sullivan, and the chapter on "Valuing Intangible Assets: The Big Pot of Goodwill" (coauthored by Weston Anson) in *Mergers and Acquisitions Handbook for Small and Midsize Companies*, edited by Thomas West and Jeffrey Jones. Reference to Smith and Parr, for their definition and discussion of goodwill, is recommended to those who wish to delve into the financial details of the topic. In this chapter we will deal with the other definition of goodwill, that is, the corporate identity or corporate umbrella brand.

---

*Note: A somewhat modified version of the materials in this chapter previously appeared in the *Corporate Reputation Review*.

As globalization continues in the world market and differences between individual markets continue to disappear, more international brands and international corporations are finding success under a single umbrella brand or corporate identity. Forward-looking management in companies like General Motors, Pirelli, Sony, and Honda recognize that their single greatest intangible asset is their corporate identity or umbrella brand.

Until recently, the valuation of a corporate identity or a corporate umbrella brand was somewhat like the weather—everyone was talking about the subject but little was being done about it. In this chapter, we focus on valuing the overall corporate umbrella brand. We also focus on why it is important and identify key elements of that corporate identity.

Why Umbrella Corporate Brands Are Increasingly Important

Whenever success is sought in consumer goods, corporate identity is critical—consider consumer goods like Polo/Ralph Lauren, Coca-Cola, or Nestlé. Among retail brand companies, such as Harrods, Galleries Lafayette, or Wal-Mart Corp., identity is also of paramount importance. Moreover, among industrial identities, witness the importance of corporate identities like Lucent, Caterpillar, or Olivetti. Finally, in services, one only has to look at UPS, Accenture, or FedEx to realize that corporate brand identity is a valuable asset. These assets are often worth far more than many companies' tangible assets.

Some of the reasons driving the importance of corporate brands are

- Increasing globalization of the business community
- A focus on return on all assets: factories, equipment, and intangible assets
- Expanding international use of trademarks, brands, and logos
- Mobile global customers: corporations and consumers
- Expanded global marketing
- Shrinking global village
- A move from tangible assets to intangible, to drive modern industry
- Improved communication: TV, Internet, telecom, international print

The corporate brand value of companies like Yahoo, Coca-Cola, General Motors, Sprint, Volvo, Pirelli, Toyota, and Starbucks is, indeed, a key asset with specific and real market value—just like fixed assets, including buildings and equipment. Increasingly, we can establish realistic market values for these corporate brand assets, as well as develop reliable methods to leverage and increase the value of those assets.

The stewardship of these assets must also play a key role in global organization today. These high-value assets are the key to corporate success on every level: they are a critical component of stock price, market capitalization, and investor perceptions. Management of these assets must be attended to on every level to maximize and reinforce corporate brand value.

Umbrella Brand

An *umbrella brand* consists of the core name and trademark plus the supporting elements. The corporate name and trademarks and the brand's supporting elements are grouped in the identity bundle. It is essential to understand that a corporate brand does not travel in a vacuum and is not just a logo, design, or piece of signage. The corporate brand must be thought of as a "bundle of assets," moving in synchronization. Some of the elements of that bundle of assets are in Table 6.1.

Determining Realistic Value: Alternative Methodologies

In earlier chapters, we described valuation methodologies. In the last 20 years, the practice of brand and intangible asset valuation has grown dramatically. Four different methodologies have typically been favored:

- Market-based approach
- Income approach
- Cost or replacement value approach
- Relief-from-royalty approach

Although there is no such thing as a single best method to be used in every case of valuation, in most cases, the best approach is market-based value when suitable data is available.

In the traditional view of corporate identity valuations, a single value is usually attached to the umbrella corporate brand—as if it were static and monolithic. The value is typically expressed as a single sum resulting from a single incremental cash flow, specific replacement cost, or some other valuation methodology. A more realistic view is to recognize that a corporate umbrella brand has two primary areas of value:

- The core brand value
- Incremental brand efficiencies: the incremental brand values it earns from its products and trademarks

The sum of these values represents the total value of the corporate brand. For example, a corporate brand standing alone may be able to earn a royalty rate of

Table 6.1 Corporate Brand Identity Assets

Corporate trademark	Corporate logo
Worldwide trademark registrations	Websites
Marketing strategy	Colors
Marketing training	Worldwide public relations
Signage programs	Labeling design and copyrights

5%, and the resulting cash flow can be capitalized and a present value calculated. However, this value does not recognize the incremental efficiencies that the umbrella brand brings to the other product-specific brands or subbrands in the company's portfolio of intangible assets.

We define the *core brand value* (CBV) as the value of the corporate brand name on a stand-alone basis. *Incremental brand value* (IBV) is the marketing and other business efficiencies that travel with the brand and benefit the subbrands under the umbrella of the corporate brand. Examples of incremental value can be expressed as efficiencies experienced across a company's portfolio of subbrands and other intangible assets, as a result of the influence of the umbrella brand value:

- Distribution efficiencies
- Sales and marketing efficiencies
- Advertising/promotional efficiencies
- Regional management efficiencies
- Purchasing efficiencies

The resulting Brand Value Equation formula ($BVE_Q^®$) states that the true umbrella brand value (UBV) can be expressed as follows:

$$\text{Total UBV} = \text{CBV} + (\text{IVE}_1, \text{IVE}_2 + \text{EVM})$$

Establishing CBV and separately identifying IBVs has only recently been accepted as an established methodology. Its logic is inescapable, and a single simple example should help to illustrate the concept. Consider General Motors; the CBV is the value of the General Motors brand in a stand-alone position without regard to, or in connection with, any of the other brands within the company's portfolio. This core value is the minimal value of the General Motors brand.

The second part of GM's brand value derives from the efficiencies, cash savings, or increased cash flows experienced by other brands within the portfolio as a result of being associated with the General Motors name. For example, each of the car brands (e.g., Pontiac, Buick, Camaro, Cadillac) experiences efficiencies in its ability to purchase advertising and promotional media because of, and in conjunction with, the General Motors brand. Therefore, there is an IVE element, or advertising efficiency, associated with the General Motors brand. Another example is the incremental value the brand brings in distribution efficiencies. The General Motors brand enables the individual subbrand nameplates to experience lower distribution costs.

One has only to look at a range of multinational brands to understand the concept of incremental brand value elements or incremental efficiencies. Whether General Motors is increasing its umbrella brand value by lowering the cost of advertising for the Chevrolet brand, Nestlé Corporation is lowering distribution costs for its Carnation products, or the IBM brand is adding value to the Aptiva and

ThinkPad brands, there are clearly incremental brand value elements that accrue to major umbrella brands beyond their CBV.

■ Case Study

Recently, an assessment of the value of an umbrella brand (Brand A) in a key country (Country No. 1) that was part of an economic marketing region of eight to ten countries. As further background, Brand A is the parent company's umbrella brand in its regional brand portfolio. The parent company is a global consumer goods multinational.

The question was: What is the value of Brand A in Country No. 1 and in the region as a whole? The objective was to measure both core value and total brand value, by establishing the incremental or "halo" value on other brands within this important regional market. In other words, beyond the CBV, what were the marketing efficiencies or IVE elements?

The first step was to establish the CBV. Market royalty rates were established that would be paid for the use of similar umbrella trademarks or corporate brand names in arm's length transactions. Multiple consumer goods transactions were referenced to establish that the cash flow directly attributable to the core brand was equal to 5% of sales. A minimum 20-year useful life remained, and cash flows were discounted at a rate of 18% to get a present value of the brand's core cash flow. On this basis, the CBV was determined to be $84M.

The next step was to identify and quantify the IBV elements or efficiencies. Several incremental efficiencies were identified, including advertising/promotional efficiencies equal to 0.75% of sales, distribution efficiencies equal to 0.35% of sales, manufacturing efficiencies equal to 0.50% of sales, and management efficiencies equal to 0.20% of sales. Incremental efficiencies totaled 1.8% of sales. The present value of the incremental efficiencies over 20 years at a discount rate of 18% was calculated for a total of $29M. Total umbrella brand value equals $113M in Country No. 1, as shown in Table 6.2. ■

Table 6.2 Sample Calculation of Brand Value

	% of Sales	NPV (in millions)	% of Value
Advertising/promotional efficiencies	0.75	$ 12.08	10.69
Distribution efficiencies	0.35	$ 5.64	4.99
Manufacturing efficiencies	0.50	$ 8.06	7.13
Regional efficiencies	0.20	$ 3.22	2.85
Total IBV	1.80	$ 29.00	25.66
Core brand value	5.00	$ 84.00	74.34
Total brand value	6.80	$113.00	100.00

Conclusion

Corporate identity as a measure of goodwill can be valued. As was mentioned in earlier chapters, however, one should always look at alternative valuation methodologies. For example, if one were to value companies in which the brand identity overarches everything else, then a market capitalization methodology might be used. Coca-Cola is a good example, because it is a company with a single umbrella brand under which virtually all other activities and intellectual property are gathered. The Coca-Cola name covers the technical know-how imbedded in the proprietary recipe, processing methods, and subbrands like Diet Coke, Cherry Coke, etc. As an alternative, therefore, one could look at the total capitalization of Coca-Cola (approximately $138B as of September 1, 2004). From Coca-Cola's balance sheet, it can be seen that their tangible assets are $29B. The remaining value when that is subtracted from market capitalization is therefore attributed to the company's intangible assets and goodwill. And, because Coca Cola has one key intangible asset— the Coca-Cola brand—virtually all of the remaining value, or $109B, can be attributed to its corporate identity.

This methodology can be used with certainty only for a handful of companies in which the brand drives all activities. Even in the case of Microsoft, with a brand that is very well known, there is still a substantial amount of value in its software, systems, etc. Therefore, total intangible asset value would have to be allocated between the globally powerful Microsoft brand and the quite valuable technology assets that it controls.

CHAPTER 7

TRADEMARKS AND BRANDS

by

A. Scott Davidson

with an introduction by Weston Anson

Introduction

In this chapter we tackle the issues in trademark valuation and pass the baton to Scott Davidson. First, it is useful to get some basic facts on the table about what trademarks are, how they are used, how they are protected, and why they are valuable.

In principle, a trademark is the only government-protected perpetual monopoly that is endlessly renewable.

The nature and definition of a trademark are changing. Historically, the trademark has always been a visual representation (e.g., a logo, a device, a character, etc.). Today, we are seeing a trend toward other kinds of trademarks—trademarks for taste, trademarks for smells, trademarks for sounds. In the United Kingdom, the trademark office has registered a few "smell marks," such as for the smell of bitter ale for impregnating darts, the smell of roses to be put on tires, and the smell of cinnamon for furniture polish. One that seems quite clever is a European Union registration for the scent of fresh-cut grass to be used on tennis balls. Taste marks appear to be a little more problematic, because tastes are more difficult to define, but even here there have been a few successful registrations. In the Benelux countries, there is at least one registration for a taste mark defined as "a trademark consisting of the taste of licorice applied to goods in class 16." On the other hand, sound marks are becoming more prevalent. In the European Union, Nokia Corporation has successfully registered the tone of its mobile phones, and in the United States and elsewhere, MGM has applied for registration of the sound of the roaring lion that introduces its productions. Most recently, Harley-Davidson lost its highly publicized campaign to register the unique sound of the Harley-Davidson motorcycle.

The point is that trademarks will continue to expand; there will undoubtedly be marks for holograms and for moving images as we make the transition from a static print society to a continuous-movement visual society. In short, trademarks will expand over the next two decades, further enhancing their usefulness and further complicating the valuation process. Trademark registration can be renewed endlessly, and some trademarks in Europe are more than 200 years old. So, the question becomes: How do you value a monopoly?

The second major change is that trademark value today has metamorphosed into brand valuation. As we point out in earlier chapters, rarely, if ever, does a trademark travel strictly on its own or in a vacuum. Almost inevitably it has a number of other marketing or brand elements attached to it. These elements add value to the core trademark (see our discussion of the Brand Value Equation in Chapter 6). As a result, the phrases *trademark value* and *brand value* have become hazy and indistinct, as trademarks increasingly become "brands."

Third, it is useful to remember that multiple, similar trademarks can exist at the same time in different classes of goods. There are 45 classes of goods and services described in international trademark law. A registration for a unique trademark in one of those classes does not mean that it is the only trademark being registered in that country, nor does it mean that it is the only trademark in that class of goods registered in the world. Put another way, one can have a trademark for Acme footwear registered in class 25 in the United States, while at the same time someone else can have Acme footballs registered in class 26 in the United States. Alternatively, Acme footwear, footballs, and other goods may be registered in the United States and owned by one owner, and at the same time in Europe, Japan, or other countries, Acme footwear, footballs, and other products could equally be registered.

The issue becomes identifying in which classes of goods the trademark will be used and, therefore, protected, and in which countries the trademark will be used and, therefore, needs protection. As to value, the simple days of excess earnings calculations or a simple relief-from-royalty calculation for basic trademark are behind us. Today's process must be more complex in order to reflect the following issues:

- The monopoly issue raised previously
- The competing trademark registration issue both by class and geography
- The expansion of the definition of trademark valuation into brand valuation

Table 7.1 gives a brief description of the 45 trademark classes available under international law. These are used throughout most industrialized countries (under the Madrid Protocol, recently approved in the United States and the European Union, potentially a single registration of a trademark in a single country in a given class of goods will apply across multiple countries in that class of goods). These are topics for legal discussion, but they need to be raised here because they have an impact on any given trademark value.

Without question, trademark valuation has become the most complex part of intellectual property values: one that is constantly changing, expanding, and becoming more complex, more subtle, and more integral to every part of an industrialized country's businesses and services.

Trademark Valuation: How, When, and Why

Trademarks are valuable assets, but placing a value on these assets can be a challenging experience. Trademarks and brand names do not travel in a vacuum. Rather, the trademark is part of a larger group of intangibles, known as the *brand*

Table 7.1 Classification and Identification of Goods and Services (USPTO)

Class number	Goods	Class number	Services
1	Chemicals	35	Advertising and business
2	Paints	36	Insurance and financial
3	Cosmetics and cleaning preparations	37	Building construction and repair
4	Lubricants and fuels	38	Telecommunications
5	Pharmaceuticals	39	Transportation and storage
6	Metal goods	40	Treatment of materials
7	Machinery	41	Education and entertainment
8	Hand tools	42	Computer, scientific and legal
9	Electrical and scientific apparatus	43	Hotels and restaurants
10	Medical apparatus	44	Medical, beauty, and agricultural
11	Environmental control apparatus	45	Personal
12	Vehicles		
13	Firearms		
14	Jewelry		
15	Musical instruments		
16	Paper goods and printed matter		
17	Rubber goods		
18	Leather goods		
19	Nonmetallic building materials		
20	Furniture and articles not otherwise classified		
21	Housewares and glass		
22	Cordage and fibers		
23	Yarns and threads		
24	Fabrics		
25	Clothing		
26	Fancy goods		
27	Floor coverings		
28	Toys and sporting goods		
29	Meats and processed foods		
30	Staple foods		
31	Natural agricultural products		
32	Light beverages		
33	Wines and spirits		
34	Smokers' articles		

bundle, that travel together. Thus, we typically start a trademark valuation by identifying any other intangible assets that may be connected with that particular trademark, such as marketing-related intangibles. The list can often be extensive. Some of the intangible assets and related Intellectual Property can be part of a brand bundle (see Table 7.2).

Testing for Value

Not all trademarks have great value—some have little or no value outside the context in which they are used. For an initial assessment of whether value exists, a series of questions or tests can be applied to a trademark before engaging in the valuation process. The purpose of going through these tests is to avoid unnecessary valuation activity and to help establish where value may lie.

- The first question is simple: Does the trademark or brand name differentiate the product or service with which it is associated? In other words, is this trademark unique enough that it actually sets apart the product to which it is connected? That differentiation can take the form of identification, imagery, or perhaps implied content.
- The second simple test is to identify whether others would be interested in using the trademark, and who those other people or entities might be. Naturally, if there is little or no interest among third parties in acquiring or otherwise using the trademark, then value exists only in the mind of the current trademark holder.
- Third, we ask the basic question of whether a third party would pay a fee to license or use the name, either on a duplicate product on which the trademark is currently being used or via extension into other product areas.

Table 7.2 Marketing Bundles of Intangible Assets

Marketing Bundle
Primary trademark
Corporate name and logo
Marketing umbrella
Subbrand names
Core brand
Worldwide trademark registration
Copyrights
Secondary trademarks
Packaging design and copyrights
Trade dress
Characters

If the answers to these three questions are yes, then there is value. The question then becomes how to quantify that value.

It is critical to understand that valuation of intellectual property is *context specific*, and trademarks are most affected by the context in which they are valued. For example, in the context of a bankruptcy, a trademark's value can drop by 90 or 95%. On the other hand, if the trademark is connected with a very successful brand and that brand is about to be acquired, then the value of the trademark can go up quite substantially. Context, as well as the time frame in which a trademark is being valued, is a critical component of the process and another key test for value.

A Brief Overview of Trademark Valuation Methods

The formal discipline involved in valuing intangibles like trademarks has been in existence for less than a generation. During the last 20 years, beginning in the United Kingdom, a number of approaches to valuing trademarks have been taken. Four primary methods of valuation have found favor over time. However, only one methodology is consistently used: the market-based approach. This is the method of calculating the market price or royalties that can be obtained by the trademark or brand based on comparable transactions. It provides values that are and should be adjustable over time, and it also relates to the system of valuation most applicable to tangible assets.

Among the other methods are the cost approach, the income or price premium approach, the comparable sale approach, and the replacement value or conversion cost approach. These are briefly discussed in the sections that follow.

Cost Approach

This method uses the *replacement cost* (the estimate of the cost to replace the asset) or *trended cost* (the historical cost of the asset) incurred in reconstructing, replacing, or re-creating the asset. It is a "physical" approach. Historical costs that can be quantified include the following:

- Legal fees
- Application, registration, and other fees
- Costs of models or drawings
- Personnel costs
- Development costs
- Infringement litigation costs

It is important to remember that cost does not necessarily represent value; a purchaser of the asset will pay only an amount that enables him or her to make a reasonable return based on expected revenue and expenses from utilizing the asset.

Income Approach

Theoretically speaking, this value is the present worth of projected future benefits. Three variations of the income approach are

- Cost savings method, which depends on the ability of the client to provide accurate cost and date records
- Relief-from-royalty method
- Allocated earnings or excess earnings method

This approach necessitates three essential factors:

1. An income stream attributable to the asset
2. The remaining life of that income stream
3. A rate of return commensurate with the risk of realizing the income

Various calculations can be made with the preceding information, and some are more appropriate than others, based on the circumstances at hand. Some techniques and considerations follow:

- Directly attributable income
- Indirectly attributable income
- Relief from royalty
- Premium pricing
- Expense reduction
- Remaining economic life
- Rate of return

Market Approach

This method uses marketplace sales or licensing transactions in identifying comparable royalty rates and prices, applying the principle that true value is what another party would pay to buy or rent the asset in the real world. The market approach is comparative in nature and is premised on the law of substitution. This approach requires extensive knowledge of comparable sales or licensing transactions. For example, once a comparable royalty rate is determined, the next step is to define a revenue stream and calculate the net present value using an appropriate discount rate, life span, and annual growth rate.

Allocation of Goodwill

This method provides a rough figure for what portion of goodwill can be attributed to a trademark or trade name in an acquisition or other transaction. It uses historical trends of purchase price allocations, along with a multiple of book value formula. It is not advisable to use this calculation alone; rather it should be used as a backup for one of the other methods discussed here.

Replacement or Conversion Value

Replacement cost is the absolute minimum value that could be ascribed to the trademark, and that minimum value is based on the cost to convert or replace the trademark within the current operation of the company. These costs include converting the company's products and physical appearance, its advertising and promotion, its subsidiaries and internal operations, and so on, to another name. This approach is very straightforward and assumes minimum value with no residual goodwill.

Summary and Conclusions

Both business and legal reasons exist for trademark valuation: bankruptcy, mergers, and acquisitions work, litigation, outright sale, or tax considerations, as in the case of a donation. All require accurate valuation, which can be attained by one of three primary methods: the market approach, the cost approach, or the income approach.

The most important element to remember, however, is this: Decide what it is that must be valued. The trademark often has accompanying brand assets, such as domain names, subbrands, marketing concepts, designs, copyrights, etc. The manager of the valuation project needs to decide whether the trademark will be valued alone, or whether all assets related to the trademark will be grouped into a single brand bundle and then valued. The difference between the value of a naked trademark and a full bundle of brand assets is substantial and affects the time, cost, and effort it takes to value, as well as the value conclusions.

Trademark/Brand Valuation

In this section, Scott Davidson of Cole & Partners, Toronto, assumes the author's role in an analysis of trademark/brand valuation methods.

Overview

Under a going-concern valuation approach, one typically looks primarily to an earnings-based method (particularly the discounted cash flow [DCF] technique, which offers the greatest precision) and to appropriate market-based comparable measures of value, both of which capture commercially transferable goodwill. This section focuses on the DCF technique and on market-based methods.

Cost-based measures of value (reproduction/re-creation cost) also provide important but secondary perspectives under the going-concern approach. Under a liquidation scenario, they are of greater importance.

Maintainable Earnings and Future Cash Flows

Determination of the earnings or cash flows a business can expect to sustain in the future is an important component of an earnings- or cash flow–based valuation approach. Reference is made herein simply to future *maintainable earnings*, but the concepts apply equally to cash flows. When valuing Intellectual Property assets under an earnings-based approach, one is typically interested in the incremental earnings that are generated by the business from the deployment of the trademark or Intellectual Property asset (i.e., incremental or above and beyond those that might otherwise be generated in the absence of the specific Intellectual Property). Accordingly, references to *maintainable* herein can be thought of as *incremental maintainable* in the context of Intellectual Property asset valuation.

Quantifying the Economic Benefit Realized from Deployment of the Trademark/Brand

This section is directed primarily at the measurement of the incremental profit advantage or economic benefit afforded by the deployment of specific trademarks. It is that incremental profit advantage that is the measure of maintainable earnings or future cash flows that must be identified, quantified, and converted to a capital sum at present in order to value the trademark.

The value of the incremental economic benefit that is realized is a function of the cash flow that can be generated by its deployment and the life span and growth potential of that cash flow. In short, it parallels the maintainable earnings and future cash flows used in a DCF methodology.

Three ways of quantifying that cash flow are

- A direct assessment from review of the relevant benefits
- Residual return on assets analysis
- Relief-from-royalty analysis

These methodologies are discussed in the sections that follow.

Direct Assessment of the Economic Benefit Realized from Deployment of the Trademark/Brand

One can consider and directly quantify a number of types of benefits, as discussed in the following paragraphs. Because these benefits are quantified with direct reference to the mark, this can be described as a "bottom-up" approach. The dollar amount of each relevant benefit must be quantified on an annual basis going forward. Simple math allows the conversion of the present value of these future benefits to a royalty rate relative to the present value of contemplated future net sales.

Premium Pricing Advantage

The nature of the trademark/brand may be such that it allows for a premium price to be charged for the subject product. That premium price is the increment in price above and beyond the price that a so-called generic product commands in the marketplace. For example, a well known soft drink carrying the mark may be able to be priced higher than an unknown or unbranded drink. The premium price advantage is quantified simply as the amount of the price per unit increment multiplied by the number of units sold.

Volume Advantage

Similarly, the trademark may be such that its use in the marketplace generates incremental unit sales of the subject product. For example, consumers may choose to buy a recognizable soft drink brand carrying the mark in preference to one that is not recognized. The volume advantage benefit is quantified as the incremental volume attributable to the mark multiplied by the per-unit dollar contribution earned on each unit of that volume.

Economies of Scale or Gross Profit Advantage

With incremental sales volume, there are opportunities to realize on economies of scale in the production process. For example, longer production runs can spread fixed costs over a larger base and thereby reduce the per-unit allocation of those costs. Similarly, higher volumes can facilitate volume discounts on the purchases of raw materials. These benefits translate into increased gross profits attributable to trademark being used. This benefit is quantified as the incremental gross profit percentage multiplied by the dollar revenues being generated from sales of the product.

Reduced Costs or Operating Profit Advantage

Similarly, additional cost savings in product promotion and administrative and other costs may also be realized because of the incremental volumes being generated. The quantum of these further cost savings is quantified and included in the measure of the economic benefit attributable to the trademark/brand being valued. Chart 1 demonstrates these four types of benefits diagrammatically.

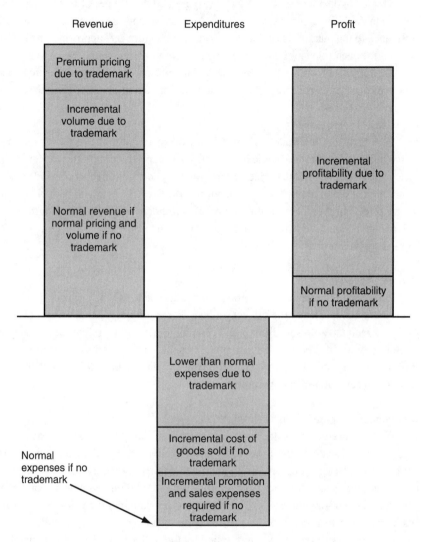

Chart 1

Incremental Profitability Due to Trademark

Residual Return on Assets Quantification of the Economic Benefit of Deployment of the Trademark/Brand

Another way to measure economic benefit that should be reflected in the value of the trademark is that derived from a residual return on asset analysis. This method is sometimes also referred to as the *excess income method*. (This method is difficult to employ in companies with multiple types of intellectual property.)

In this context, the valuator makes a review of all of the assets, tangible and otherwise, that are deployed by the business in the sale of its products. Having determined appropriate returns that need be earned on all of the tangible and other assets deployed (based on market rates of return), the remaining portion of the total profits generated can be attributed to the trademark/brand (and other Intellectual Property as applicable). That residual return is then the measure of the economic benefit of that asset.

In the context of a branded soft drink carrying a well known trademark, part of the total profits earned must first be allocated to such assets as the working capital deployed in running the business and the fixed assets used in the production and bottling process. The distribution assets, and likely other assets, would similarly be entitled to some appropriate return. The residual profits after these allocations can be attributed to the trademark/brand. Presumably, this measure of economic benefit should be reconcilable to other measures of benefit after these allocations, such as premium pricing, volume, and reduced cost advantages afforded by the trademark/brand.

Chart 2 demonstrates this returns analysis diagrammatically. The *Residual return due to trademark* box in the third column of Chart 2 is conceptually the same as the *Incremental profitability due to trademark* box in Chart 1. Conceptually, these two measures of the economic benefit should be equivalent. Practically speaking, however, because they are derived from different analyses using inputs that are subjective and unique to the business operations of the subject Intellectual Property, it is unlikely that they will be precisely equal. A comprehensive analysis using both methods would also include a reconciliation of the differences.

Relief from Royalty

An alternative measure of the economic benefit that may be attributable to a particular Intellectual Property asset is often referred to as the *relief-from-royalty method*. This method is a top-down analysis in the sense that it uses a market-based royalty rate as the starting point for quantifying the economic benefit.

Under the relief-from-royalty method, the valuator must determine what arm's length royalty would likely have been charged if the owner of the mark had to license that asset from a third party. The quantification of the benefit is the product of that royalty rate and the revenues generated from sales of the product. Chart 3 demonstrates this diagrammatically. Conceptually, the relief-from-royalty–based measure of the profitability attributable to the trademark/brand shown in Chart 3 should be equivalent to the boxes in Chart 1 and Chart 2 that represent the economic benefit of the trademark/brand.

Again, a comprehensive analysis should include both a bottom-up analysis and a top-down analysis, with a reconciliation of the results under each. Significant

Chart 2

Returns Analysis

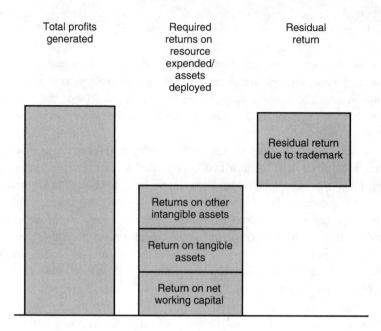

Total profits generated

Required returns on resource expended/ assets deployed

Residual return

Residual return due to trademark

Returns on other intangible assets

Return on tangible assets

Return on net working capital

Chart 3

Relief from Royalty

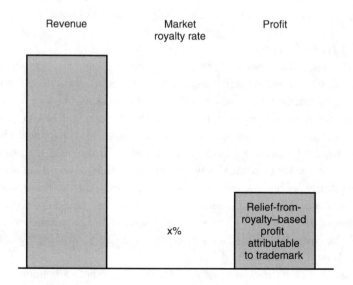

Revenue

Market royalty rate

Profit

x%

Relief-from-royalty–based profit attributable to trademark

differences may indicate unusually high or low profitability from the mark/brand or the use of external market-based royalty rates that are not appropriately comparable.

Terminal Value

Under a DCF analysis, the trademark asset will typically have a residual or terminal value at the end of the forecast period. A capitalized earnings/cash-flow method is typically used to determine the terminal value. For example, if at the end of the forecast period the cash flows relevant to the Intellectual Property assets being valued will stabilize at $3M per year, the capitalized cash-flow method would capitalize $3M by an appropriate multiple. This amount must be present-valued to the valuation date, using a discount rate commensurate with the risk that the terminal value will be different come the end of the forecast period.

CHAPTER 8

PATENTS

Valuation of Patents and Technology

For two centuries, technological innovation has been the cornerstone of the success of the American economy. The technology can take the form of patents issued, patents applied for, or other processes, systems, supporting knowledge and know-how. Taken together, all this is known as a company's *technology*. The word technology is used today in its broadest sense to encompass both patented and unpatented technical achievements.

A subset of this technical achievement is a component of value known as *trade secrets*. Trade secrets are, as their name implies, bundles of proprietary knowledge known only to one or a very few users, such that there can be protection of the knowledge even though a patent has not been applied for. This whole subject of whether to apply for patents, versus keeping the technology or technical innovation in the form of a trade secret, is worthy of a book in itself—in fact, several such books have been written. This book deals with trade secrets separately, and the reader will find an excellent presentation in Chapter 9. Here, we will concentrate on the technical bundle without trade secrets.

Patents

Patents are granted by governments and provide legal protection for a fixed period of time, currently 20 years from the earliest date of filing in the United States, as well as in most industrialized nations. Patent protection offers an incentive to a developer or innovator to work to perfect his or her innovation and then to offer it under protection of the law to other users. This process of offering the patent to others gave rise to the discipline of licensing (but also can take the form of outright sale, etc.).

In this chapter, we will first review the following questions: What is a patent? Why is a patent important? Under what circumstances, and why, does one need to value a patent or technology? What are the methods to value these pieces of intellectual property? We will close out the chapter with an actual case study.

First, let's deal with what patents are. Under United States law, a patent is the process whereby a technology is turned into a specific piece of intellectual property using due process and the legal system. The patent defines who the owner is and is granted by the U.S. government, typically to the inventor or to someone to whom the inventor assigns the rights. The U.S. Patent and Trademark Office (PTO) issues patents and trademarks. The basic patent establishes the ownership rights of the inventor, as a piece of property, and also establishes that no one else can use that patent or piece of intellectual property without permission. There are several types of patents, and these are discussed next.

Utility Patent

A utility patent is the most common type of patent. It is for any method or process, machine or manufacturing implement, combination or composition of matter, or any new or useful improvement upon earlier processes. The utility patent protects functionality and is designed to cover new methods and machinery, etc., used in the manufacture or production of any type of item (or "composition of matter"). Two types of utility patents are of particular interest, the animal patents and business method patents. Although they are just a type of utility patent, their popularity often encourages people to refer to them by these special names.

- ### Business Method Patent

Business method patents (BMPs) have become popular in the United States. The European patent authorities have thus far rejected the concept of business method patents—at least for now and in the form that we have them in the states. This is changing, and there are other possible ways to protect these inventions in Europe. BMPs cover a unique approach to processing information. Perhaps the best example and one of the most controversial was decided in the courts in the recent past: the so-called One-Click process developed by Amazon.com for customers to purchase products on-line. Amazon.com filed for a business method patent protecting the one-click process, and, in a highly awaited decision by the courts, the one-click patent was upheld. Thus, all other on-line sellers would need to take a license from Amazon.com to use the one-click approach, or their consumers would have to adapt to a two- or three-click method of purchasing products.

The process and existence of the BMP is under debate. It is possible that in the near future the business method patent will be modified or will essentially disappear and be subsumed into one of the other patent classifications.

- ### Animal Patent

For more than two decades, the United States has been issuing animal patents, which cover any living matter that has been designed or engineered with human intervention. This coverage varies from country to country.

Design Patent

A design patent differs from a utility patent in that it has a short life of only 14 years and is used to protect ornamental designs for an article of manufacture. Design patents essentially protect the appearance of a thing rather than its functionality. A hypothetical example of a design patent would be a new and unique toothbrush design.

The process and existence of the BMP is under some threat and debate. It is possible that in the near future the business method patent will be modified or will essentially disappear and be subsumed into one of the other patent classifications.

Important Issues in Valuing Patents and Technology

In a much different way than trademarks, copyrights, and other intellectual property, the value of patents is very much affected by the relative maturity of the technology. As one goes from very early stages, technology and patent applications, to fully mature and fully commercialized patents and technology, value rises on a nonlinear but fairly predictable curve from low to high as shown in Table 8.1. One of the most important considerations in patent and technology development is *stage of development*. Of course, there are other important considerations. Included among those are the following:

- The uniqueness or novel nature of the patent or technology
- The breadth and depth of the technology
- Competing or existing technologies
- Time and processing costs required to commercialize a technology fully
- The ability to protect the technology with various patents
- Size of the market and future prospects for that market
- Strategic or econometric influences on the future of the technology

From this we can see that value is truly situation specific and context driven when it comes to valuing patents and technology: developing versus developed technology, competitive versus noncompetitive patent, internal development versus external development, and so on. The breadth of the technological package is also important to value.

Table 8.2 is a review of some of the key elements that *could* be included in a bundle of technology rights. One would normally expect to find at the top of the pyramid either a patent or a truly unique trade secret (see Chapter 9). From this

Table 8.1 The Value of a Technology Bundle

Status	Value
Mature/fully commercialized	High
Developed/market introduction	
Developing	
Early stage	Low

would then flow the supporting elements, processes, know-how, formulas, blending information, manufacturing databases, and so on. Depending on the environment in which the technology is being valued, and for what purpose, some or all of these elements will be included in the specific valuation.

Why and How Can Technology Assets Be Valued?

As with most intellectual property and intangible assets, the primary reasons for valuation can be either legally based or business based. On the legal side, valuation may be necessary because of legal challenges to a patent or other ownership, or there may be litigation over possible infringement or unauthorized use of the technology or issues of valuation in bankruptcy, company reorganization, or company transfer. On the business side, the normal deal-making drivers of the valuation process exist: mergers, acquisitions, spin-offs, licenses, etc.

Most often in litigation, individual patents will be valued, although portfolios and technological bundles can also sometimes be valued. On the business side, the bundle of technology, including a patent and other elements, will more often be valued, because more typically the entire bundle of rights would be transferred in a merger, acquisition, or other deal. Depending on the context, therefore, the valuation changes.

As a brief background based on earlier chapters on methods of valuation, the primary methods fall into four areas:

- The cost method, which can include replacement and/or reproduction costs
- The market-based method, which looks at similar sales and transactions

Table 8.2 Some Key Elements in a Bundle of Technology Rights

Technical Bundle
Key patents
Trade secrets
Formulas
Packaging technology and sources
Shapes and sizes
Process technology
Design technology
Proprietary test results
Plant and production design
Product specifications
Operating platforms

- The income method, attributing levels of earnings or excess income to the patent or technology
- The relief-from-royalty method, which is an extension of the income method

In general, as the patent or technology becomes more mature and more fully developed, the market method of valuation can be used. In early and developing stages of technology, different approaches should be used—cost, reproduction, replacement, and/or relief from royalty. In Table 8.3, we lay out a visualization of the valuation methodology to be used, both the preferred methods and the relative precision of the expected valuation result (in other words, the more mature, fully developed, and market based the patent and technology bundle is, the simpler and more predictive it is to value). In very early stages, the precision of the valuation conclusions will be relatively much lower than for mature technologies. Also, in the early stages one may choose the cost or reproduction approaches to value, whereas at the upper end of the scale in developed or fully mature technologies, the market or income approaches would be used. Briefly, we review them in the sections that follow.

The Cost Approach

The cost approach is used less often on fully commercialized Intellectual Property than other stages and is most typically used in the very early stages of development. The reason for this is straightforward—the cost invested in a technology does not typically represent its true value. However, in the very early stages, value is problematic at best, and the cost or replacement method can work well.

Replacement or Reproduction Cost Approach

As an early stage of technology develops and identifiable value begins to appear on the horizon (not easily quantified but still apparent), the cost to reproduce the asset to its current stage may be an appropriate way to value.

Relief-from-Royalty Approach

The relief-from-royalty approach is useful when the developing technology is ready to go to market and one can identify the value or stream of income that can be imputed to the technology. In other words, a "market royalty" can be established as the developing technology goes to market.

Market Approach

In its simplest terms, the market approach requires finding transactions for other and similar technologies (either licenses, sales, joint ventures, or others) and then comparing those market transactions to the technology value. Although one gets the greatest sense of true market value and reality using this method, the typical problem is finding comparables that are close, if not exact.

Excess Earnings or Residual Method Approach

This method is also known, when used in a tax environment, as the *formula method* and is best applied to a fully developed or mature technology. This approach can be thought of as the earnings that are applicable to the technology, in excess of the returns a company needs to earn on all other assets. In other words, the valuation assigns an average annual percentage return on a company's tangible assets using accepted business models, and the amount is deducted from a company's average annual income, with the remaining amount attributed to the intangible assets. This annual return is then capitalized, using the present value formula discussed in Chapter 4. This method, known as *excess earnings*, *residual method,* or the *IRS formula*, has a number of variations.

Technology Factor Method (TFM) Approach

This method was originally developed some two decades ago by the Dow Chemical Company, supported by the Arthur D. Little consulting firm. Since then, substantial work has been done to refine and improve the method, and variations on TFM are being used by most reputable valuation and appraisal firms today. Much of the credit for developing, extending, and refining this approach can be attributed to Dr. Sam Khoury, formerly of Dow Chemical, and to Michael Patin, formerly of Intecap.

In briefest terms, the technology factor method is essentially a modification of the income approach to valuation. However, it attempts to measure the contribution of the specific technology or patents to the total revenue of the business. Therefore, even if a user is losing money, the method can identify how the technology would contribute to the profitability in another environment. TFM puts weighted values on 10 utility attributes and on 10 competitive attributes for that same technology. The combined weighted score is then used as a multiplier against projected cash flow, and the net present value of that calculation becomes the value of the technology. Elegant in concept, but requiring specialized knowledge to execute the technology factor matrix, TFM can be quite valuable in many instances.

Table 8.3 Visualization of Valuation Methodology

Value	Stage	Method(s)	Precision
High	Mature	Market and/or Residual	High
↑	Developed	Income and/or Market	↑
	Developing	Replacement and/or RFR	
Low	Early Stage	Cost and/or Reproduction	Low

■ Case Study

This case study looks at an actual company. Some three or four years ago, the client was to make a decision whether to develop internally or sell. Tables 8.4 through 8.11 lay out the process and progress of the value calculation. This detail offers a useful way to look at valuation using the relief-from-royalty method, not only for patents and technology, but also for other intellectual property. We hope the reader will return to this case study whenever she or he wishes to review the steps in a relief-from-royalty valuation. ■

Table 8.4 Technology Value Is Context Specific

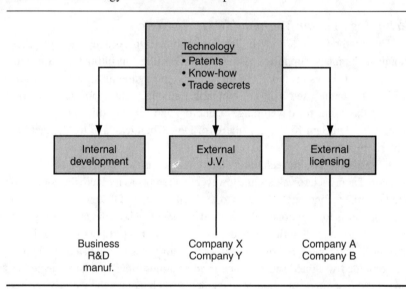

Table 8.5 Biotech Technology Bundle

Company:	Confidential
Context:	Fair market value
Components:	Organ transplant process
	Two primary patents
	Apparatus patent
	Research and know-how
Cause:	Make or sell decision
Approach:	Income approach/relief from royalty
Concept of value:	Bundled components

Table 8.6 Biotech Market Review

Three applications have been identified:

---

1. Laboratory research

2. Transplant organ transportation

3. Ex vivo organ treatment

Convoyed sales of disposables as a revenue stream.

Two applications are considered viable.

Market size, growth, share, and revenues established.

Seven-year market life, 20% discount rate.

Table 8.7 Market #1: Laboratory Research

Potential market in year = 28,000 units

Growth in market = 5% per year

Market share = 10% after 5 years

Sales growth = 10% per year thereafter

Price = $30,000 per unit

Disposables = 12 sets per year/$400 each

Table 8.8 Market #2: Transplant Organ Transportation

Transplant operations in year 1 = 46,000

Estimated growth = 15% per year

Market share = 33% after 4 years

Sales growth = Maintain 33% share

Price = Units free: $2,000 per use

Disposables = 100% of usage for the first five years,
    75% of usage thereafter: $500 per set

Table 8.9 VALMATRIX® Analysis of Comparable Royalty Rates

Licensing Entity	Royalty Rate Range			Licensed Product
Biotech company	1.00%	–	4.00%	Scientific instruments
Surgeon		3.50%		Surgical device
Tech. manufacturer		5.00%		Medical device
Hospital		4.00%		Medical method
Tech. manufacturer	2.00%	–	5.00%	Surgical devices
Biotech company	1.00%	–	4.00%	Medical products
Tech. manufacturer	3.00%	–	4.00%	Scientific instruments
Biotech company		3.00%		Medical technology
Concluded rate		3.50%		

Table 8.10 Risk Variables

- Discount rate: 20.0%
  - Average equity return = 12.5%
  - Premium needed for asset class
  - Start-up, biotechnology industry

- Duration: 7 years
  - Broad claims in the patents
  - Current lack of direct competition

Table 8.11 Valuation Conclusion: Revenue × Royalty Rate × Discount Factor = Value

	Estimated Revenues	Avoided Royalty Payment	PV of Cash Flows
2000	$451,300	$15,796	$13,988
2001	5,979,800	209,293	154,448
2002	36,057,300	1,262,006	776,084
2003	89,780,479	3,142,317	1,610,334
2004	131,532,425	4,603,635	1,966,010
2005	166,148,483	5,815,197	2,069,513
2006	205,114,793	7,179,018	<u>2,129,058</u>
Value of technology			**$8,719,434**

Summary and Conclusions

This chapter began by pointing out that the valuation of "technology" is a very loose term because of the potential breadth or narrowness of the bundle. A technology bundle can be as simple as a single patent or as complex as a family of patents applied for processes, technical know-how, etc. So, the first consideration is the size and breadth of the patent and technology bundle. Second is stage of development. Is this technology brand new? Developing? Fully developed? Mature? The stage of development has an impact on both valuation methodology and value. Third are other contextual impacts on value, such as the competitive environment, the cost to bring to market, the legal environment, strategic positioning, and econometric impact.

All of this tells us that context, particularly with technology valuation, is all important: a large portfolio versus a single patent, trade secrets and technical know-how versus a patent, early stage versus fully developed technology, competitive versus noncompetitive marketplaces. These contextual issues affect which method to use for the most accurate valuation of the technology.

Gordon Smith and Russell Parr are pioneers in the area of intellectual property valuation. In fact, their books have become industry standards. At an International Licensing Executives Society meeting and presentation attended by several hundred people, Russell Parr was asked a critical question: "Tell me, Mr. Parr, what is the best method to value technology?" Russell replied, quite rightly and intelligently I believe, "I don't know what the best method to value technology is, but I do know that in any given situation I can find and adapt the best method to value that *particular* technology."

CHAPTER 9

THE ECONOMIC VALUATION
OF TRADE SECRET ASSETS

by

R. Mark Halligan and Richard F. Weyand

with an introduction by Weston Anson

Introduction

In this chapter, Mark Halligan and Richard Weyand do an excellent job not only of explaining how to approach the subject of valuation of trade secrets, but also of laying out what a trade secret is. First, they take us through the four proofs of ownership in order to assert trade secret protected status. Second, they take us through the six factors defining a trade secret. They then proceed to the valuation conundrum—what is the best method of valuing trade secrets and how is it done?

Not only is this an excellent legal review of trade secrets and their value, it is also an outstanding review of the business and economic issues involved in valuation of this unique intangible asset group. A key point to be made with trade secret valuation is that, by definition, there can be no market comps; neither does cost/replacement value play a part: how does one replace a brilliant thought or a truly unique process? Also, because the context of value for a trade secret is usually done in litigation (and far less often in a business transaction), the definition of value is equal to damages, which in turn is equal to loss of future income or loss of current and future competitive value. The authors emphasize a key point: a trade secret can only be validated in a litigation environment.

As to the conclusions of value for a trade secret, the context again is different, since value is usually established in a litigation context. The value of the trade secret is an implied value with no tangible proof that the value would have or could have been realized. This is value expressed as competitive advantage value, and it is measured by imputing a company's competitive position or competitive value with and without the trade secret.

Because of the nature of this conundrum, we have developed a unique approach to trade secret valuation called *snapshots of value* (see bibliography). Table 9.1 illustrates the difference in value between snapshot 1 and snapshot 2. That difference in value then becomes the value of the trade secret.

Table 9.1 Valuing Trade Secrets: Snapshots of Value

Snapshot #1		Snapshot #2	
Value of trade secret given absence of effective technical competition		Value of trade secret given presence of effective technical competition	
Total market size (10 years)	1,900,000 units	Total market size (5 years)	950,000 units
Market share	100%	Market share	70%
Pricing	$250/each	Pricing	$200/each
Total revenue	$475M	Total revenue	$135M
Royalty attributed to trade secret	10–12%	Royalty attributed to technology	5–6%
Total value	$47–56M	Total value	$9–12M

Net difference in value: $35–45M

The Economic Valuation of Trade Secret Assets

The economic valuation of trade secret assets has perplexed the intellectual property bar for years. The economic and legal issues seem inextricably intertwined. We present here a method for valuation of trade secret assets that decouples the economic and legal issues, rendering the problem tractable.

Several accepted methods exist for the valuation of a property. Depreciated cost, replacement cost, fair market value, and net present value of future cash flows are all proper measures in specific circumstances.

For intellectual property, however, depreciated cost is not appropriate. The direct acquisition cost of intellectual property may be insignificant, as when the intellectual property results from a flash of insight. However, that same insight may result from the sudden emergence of an idea after years of study in the field and years of experimentation in the laboratory. Which, then, is the true cost: the negligible cost of a moment's insight or the sum total cost of the education and experience of a lifetime?

Similarly, replacement cost is problematic. How does one replace a flash of insight? By what means can one predict the machinery of invention? For patents, trademarks, and copyrights, injunctive relief is true replacement, that is, the restoration of the exclusive use of the intellectual property. But trade secrets, once lost in the public domain, are lost forever. The bell cannot be unrung. How, then, can a replacement cost even be conceptualized, much less determined?

As for fair market value, there may be no marketplace for the intellectual property in question. An advance in the method of manufacturing a proprietary product, a unique corporate organizational structure or compensation plan, negative know-how (knowledge about what doesn't work)—none of these intellectual properties has a marketplace from which a fair market value may be obtained.

What we are left with, then, for trade secrets is the *net present value of future cash flows*. This is a particularly appropriate measure for trade secrets, because the very essence of a trade secret anticipates future cash flows. A trade secret is any information not generally known in the trade, which the owner has made appropriate efforts to keep secret, and which confers a *competitive advantage* from being kept secret. The net present value of future cash flows resulting from that competitive advantage is an appropriate method for placing a dollar amount on the current value of a trade secret asset.

Future Cash Flow

Net present value of a future cash flow requires an evaluation of three factors:

- The total amount of future cash flow
- The discounted basis of that future cash flow as a present value
- The probability that the future cash flow will occur

If values can be assigned to these three factors, then the economic value of a trade secret can be calculated by multiplying these three factors together.

Total Amount of Future Cash Flow

The total amount of the future cash flow is the total amount of income over time that will be derived from keeping the information secret, as compared to the expected income over time if the information were in the public domain. This is analogous to the valuation of patents, where the economic value of the patent is the value of the exclusive use of the invention as compared to the situation in which the invention is available for use by all.

It may legitimately be asked whether there isn't a broader altruistic value in discovering new knowledge for the use of all, to the benefit of everyone. There is such value, but it is not economic value, that is, it is not a value on which a price can be put, as in the sale or license of a technology. No one will pay for the use of public-domain knowledge, so the fair market value of such knowledge is zero.

Note that there may be more than one legitimate possessor of a trade secret in the marketplace. Calculation of the net present value of trade secrets is much easier if the trade secret is an invention not known at all in the trade. Because in practice it is impossible to determine whether one's competitors already have legitimate possession of the same information and are also holding it as a trade secret, the simple calculation of value comparing the situations of exclusive possession to public-domain exposure is appropriate.

Misappropriation creates another possessor of the trade secret without the trade secret owner's authorization or consent. Under these circumstances, the damages evaluation compares the premisappropriation market to the postmisappropriation market, and plaintiff can obtain its lost profits and disgorgement of the misappropriator's ill-gotten gains to the extent not already taken into consideration in calculating the trade secret owner's losses. If other competitors remain ignorant of the information, the damages so calculated will be some portion of the total value calculated when comparing the situations of exclusive possession and public-domain exposure.

Discounted Basis of Future Cash Flow as a Present Value

The second factor in the trade secret valuation model, the discounted basis of a future cash flow, is that percentage of the future cash flow that must be invested now as principal to realize the calculated future cash flows over the expected life cycle of the trade secret. This is a traditional accounting method for the calculation of the present value of a future income stream.

Probability of Future Cash Flow

The last factor in the trade secret valuation model is the probability of future cash flow derived from the trade secret asset, which can be calculated by evaluating and determining the probability of prevailing in a civil lawsuit to defend the trade secret asset. This has been the critical barrier preventing the economic valuation of trade secret assets, because it has been widely held that the probability of prevailing in a future litigation cannot be calculated. The authors disagree with this general opinion.

A trade secret can only be validated in litigation. Until there is a judgment entered in a civil lawsuit that the plaintiff possesses a trade secret, there is no legal trade secret status. In contrast, there is a presumption of validity when patent, copyright, and trademark certificates are issued by the U.S. government. An official certificate defines the specific intellectual property right that exists.

Trade secrets, however, remain inchoate and subject to the vagaries of the litigation process. The burden of proof is on the trade secret owner to show the existence of a trade secret as plaintiff in a misappropriation lawsuit. The plaintiff cannot rely on presumptions flowing from a prior *ex parte* examination by the federal government.

Essential Proofs for Trade Secret Assets

Four proofs are required to prevail on an assertion of trade secret protected status in court:

- **Existence:** The information must qualify as a trade secret asset.
- **Ownership:** The plaintiff must be able to prove ownership of the information.
- **Access:** The plaintiff must prove the defendant had access to the information, that is, that the defendant did not independently reinvent the trade secret.
- **Notice:** There must be actual, implied, or constructive notice of the trade secret status of the information prior to the misappropriation.

Failure of any of these four essential proofs puts the trade secret assets at risk.

Existence

The identification of the *res* is critical to proving existence in trade secret litigation. What is "it" that is alleged to be a trade secret? Any information, technical or nontechnical, can qualify under the modern definition of a trade secret if the information is not generally known in the trade, if there have been appropriate steps taken to protect the secrecy of the information, and if there is an actual competitive advantage derived from the secrecy of the information.

These inquiries inevitably require a careful consideration of the following six factors derived from the original definition of a trade secret in the United States in §757 of the First Restatement of Torts:

1. The extent to which the information is known by outsiders
2. The extent to which the information is known by insiders
3. The measures taken to guard the secrecy of the information

4. The value of the information to the information owner's current operations and the value if obtained by competitors
5. The amount of time, effort, and money expended to obtain the information
6. The ease or difficulty of reverse-engineering the information

All six factors need not be present. However, the six factors will be considered by the trier of fact, and the probability of the existence or nonexistence of a trade secret can be determined only after all six factors have been evaluated and considered. See *Learning Curve Toys, Inc. v. Playwood Toys, Inc.,* 342 F.2d. 714 (7th Cir. 2003).

In litigation, the defendant will dispute all six factors, and further argue

1. That the information is generally known in the trade
2. That it was not reasonably protected
3. That it confers no competitive advantage

Plaintiff need not prevail on all six factors, but plaintiff *must prevail* on the three essential elements of the modern definition of a trade secret outlined previously. Failure of proof on any one of these essential elements will invalidate the existence of a trade secret.

With regard to the first prong of the modern definition, not generally known in the trade, experience in trade secret misappropriation cases has shown that an "everyone knows it" defense does not prevail absent evidentiary substantiation. The defendant must come forward with evidence from industry publications or present evidence from persons skilled in the art to convince the trier of fact that the information is generally known and used by the other competitors in the marketplace.

The second prong of the modern definition causes the most trouble in real situations. What are appropriate measures to protect the trade secret? The test is defined as relative secrecy, not absolute secrecy. Measures approaching absolute secrecy would prevent exploitation of the trade secret to obtain the resulting economic advantage. Relative secrecy means taking reasonable measures under the circumstances. For example, if a company has already suffered a computer theft of trade secrets, the courts expect a higher level of security in the face of this established and known threat. Courts also apply a sliding-scale analysis to corporations based on size. Larger corporations are expected to have more sophisticated trade secret protection measures than a "Mom and Pop" business.

The burden of establishing reasonable security measures rests upon the plaintiff. Security measures help the courts define what "it" is that is being protected as a trade secret. For example, if a lock box is the security measure, then the contents of the lock box must be the trade secrets. Second, reasonable security measures establish the property interests in the trade secret. Stated differently, why should the courts protect the alleged trade secret if the plaintiff has failed to protect it? The standard of care in the industry comes into play with respect to this prong. Courts will look to the security measures of competitors in the industry to determine whether the plaintiff has executed the requisite amount of reasonable care.

Finally, the third prong of the definition requires competitive advantage, that is, an economic advantage. This advantage can take the form of increased revenues or profits for the owner of the information, but it can also take the form of a reduced ability of other firms to compete effectively against the owner of the information. That is, either the trade secret owner's competitive position is enhanced by the possession of the information or the competitors' position is diminished by lack of knowledge of the information. Trade secrets also deter entry of new market entrants who must spend the time, effort, and money, go down all the blind alleys, and engage in all the trial and error necessary to compete against the existing competitors in the market.

Ownership

The second required proof, ownership, has been implied but has not often been litigated, probably because the word *ownership* is not expressly included in the definition. However, it is critical that the possessor of a trade secret has ownership or be a licensee of the owner. The intellectual property laws in the United States protect the creator with few exceptions (e.g., the work-for-hire doctrine in the copyright statute), and the plaintiff must show ownership of the trade secret. Absent an employee-assignment clause in a valid and enforceable employment contract, the result in litigation may be that a trade secret does in fact exist, but it was created and owned by the employee. The company may retain no more than a shop right to practice the inventions embodied in the trade secret because it was created with company tools on company time.

Access

Access is an important proof to secure plaintiff's trade secret rights. There is no monopoly right in trade secrets. If the defendant can show that the trade secret was independently developed, without access to or use of plaintiff's information, then the defendant has the right to practice the inventions or improvements embodied in the trade secret. Trade secret protection can only be extended to prevent actions by employees or third parties who obtain access to the information in confidence and breach that obligation of confidentiality.

Notice

Finally, notice of the trade secret status of the information is necessary. The courts will imply constructive notice in a principal–agency relationship under certain circumstances. With respect to third parties, however, failure to provide notice and to obtain an agreement to maintain the information as confidential *before* actual disclosure may result in forfeiture, and therefore be fatal to the trade secret claim. This is why nondisclosure agreements (NDAs) and confidential disclosure agreements (CDAs) must be executed before third-party disclosures. Although writing is not required to establish notice, it is clearly preferred to the conflicting testimony of witnesses in a subsequent court hearing.

Notice can take the form of *confidential and proprietary* labels on sensitive documents, a high-level description of the trade secrets on a trade secret exit interview form, or password-protected access on a computer. The failure to mark a document as confidential is not fatal, however, if it can be independently established that the recipient knew or had reason to know that the information was confidential and that the recipient was not authorized to take and use the information for his or her own benefit or the benefit of others without the trade secret owner's consent.

It is important to note that this required notice cannot take the lackadaisical form that "everything we do is a trade secret." A failure to differentiate the trade secret information from the public-domain information within the company places all information in the same class. Companies have found that when they claim that "everything" is a trade secret, the courts conclude that "nothing" is a trade secret. There is no substitute for the specific identification and protection of trade secret assets by a company.

Where does all this leave us with regard to the economic valuation of a trade secret? There are two important observations to make at this point.

First, the total value of all the potential trade secret information of a company that has failed to meet the evidentiary criteria outlined previously should be set at *exactly zero*. There is no inherent right to obtain trade secret status for information absent proper stewardship, and, absent such stewardship, the probability of prevailing on the merits in future litigation alleging trade secret status for the information approaches zero.

Second, the valuation of a trade secret is not confined to the value of the information content *per se*. *The valuation of a trade secret asset is a function of both the content of the trade secret information and the stewardship and protection of the trade secret asset.*

This fundamental principle of trade secret asset valuation presents good news and bad news scenarios to corporations faced with the task of performing an economic valuation of their trade secret assets.

It is certainly bad news to the well meaning but poorly prepared client, after the misappropriation and on the brink of litigation, that their suit has little chance of success due to poor stewardship. The good news is that the implementation of procedures for the proper stewardship and protection of trade secrets *before misappropriation* can both ensure and increase the economic value of those assets.

We present the following case study to illustrate these principles. Because trade secret cases are by definition very sensitive, this case study is necessarily hypothetical. We have combined certain common issues that we have seen in actual cases in order to construct a likely scenario.

■ Case Study

In our example, the owner of a closely held company has contacted you to perform an economic valuation of its trade secret portfolio. You perform an initial investigation and find the following:

- There is no inventory of the alleged trade secrets.
- There are no employee agreements beyond the statutory fiduciary obligations.
- There are no contractor or visitor agreements.
- Alleged trade secret information is not secured in locked file cabinets, and such information is often left out in the open on company desks in unlocked offices.
- Alleged trade secret information is stored on personal computers on which login protections have not been implemented.
- Documents containing potential trade secrets are not stamped or labeled *confidential* or *proprietary*.
- There is no secure method for destroying confidential documents.
- No method is in place to track the time, effort, and money expended in creating and developing the alleged trade secret information.
- Employee, contractor, and visitor badges are not required.
- There is no security at the front door.
- The manufacturing processes are not hidden from public view.
- Temporary workers are often hired during peak periods and exposed to the alleged trade secrets.
- There is no policy handbook on trade secrets and no training in trade secret–handling procedures for employees.
- There are no trade secret exit interviews of departing employees.

You inform the business owner that the valuation of his trade secrets has been performed, at far less expense than he had hoped. That's the good news. The bad news is that the economic value of his trade secret information is exactly zero. Although the content may or may not have economic value from not being generally known in the trade, there is little probability that the company can or will prevail in litigation. Why should the courts protect information that the company itself has not protected? The company risks forfeiture of its trade secret rights to anyone exposed to such information, who can then legally appropriate them for his or her own benefit.

The owner of the company is appalled by the results of your valuation study, shared in confidence with the client. How can this information, developed over many years at great expense, have an economic value of zero? The answer is clear. There is no inherent right or title to trade secrets absent proper stewardship. There is undoubtedly information that provides an economic advantage, but the company has voluntarily exposed it to the world, without restriction, and any trade secret rights in this information are at immediate risk of forfeiture.

The case law is replete with examples of this hypothetical situation. Many information owners find out, when it is too late, that the courts will not protect their information assets as trade secrets because the company has taken inadequate measures to protect such information or a forfeiture of any trade secret rights in such information has occurred. Information is either a trade secret or not a trade secret. Absent a patent, if the information is not a trade secret, then the information can be legally appropriated and used by others for their own benefit or the benefit of others.

However, in our example case, it is not too late to change the economic value of the assets, because there has been no misappropriation yet. In our report, we recommend, *inter alia*, that the following steps be taken immediately:

- An inventory of the potential trade secret assets should be conducted immediately. In practical terms, this will involve the preparation of a list of trade secrets with documentation of the dates of creation, places of storage, places of use, and other key information necessary for the maintenance of these assets on an ongoing basis.
- Employee, contractor, and visitor agreements should be implemented. Careful attention should be paid to both confidentiality and ownership issues, with contractual assignment clauses being implemented where necessary.
- With respect to paper documents and tangible items, procedures for locked file cabinets or other security measures should be implemented.
- Electronic security procedures should be implemented, including, at a minimum, the implementation of login protections on personal computers.
- Access to information should be on a need-to-know basis. Sign-in/sign-out procedures should be used. Confidential documents should be marked *confidential*. Super-confidential documents should be marked *super-confidential*, and access should be severely restricted.
- Locked bins should be used to discard confidential documents, and these bins should be maintained by an outside company performing onsite document destruction.
- Accounting procedures should be implemented to track the time, effort, and money expended on the creation and development of trade secret assets.
- All persons should wear prominently displayed badges while on the premises. A visitor sign-in/sign-out badge system should be implemented.
- Manufacturing processes should be restricted from public view.
- The company handbook should devote an entire section to trade secrets. There should be ongoing employee education on the importance of identifying and documenting the existence of trade secret assets, with employee economic incentives for complying with this policy.
- The company should implement a strict procedure for trade secret exit interviews.

Once the information is secure and ownership, access, and notice issues are under control, we change the zero probability of being able to defend the trade secret information and its resulting future cash flows to a near certainty that protected status will be granted. At this point, the evaluation of the economic value of the *content* of the trade secret information can be performed in the same manner as currently practiced for patents, as described in Chapter 8. Finally, the current economic value of the trade secret information can be calculated by multiplying the three factors described previously. ■

Conclusion

We conclude with a short discussion of an important further distinction between trade secrets and the other intellectual properties—patents, copyrights, and trademarks—and the implications of this distinction. The actual number of patents, copyrights, and trademarks owned by most companies is small, is numerable, and changes slowly over time.

In contrast, even small companies may have a very large number of trade secrets. These trade secrets are not so well bounded and defined as patents, copyrights, and trademarks, so they tend to blend into each other, forming an interlocking mesh of information that does not easily divide into separate, countable, and distinct trade secrets. Finally, trade secrets are created and destroyed rapidly in an information economy, making the management of trade secrets a dynamic process.

The dynamic trade secret environment of firms in our modern economy has led many to conclude that it is simply too difficult, even overwhelming, to address all of these rapidly changing assets on any organized basis. However, the marketplace demands an accounting system to track and value intangible information assets. We therefore must provide appropriate solutions for the management of trade secrets by our clients.

The computer revolution that is driving the dynamic trade secret environment holds the promise of a solution as well. Automated systems for the inventory, tracking, and life-cycle management of trade secrets are becoming available, and we must incorporate these solutions in providing quality intellectual property legal services. As these systems come into wider use, the relative standard of appropriate care for trade secret information will come to include such systems as a necessary element of proper stewardship.

CHAPTER 10

VALUATION OF INTERNET ASSETS

The value of domain names and Internet assets has become more accurate over the last decade, as users and appraisers have become more familiar and realistic with market value of these assets and the methods to arrive at that value. From a start in the 1980s, when Internet assets and domain names were relatively new and little valued, through the enormous boom of the late '90s and the subsequent collapse in 2000–2001 to today, the value of domain names has stabilized and begun to rise again as the market and our dot-com economy have returned to reality. The values and methods of valuation of the assets have also returned to reality.

What are Internet assets? They are not simply a domain name; instead, as the Internet is increasingly used by all companies and many individuals, and as the sophistication of both the usage and the quality of the assets has increased, the value and the range of assets connected to the Internet have also increased. Table 10.1 shows a partial list of Internet assets. They range from linkages to website design and from domain names to architecture and structure. Domain names remain the primary element of value in an Internet asset bundle. However, that same domain name needs a supporting Internet infrastructure, website architecture, and development to maximize value. Once again, the issue of context affects value. For example, the domain name *men.com* sold at the end of 2003 for $1.5M. Five years earlier, it might have sold for two or three times that amount.

Table 10.1 Bundle of Intangible Assets

IT Bundle	
Enterprise solutions	Data mining
Custom applications	Domain names/URLs
Data warehouses	e-Commerce sites
Master licenses	Third party software tools
Source code	Credit/payment systems
Databases	

What Are Domain Names?

First, let's review what domain names are and how they came into being. At the height of the Cold War in the late 1960s and into the early 1970s, the U.S. Department of Defense and Intelligence Agencies spent money to develop a secure communications network that could be used in times of disaster. The U.S. government was looking for a foolproof way to communicate among military groups, bases, and facilities should an attack take place. The network had to be wireless and could not function through a single center but rather had to be dispersed, with funneling of communications through multiple stations and multiple networks—in other words, the Internet cannot be on one or two central switching stations. Through the 1980s, more universities and scientific establishments began to participate in the development of the Internet. As a consequence, members of these institutions began to use the Internet and communicate via e-mail more frequently.

By the late 1980s and early 1990s, private individual users had learned to log on to the Internet, and this led to an explosion of usage in the early 1990s. By 1993, usage grew geometrically each month. The dot-com boom in the late '90s was essentially premised on the fact that domain names and Internet sites would be the business platforms for virtually all types of commerce. There was talk of strategic alliances eliminating competition, the death of retail stores, the demise of cable television and telecommunications, and the often-foretold imminent loss of privacy. At the height of that frenzy, some domain names were selling for eight figures, and it was not uncommon to hear of domain names selling for millions of dollars.

This, of course, was followed by the total collapse of prices and the dot-com boom companies at the beginning of the new millennium. Today, we see a rejuvenation of values because domain names, websites, and Internet assets are absolutely integral to every corporation's communications, marketing, and branding. The lessons learned from the dot-com "boom–bust cycle" were (a) that the assets were overvalued, but (b) that domain names and Internet assets did have value and would essentially continue to increase in value over time—it was simply a matter of drastically readjusting the base or floor value for these assets. Once this market adjustment was accomplished, we could move into a more rational marketplace, as that found in early 2004.

A domain name is essentially an address, expressed in up to 26 numbers, and the domain name itself is an alphabetized or alphanumeric format to describe that address for ease of use and identity. In other words, the domain name and e-mail address *consor.com* could also be expressed in numerals, such as *209.862.511*. Just like a phone number, this address, whether numeric or alphanumeric, identifies who or what the entity is and where they are. Finally, there are many endings to domain names that include .com, .org, .co, .uk, etc. These designations or *domains* are simply a way to subdivide the "Internet telephone numbers" represented by domain names. These various domain names enable a much greater number of registrants with easily understandable identities. Without these additional domains, we would end up with domain names that might look like the following: XQPTTDZWXRSTVBCGJIL.com. More domain descriptions are the answer to multiplication of domain names and websites.

Valuation of the Assets

To get an accurate valuation, some questions must be asked:

- Is the value of a domain name an intrinsic part of its parent trademark and therefore imbedded in that trademark value, or does a domain name produce purely incremental value?
- Does the value of a domain name depend on whether it comprises all or most of the value of the underlying trademark, as opposed to domain names that only support existing trademarks?
- Do domain names travel in a vacuum or are there other Internet assets connected to them when valuation takes place?
- How frequently should a domain name be valued—annually, every two years, monthly?
- Are the traditional methods of valuation useful for these assets, and what are the most effective and defensible methods to value domain names?

When valuing these assets, there are two different groups of value that are often taken together but can be separated:

- The domain name itself
- Its accompanying Internet assets

Let us look at each in turn.

Methods of Valuing Domain Names and Websites

Traditionally, patents, trademarks, and other intellectual property assets have been valued using one of three different methodologies: the income approach, the cost approach, or the comparables (or market-based) approach. In most cases, the comparables approach is the best way to establish true market value for intangible assets like trademarks or brand names. This methodology requires that specific royalty rates or cash flows be established that are attributable to that given trademark or brand (or to similar or comparable brands).

The approach to domain name valuations can be slightly different. Unlike other intangible assets or other intellectual property, domain names share much in common with real estate, where location is often equivalent to value. In other words, the location or description of a domain name—its exact spelling—gives the domain name some of its intrinsic value. In electronic marketing or cyberspace, domain name values are determined at least partially by consumers' ability to recognize and access the domain name easily and with great familiarity. This can be achieved using the simplest and most accurate name and identification. For example, a 10-year-old child can easily type in the domain name BARBIE.com and find the Website that he or she is looking for. However, if Mattel were forced to use a variation, such as BARBYE.com, that child would be less likely to recognize the domain name and find the location.

As in a real estate transaction, we would look at comparable pieces of property selling in similar locations. Although this principle holds true for most intellectual property valuation, in these early stages of domain names we often must look beyond comparable transactions. Most times there are no exact comparables for a sale or valuation of a given domain name. In the process of valuation, five different methodologies may be appropriate, depending on specific circumstances. Those five concepts and methodologies are as follows:

The concept of relative value: This approach is based on the premise that the domain name will represent some percentage of value of the underlying trademark or brand value. For example, if the underlying trademark or brand has a market value of $10M, one could assume that the domain name accounts for 5% of that value, or $500K.

The concept of comparable value: It may be appropriate to look at comparable transactions for the sale of domain names or similar intangible assets, such as alphanumeric trademarks. Trademarks such as 1-800-DENTIST or 1-800-DOCTORS can be used to help establish the relative value of the domain name.

The concept of replacement value: This approach answers the question: What would it cost to duplicate or replicate a specific domain name or website?

The concept of cost: In this approach, the value is based on the costs that were incurred to develop a given or similar domain name. Although it captures historical costs, this methodology does not take into account any appreciation already experienced or potential future appreciation in the value of the domain name.

Imputed income: In some cases, domain name value can be established by looking at its activity. A domain name site for a company might be receiving 5,000 inquiries (known as *clicks* or *hits*) in a given month. Assuming that these inquiries have a market value to the brand of perhaps $4 each, the income of the domain name can be established, based on projected annual levels of inquiry, income, remaining life span, discount rate, and so on.

An Approach to Internet Asset Valuation

The Internet brand value equation (IVE) is an effective way to value an Internet brand. The traditional view of a brand as having a single core value does not recognize the incremental values and efficiencies that an Internet brand gathers from all elements of its business model. An Internet brand, particularly one that is extending itself via alliances, licensing, and other leveraging techniques, has incremental value not found in traditional brands. An example follows:

Table 10.2 Internet Asset Bundle

Value Element	$M
Domain name	1.0
IVE1 = Exchange platform	1.5
IVE2 = Software assets	1.8
IVE3 = Linkages	2.0
IVE4 = Alliances	0.5
IVE5 = Databases	1.7
IVEN = Total value of IPN Brand	$8.2

$$CV = \text{Domain name}$$
$$IVE_1 = \text{Technology platform}$$
$$IVE_2 = \text{Databases}$$
$$IVE_3 = \text{Patented/proprietary business methods}$$
$$IVE_4 = \text{Etc.}$$
$$\text{TOTAL IVEQ} = CV + IVE_1 + IVE_2 + \ldots\ldots IVEN$$

The IVE recognizes that a company's Internet assets have two primary components of value: the core value and the incremental value elements. To illustrate this, we take a look at an Internet brand valuation for one of our B2B clients. The client is one that we helped to develop and that we have counseled through its successful initial phases of growth. We will refer to this as the *IPN brand*. The IVE for the IPN brand is shown in Table 10.2.

Why Should Domain Names Have Value?
Price versus Value, Now versus Tomorrow
The market for domain names can be compared to the current Southern California real estate market. Everyone has something for sale, and every asset has a price. One of the hottest games in the dot-com boom was "Can I sell you my domain name, and if I can't, can I buy yours?" One had only to tap into the nearest website for domain name brokers to see just how widespread the practice had become. Dozens of domain name brokers sprang up in the U.S. and overseas.

Registration and nurturing of domain names is critically important for key trademarks and brands. However, careful management of the domain name and its use on various websites can induce real growth and market value. This growth accelerated as we moved into the 21st century, and its acceleration continues as we depend increasingly on our digital assets, electronic marketing, and the Internet.

The very concept of valuing domain names and other digital assets, particularly ones linked to an established trademark or brand, is increasingly a major issue, not only on the Internet but also on Wall Street and in other financial and legal circles. As domain names grow in importance to corporations, service providers, retailers, and associated brands, the establishment of accurate domain name values will increasingly be necessary.

Just as in a real estate transaction, the single most important factor is location, location, location. In other words, the domain name *intel.com* is worth millions of dollars, whereas the slightly different domain name location *intele.com* is worth substantially less. In negotiating the purchase, the first consideration is of course cost: cost to acquire, cost of the seller's changeover to an alternative e-mail address, and any associated marketing costs. The second consideration is whether the seller will be allowed to maintain some signage or indication of transference in connection with the domain name and website. Another important consideration is whether the buyer wishes to acquire rights in any trademarks that are similar to or associated with the domain name. Ideally, the purchaser of a domain name, in order not only to avoid confusion but to be sure that any goodwill associated with the domain name, via the trademark, is acquired at the same time as the domain name.

There are other considerations, but one final question is appropriate here: Will the seller of the domain name promise not to adopt another, similar domain name? For example, if the seller were selling the domain name *united.com*, we feel that it would be important that the seller agree not to register similar domain names, such as *united.org*. As in real estate, however, the rule of buyer beware is very much in force. This area of asset acquisition and valuation is in its early stages of development and still has some of the attributes of the wild west.

Summary

To illustrate just how far Internet values have dropped, as represented by domain name prices, Table 10.3 is a list of domain names available for sale at the beginning of 2004. This is intended simply as a sampling and to give the reader a sense of relative value at this point in time. Values have stabilized, and we believe they are no longer dropping for those domain names that have some reasonable sense of place and appropriateness for potential users.

Table 10.3 Domain Name Asking Prices, March 1, 2004

Indiana.com	$50,000
Dj.net	45,000
Musicals.com	40,000
Granny.com	19,500
Horror.com	15,000
Friendships.com	9,000
Slots.net	7,000
Crimes.com	6,500
Soccerfans.com	6,300
Figure.com	5,888
Darts.com	5,000
Projector.com	5,000
Mrcoupon.com	1,600
Lazy.net	1,990
Enhance.com	2,000
Loveourkids.com	315

CHAPTER 11

COPYRIGHTS, VALUATION, AND LITIGATION DAMAGES

by

Weston Anson and Jennifer Sickler

with an introduction by Weston Anson

Introduction

The introduction to this chapter briefly examines what a copyright covers, why it was created, for what use it is intended, and how long the coverage of protection lasts. In addition, we look at how businesses use copyrights, what they are, and what they can or cannot be. We go on to show the value of copyrighted databases, software, and artwork in the context of a corporate or business environment. The introduction includes three brief case studies: a database, a software program, and apiece of art.

In the rest of this chapter, Jennifer Sickler covers the value of copyrights in litigation—in other words, a value based on damages award. This section also deals with the legal definition of damages to copyrights, how to document statistically those damages and the range of dollars under statutory damages that can be awarded. The chapter also briefly reviews actual damages cases based on an infringer's profits, imputed royalty rates, or income. Finally, the chapter touches on excess or exemplary damages as the measure of value for copyrights in litigation.

Copyrights Valued in a Business Environment or Transaction

What is a copyright? In simplest terms, a copyright is legal protection granted by a government for a creative idea or expression. It is specifically defined in the Federal Copyright Act as providing protection for "original works of authorship and any tangible means of expression." Many different types of intellectual property or intangible assets that are based in creativity can be and are covered by the Copyright Act. Included are the following:

- Art and artwork
- Logos and graphics
- Music
- Books
- Databases
- Cartoons
- Photography
- Software

- Characters
- Poetry

In getting copyright protection for a piece of creative expression, one is granted the broadest and longest possible protection afforded by the law. In recent changes to the law, copyright protection was extended so that material is protected for 95 years from the first date of publication or 120 years from the date of creation, whichever is shorter. These terms of protection were recently extended because of pressure exerted by the Walt Disney Company (in great fear that Mickey Mouse would fall into the public domain) and other powerful corporate interests in the music, art, and entertainment worlds.

Methods for Valuing Copyright Materials

Economic analysis of the value of copyrighted works falls into three overall categories:

- Traditional valuation (e.g., for taxes or financial reporting)
- Transfer pricing (e.g., for determination of a license fee or sales price)
- Litigation (e.g., damages)

Accounting firms and other financial service companies provide sophisticated valuation services, so only general concepts will be covered here.

Valuation methods are complicated and include, for example, the cost or market approach methods and the income approach method. Copyright value is based on a number of components, including the following:

- The current value of the intellectual property based on sales, licensing fees, and/or internal company benefits from its use
- Possible future new uses of the intellectual property

In essence, the valuation question comes down to the fair market value of the copyrighted work between a willing seller and a willing buyer. However, a copyrighted work may be valued differently by accountants and other accounting professionals in situations not involving commercial transactions, such as bankruptcy, financial reporting, federal tax, state and local taxes, and litigation situations.

How does one value the diverse range of copyright assets? In most cases, one can rely on one or more of the three traditional valuation methods: cost, market, or income/relief from royalty. Next we look at market and cost approaches in three different case studies.

■ Case Studies: Database, Software, and Artwork Valuations
Database

If the copyright act protects only creative materials, how does a database come to be protected under that act? If the database were, in fact, just a collection of facts, it would not qualify for protection. However, it is clear from the interpretation of the Copyright Act that compilations of facts, including works that are formed by the collection and assembling of preexisting materials, or data, and that are coordinated, arranged, or selected in a way that makes the resulting work an original work of authorship, are in fact protected. Although individual facts are not protectable, if the facts collected in a database involve creativity, then the resulting database as a whole is covered by the Copyright Act.

Valuations can be quite straightforward based on market comparables. The following case study show the simplest way to value a database:

- Company X owns a database with 1 million names.
- Competitive and comparable databases can be acquired for $2.50 per name or can be rented on a one-time basis for $0.50 per name.
- The average database in the industry of Company X rents its names 6–8 times before they are obsolete.
- A value can be $2.5M based on the cost method to acquire 1 million names at $2.50 each; or a value can be calculated using the income method, where the net present value of 6–8 rentals of the 1 million names at $0.50 each is discounted back to value in today's dollars, or $3 to $4 million.

Software Valuation

There are two types of software: application software and product software. With product software, we would typically use a market comparable or income approach based on data from the marketplace. With application software, we would most often use the cost approach to establish value, based on reproduction or replacement value for the particular application. Table 11.1 shows a simple cost-based valuation of a large installed application software system.

Table 11.1 Software Valuation by the Replacement Cost Method

Application	Active lines of code	Lines of code/ function point	Number of function points	Total hours	Fully burdened salary/ hour	Implied value of software
Software Categories:						
Business	1,500,000	75	20,000	500,000	$50	$25M
Operations	1,125,000	75	15,000	375,000	$50	$18.75M
					Fair market value of software	**$43.75M**

Art Valuation

Much of today's art is created specifically for consumer applications and consumer paper goods—greeting cards, posters, notepads, etc.—or for use in humorous paper goods or cartoons. In simplest terms, the valuation of a piece of artwork can be based on a stream of income received from the publishers who use that art. Therefore, identification of potential fee-based income for the artwork based on the history of other pieces of artwork should provide comparable income streams, which can then be used to calculate the net present value of the potential income for the piece of art.

For original or fine art, there can be two components of value. First, income value as described immediately above, and second, replacement or market value of the piece itself. The total of these two components of value represent the most accurate value of the artwork. ■

Copyright Value Measured as Damages

In the next few pages, we will look at valuation of copyrighted materials in a different context: litigation. Unfortunately, all too often today, copyright material is valued because it is in litigation because of alleged misuse. Basically, there are two approaches to establishing damages, and therefore value, in a litigation context: statutory and actual damages. As explained below, value based on statutory damages calls for the application of a fixed amount, ranging from $750 to $30,000, for each misuse of the copyrighted material. In unusual cases, the $30,000 can even be quintupled up to $150,000 per infringement.

The second approach to value, and therefore damages with respect to copyrighted material, is to look at the actual damages and the alleged infringers profitability. As in most litigation, it is our experience that measuring actual damages and/or establishing an infringer's true profitability is difficult if not impossible. The reasons are many—the owner and infringer of the copyrighted material may, for example, operate in a different geographic market, at different price points, or on different types of goods. Secondly, the infringer may, in fact, show no profits whatsoever from the infringing sales. Third, in many cases it is difficult for the owner of the copyrighted material to prove actual damages in any form. One thing we have found is proving profit margins in any instance of litigation between a plaintiff and defendant, on sales of infringed work, are extremely difficult to pin down.

While in principle a plaintiff that has had its copyrighted material infringed is entitled to recovery not only of the actual damages it suffered but also of the infringer's profits. However, most often putting firm, identifiable, and agreed-to numbers in place is difficult. As a consequence, an alternative approach has grown in calculating value for damages in infringement of copyrighted materials. That approach is the relief-from-royalty rate, or income approach.

Many courts are now defining damages as the value of the work in use or under license. In other words, damages would be established as the amount of avoided royalty the infringer did not previously have to pay. That amount would then be payable to the owner or forced licensor of the material, as well as any penalties, attorney's fees, etc. the court may decide on.

Copyright Infringement Damages

Digital technology has expanded the scope and frequency of copyright infringement litigation. The Internet is used regularly, for example, to pirate software, music files, and videos, leading to actions under the Digital Millennium Copyright Act. The Copyright Act, found at 17 U.S.C. §§ 101 *et seq.,* governs copyright infringement actions and preempts state law and other federal claims. Remedies for infringement are found at 17 U.S.C. §§ 502 to 507. Civil actions under the Act must be filed within three years from the date the claim accrues or they are time barred.

Statutory Damages

A prerequisite for recovering statutory damages is registration of the copyright work in question prior to the infringement. For unpublished works, statutory damages may not be recovered before the effective date of the registration. For a published work, statutory damages may not be recovered after first publication and before the effective date of its registration, unless the work is registered within three months of first publication. Thus, copyright owners are well served to register their important works as soon as possible.

Under the Act, a copyright owner may elect to recover statutory damages at any time before final judgment is rendered. The dominant view is that statutory damages are determined by the judge, not the jury.[1] The Copyright Act of 1976 provides a range of damages that the court may award. For all infringements of any one work, the court has discretion to award damages in the range of $750 to $30,000, as it deems just under the facts of the case.[2] If the copyright owner proves that the infringement was willful, the court has discretion to increase the award to an amount up to $150,000. On the other hand, if the infringer proves that it was unaware that its acts constituted infringement of copyright, the court has discretion to reduce the damage award to $200.

Statutory damages may be avoided in certain situations in which the infringer believed, not unreasonably, that his or her use of the work was a "fair use" under the law. An exception applies when the infringer is an employee or agent of a nonprofit educational institution, library, or archives. Another exception applies when a public broadcasting entity infringes (during its nonprofit broadcasting activities) by performing or broadcasting a published nondramatic literary work.

---

[1] See *Feltner v. Columbia Pictures Television, Inc.,* 523 U.S. 340, 345 (1998). But see, e.g., *Superior Form Builders v. Dan Chase Taxidermy Supply Co.,* 881 F. Supp. 1021, 1024 (E.D. Va. 1994), *aff'd,* 74 F.3d 488 (4th Cir. 1996), *cert. denied,* 519 U.S. 809 (1996).
[2] Under the 1909 Act, statutory damages ranged from $250 to $5000 immediately prior to enactment of the 1976 Act.

Factors considered by courts when determining statutory damages include the infringer's knowledge, profits of the infringer, the magnitude of the infringement, and revenues lost by the plaintiff.[3] Moreover, if multiple works are infringed, the applicable statutory damages can be multiplied by the number of infringed works. In cases in which the defendant has infringed vast numbers of works, statutory damage awards have ranged at least as high as $53,400,000.[4]

Actual Damages and the Infringer's Profits

The determination of actual damages is an issue for the jury to decide. The Copyright Act provides no guidance, however, about how to calculate "actual damages." The courts have construed actual damages to be the degree to which the market value of the work has been destroyed by the infringement.[5] That value may be destroyed completely or just in part.

One method for determining the damage to the market value of a work is to identify the revenue the plaintiff would have gained but for the infringement. The plaintiff has the burden of proving the causal connection between the infringement and the loss of revenue.[6] Once this burden is met, the burden of proof shifts to the defendant to try to show that the revenue would not have been received, even if there was no infringement.[7] Plaintiff's damages are usually limited to the net profit from the lost revenue.[8] This method of determining actual damages is often difficult, so courts also look at circumstantial or indirect evidence.[9] In addition, some courts, such as the Second Circuit, have developed more complicated methods for determining damages.[10]

Because of different manufacturing and sales costs, the profit margins of the plaintiff and defendant on sales of the infringed work are likely to be different. This is important because a plaintiff is entitled to recover not only actual damages, but also the infringer's profits, so long as those profits are not already taken into account in a recovery of plaintiff's lost profits (to avoid double recovery). Thus, if plaintiff's lost profits exceed defendant's actual profits, the damage award will normally be limited to plaintiff's actual damages.

Further, in determining plaintiff's lost profits, it is necessary to deduct the increase in costs, if any, that plaintiff would have incurred if the sales had been made.[11] In contrast, when establishing the infringer's profits, "the copyright owner

---

[3] *N.A.S. Import, Corp. v. Chenson Enters., Inc.*, 968 F.2d 250, 252 (2d Cir. 1992); *Video Cafe, Inc. v. De Tal*, 961 F. Supp. 23, 26- 27 (D.P.R. 1997).
[4] *UMG Recordings, Inc. v. MP3.COM, Inc.*, 109 F. Supp.2d 223 (S.D.N.Y. 2000).
[5] *In Design v. K-Mart Apparel Corp.*, 13 F.3d 559, 563 (2d Cir. 1994).
[6] *Montgomery v. Noga*, 168 F.3d 1282, 1294-95 (11th Cir. 1999); *Data Gen. Corp. v. Grumman Sys. Support Corp.*, 36 F.3d 1147, 1171 (1st Cir. 1994).
[7] *Harper & Row, Publishers, Inc. v. Nation Enters.*, 471 U.S. 539, 567 (1985).
[8] *Id.*
[9] *On Davis v. The Gap, Inc.*, 246 F.3d 152, 167 (2d Cir. 2001).
[10] *Stevens Linen Assocs., Inc. v. Mastercraft Corp.*, 656 F.2d 11 (2d Cir. 1981).
[11] *Taylor v. Meirick*, 712 F.2d 1112 (7th Cir. 1983).

is required to present proof only of the infringer's gross revenue, and the infringer is required to prove his or her deductible expenses and the elements of profit attributable to factors other than the copyrighted work." (17 U.S.C. § 504(b).)

What if these traditional measures of damages leave the copyright owner with no recovery and statutory damages are not available? An imputed license fee may be assessed by some courts, if the defendant acted willfully.[12] In *Deltak*, for example, the Seventh Circuit defined damages as the "value of use" of the work to the infringer, reasoning that the infringer had reduced its costs by not paying a royalty to the copyright owner. (*Id.* at 361.) In determining value of use, a court may look to prices previously set by the parties for the same or similar works.[13] Exemplary damages are available sometimes where the defendant's conduct is found to be willful.

Attorneys' Fees, Costs of Suit, Prejudgment Interest

Under 17 U.S.C. § 505, the court also has discretion to award court costs and a reasonable attorneys' fee to the prevailing party. Prejudgment interest may also be available in a number of Circuits.[14] A nonexclusive list of factors to be considered in deciding whether to award attorneys' fees and costs includes deterrence, intent, frivolousness, and compensation.[15]

■ Case Study One

This case study illustrates how a willful and sophisticated business infringer can be exposed to significant copyright infringement liability. A commercial real estate company infringed weekly issues of a newsletter of a commercial real estate broker for more than two years. Moreover, its infringing publications were distributed widely to its customers and potential customers, which customers overlapped with the copyright owner's own market.

The jury found the infringement willful and awarded $18.6M in statutory damages. On appeal, the defendant argued that the award was excessive in light of the actual damages to the copyright owner. The plaintiff countered that, due to the difficulties in calculating actual damages, the exemplary damages were within statutory limits, meeting the standard set out in *BMW of North America, Inc. v. Gore*, 517 U.S. 559 (1996). The appellate court agreed and, moreover,

---

[12] *Deltak, Inc. v. Advanced Systems, Inc.*, 767 F.2d 357 (7th Cir. 1985); *Estate of Vane v. The Fair, Inc.*, 849 F.2d 186 (5th Cir. 1988), cert. denied, 488 U.S. 1008 (1989).
[13] *Sid & Marty Krofft Television Prods., Inc. v. McDonald's Corp.*, 562 F.2d 1157 (9th Cir. 1977); *On Davis*, 246 F.3d 152, 161 (2d Cir. 2001). But see *Business Trends Analysts, Inc. v. Freedonia Group, Inc.*, 887 F.2d 399 (2d Cir. 1989).
[14] *Kleier Adver., Inc. v. Premier Pontiac, Inc.*, 921 F.2d 1036 (10th Cir. 1990); *Frank Music Corp. v. Metro-Goldwyn-Mayer, Inc.*, 886 F.2d 1545 (9th Cir. 1989), cert. denied, 494 U.S. 1017 (1990); *Gorenstein Enters., Inc. v. Quality Care-USA, Inc.*, 874 F.2d 431 (7th Cir. 1989).
[15] *Fogerty v. Fantasy, Inc*, 510 U.S. 517, 534 (1994).

found that a jury instruction permitting the infringer's wealth to be considered was not erroneous.

Nonetheless, attorneys' fees were not awarded to the prevailing plaintiff due to the size of the damages award, which already served the purposes of deterrence and compensation. In addition, the defendant had presented some defenses at trial that were not persuasive on liability but were considered by the court in assessing the adequacy of the award.

Large statutory awards are possible when multiple works are infringed willfully. The Act permits an award of up to $150,000 per work infringed willfully, which may be multiplied by the number of works infringed. ■

■ Case Study Two

A small U.S. company named Chang Imports bought stationery from China for resale. The stationery appeared to be authentic and noninfringing. Nonetheless, some of the stationery works were later alleged to infringe the copyright of a well-known paper goods company. After discovery, the evidence showed that although thousands of the cards were sold, only three different copyrighted works were infringed.

Because the defendant lost money on the sales, plaintiff was not able to prove damages based on defendant's profits. Secondly, plaintiff and defendant sold their goods in different markets. Plaintiff sold its paper goods in high-end retail stores, whereas defendant sold its stationery in dollar stores. As a result, plaintiff was not able to show that it lost sales due to the sales of the defendant. Failing to prove actual damages or defendant's profits, plaintiff finally sought statutory damages and alleged that it should receive $150,000 per work infringed due to the willful nature of the infringement.

The jury awarded $2,200 in damages, the statutory minimum. There was no proof that defendant knew or should have known that the works were protected by copyright. The jury also did not award attorneys' fees to the plaintiff, in light of plaintiff's failure to show actual damages and the defendant's seeming inadvertent infringement. Plaintiff therefore had to absorb its attorneys' fees in the amount of $215,000.

This case study illustrates how a plaintiff should focus early in a case on damage evaluation, so that the attorneys' fees spent do not exceed the settlement value of the case or the benefit of any permanent injunction. ■

CHAPTER 12

VALUATION OF COMPUTER SOFTWARE

by
Donna Suchy
with an introduction by Weston Anson

Introduction

This chapter covers both application and product software and does so concisely, clearly delineating one from the other. It also addresses the methodologies and considerations in valuation under a going-concern context. The going-concern or business scenario of valuation context is one that usually applies. As with other intellectual property, different contexts clearly affect the value of software assets. The chapter also briefly addresses mask works, some of which are best described as the series of images imposed on a semiconductor chip to create various kinds of circuitry.

Valuation of these assets is done primarily by using either the market or the cost approach to valuation. However, one aspect of valuing software that needs to be addressed in this Introduction is the chameleon-like nature of the value of software. Software, particularly application software, has one value when used by a company, and an entirely different and possibly much lower value should the assets be sold, transferred, or liquidated. For that reason, true market value is the toughest to identify for software.

An additional difficulty in valuing software is that, with the increasing sophistication of desktop computers, the line between application software and product software is quickly becoming blurred. A simple example serves to illustrate this phenomenon. When retailer Montgomery Ward was being liquidated by its creditors in bankruptcy, they requested that a value be established for the software assets and other intangibles, and then to determine the disposal value and to install a liquidation plan. The operating platforms owned by the company had been purchased from large outside suppliers. The situation was as follows:

- Original acquisition cost: $110M
- Fair value to the company in place: $140M
- Value in an orderly disposal: $5–25M
- Ultimate value in liquidation: Less than $5M

When looking at software, the issues of value usually depend on the context: Is the company solvent and using the software? Is the software being acquired in a merger by another company? Is the software being sold or liquidated? Another example of the great range of values in software can be found by looking at product or *shrinkwrap* software. In the same situation cited previously, Montgomery Ward had two well-known shrinkwrap software packages, each with approximately 20,000 seats or users scattered throughout its retail network from coast to coast. Value for these was as follows:

- Cost to acquire software: $1,000 per seat/$20M
- Cost to reproduce software: $10M
- Ultimate sale value to another retailer: $2M

As in many other situations and as with many other types of intangible assets, we find that context is very important. Although the term *market value* is a useful measure of value when, for example, application software is being used by a company, that same market value can decline substantially should the software be offered for sale.

Valuation of Computer Software

Computer software is a chameleon in the area of intellectual property because a patent, a trademark, a copyright, or even a trade secret can protect it. This chapter describes the valuation of two main classes of computer software:

- Application software, which is the software a company uses to control and operate its business
- Product software, which is the software developed by a company to be sold

Computer software[1] can be considered a type of intellectual property that has a physical form, because it may be listed on paper or magnetic tape, CD or disk. However, it is essentially still an intangible. A patent, through the use of method claims or process claims, can protect computer software, as can a copyright. When software is copyright protected, that protection does not prevent development of a different program that would perform the same steps.

The term *software* is often used interchangeably to refer to both the computer operating software and the information contained in or described by the computer software. For example, a database consists of both the software and the compilation of the data themselves. The compilation of data is basically a "literary work" similar to that found in dictionaries and catalogs and can be valued using similar methods, as discussed in Chapter 14. Similarly the valuation of other data contained or described by computer software should be approached in a manner similar to that used for the data as if these were independent of the soft-

---

[1] The Copyright Act (17 U.S.C. Section 101) defines a computer program as "a set of statements or instructions to be used directly or indirectly in a computer in order to bring about a certain result." For this discussion, I define computer software to include source code, object code, program documentation, user instructions, and operating manuals.

ware. The following discussion focuses on the computer software itself, not the data contained and manipulated by the software.

This chapter will not discuss the valuation of all mask works. This discussion could be applied to new types of mask works, such as the software application referred to as *smartcard* software, in which both the operating system and higher-level applications are packaged together as mask works. These types of mask works often can be valued in a manner similar to software; that is, similar to computer hardware and software. Neither do these remarks specifically apply to the type of mask work that includes the series of images used in making semiconductor chips. This type of mask work can be valued both as computer hardware and as computer software. It should be noted that the second type of mask work is eligible for protection under the 1984 Semi-Conductor Chip Protection Act. This protection currently lasts for 10 years but terminates if the registration is not made within two years of exploitation.

Intellectual Property Valuation Methods

For purposes of this chapter, I have used the definitions of the most common methods of Intellectual Property valuation (cost, market, income) that were discussed earlier in this book. Please refer to those discussions in Chapters 3–5 for more details on these methods.

The most common methods of Intellectual Property valuation currently being used by corporations to value Intellectual Property can be grouped into the three categories of cost, market, and income approaches to Intellectual Property valuation. These approaches include methods for discounted net cash flow, direct capitalization analysis, comparative income differential method, split profit method, Monte Carlo programs, and other simulation methods. The market approach includes methods such as industry standards, market comparables, ranking/rating methods, pricing multiples, relief from royalty, market replacement, allocation of business enterprise value, and others. The cost approach includes methods such as costs savings, replacement costs, reproduction costs, replacement/reproduction costs less depreciation (actual cash), and design-around costs. It is possible to combine these approaches to suit both the subject matter being valued and the information, tools, and resources available. In the experience of many Intellectual Property valuation experts, the convergence of multiple methodologies applied to a particular situation produces the most reliable valuation results.

Application Software

To many, application software is the software that a company buys off the shelf. To a typical information technology (IT) person, an application program is a program that operates in conjunction with and is controlled by an operating system, regardless of how it is packaged and whether it is a proprietary application or an off-the-shelf product. I will address valuation of application software that is generally the software that a company buys off the shelf. It is the type of software that most people would use in a company or personally, and it is the type of software that is most often valued by a company. For example, application software is the software that companies use to provide management controls, such as inventory control, payroll, accounting programs, sales analysis programs, personnel data, and other programs.

It is common for people who are unfamiliar with the value of application software to think that it does not add significant value to the company unless it includes extensive modifications or additions. In actuality, much of the application software a company uses, such as for human resources, is very expensive. Often a company will pay a large amount of money for the software that it needs. The company may or may not have to make extensive modifications or additions to the software for the company's specific application.

For the purposes of this chapter, I will concentrate on application software that has not been extensively modified. Although I will focus on the valuation of purchased (off-the-shelf) software, many of the concepts could be easily applied to proprietary software developed within the company.

When valuing application software, especially software used to manage a company, it is generally reasonable to use a combination of the cost and market approaches. This combination approach is reasonable because many companies purchase a base product and then make modifications as required. The income approach is not used as often because it is difficult, if not impossible in many instances, to assign specific economic benefits to specific application software. An exception to this rule would be software such as workforce management software that can, at least to some degree, be correlated to improved sales or reduced labor costs.

The market approach is favored when valuing application software because the retail price of similar software can often serve as a foundation or basis for the value of a software package. However, these costs are not applicable to an internally developed application and thus would not be included when determining the value of an internally developed, proprietary application.

The first step in determining an approximate value is to determine the base cost by estimating what would be spent in current dollars to re-create or purchase the existing asset. Certain costs that should be considered when valuing application software are as follows and should include any necessary maintenance:

- The cost of project coordination
- The purchase of a program package from a software vendor
- The costs that would be necessary to re-create the custom programs for use with, or control of, the purchased software that is being valued, including the salaries, benefits, and overhead costs to dedicate one or more programmers to such a project

- The cost to install the software on the company's computer (note that this may be considered a duplicate cost because a licensee would also have to install the application software on his or her system)
- The cost of contracting supply-company or third-party expertise to install and test the software
- The cost of in-house personnel necessary to assist the outside contractor with the installation, which include provisions for debugging and customizing the installed software
- The cost of preparing operating manuals
- The cost reflecting the depreciation in value due to obsolescence

When many of these items are not taken into account, the application software is undervalued.

Another method of applying the cost approach to the valuation of application software is to estimate the efforts and costs to create a similar asset. This can be also achieved by estimating the costs associated with the salary and benefits that would be paid to the computer programmers who would create similar code to meet similar specifications and then subsequently test the installed software. For such a project completed in-house, it is important to include office space, utilities, clerical support, and finally, the cost associated with the installation and debugging of the program on company computers. A simple example of a software asset valuation is shown at the end of this chapter.

Because the approach described here provides only an indication of the costs necessary to reproduce the intellectual property in a form that is brand new, it is necessary to adjust for obsolescence. This adjustment would be subtracted from the value assigned to the software. In determining the fair market value of computer software, it is important to reflect obsolescence, because the fair market value of computer application software can be significantly degraded when the software is devoted exclusively to a particular business. Unique application software is an asset that may have very little use outside a particular business or corporate entity and has a higher functional obsolescence and thus a lesser value.

Other elements can be considered when valuing proprietary software, including the following:

- Cost savings by the licensee resulting from the use of the licensed application, as compared to those costs for developing the proprietary software
- Time-to-market
- Potential sublicensing rights

Other valuation methods can be used besides the cost or the cost and market approaches I have discussed in this section, but the cost and market approaches are the most commonly applied. Sometimes it is possible or even desirable to use income valuation techniques.

Product Software

Product software is the software produced by a company for sale. Because it may represent a significant portion of the company's inventory, product software is more easily recognizable as software that must be valued. An example of product software would be a word processing program or database program produced to be sold as application software. Product software can be valued using various methods, including a market approach to the extent it is possible to ascertain the value of the Intellectual Property in other, similar transactions. The market approach is often favored because companies set the price of the product software based on market demand and available supply (or suppliers). This standard pricing technique is often referred to as market *comparison pricing*. I will discuss the market approach of valuing product software assets, because the price of most product software is set by the demand supply curve.

First, here is a general comment on the market approach when used for valuing computer software and, specifically, product software: in order to utilize the market approach, it is necessary to ascertain the value of similar product software in comparative deals, hereafter called similar *transactions*. Although all intellectual property (including software) is unique, key insights can be gained in developing a database of comparable transactions. Key elements to understand include the following:

- The industry in which the transaction took place
- The nature of the Intellectual Property licensed
- Rights transferred and retained
- Other nontransactional information (such as settlement of litigation),
- Many other factors

It is difficult for a company to have this level of understanding unless the company has licensed or transferred similar intellectual property in the past. When the market approach is applied in this manner, using a few past experiences, it is sometimes referred to as a *quasi–market approach*. This approach is often quite effective. Although it is true that finding and relying on public information about similar licensing transactions is difficult, most companies can build and use a database of historical transactions. Eventually, a company can do a real market valuation utilizing the company's historical licensing information. It is possible to combine valuation approaches to suit both the subject matter being valued and the information, tools, and resources available. In the experience of many Intellectual Property valuation experts, the use of multiple methodologies applied to a particular valuation problem produces the most reliable valuation results.

For example, a company develops software for the marketplace and charges $1M for that development because it is considered to be the "market" value. The following discussion considers the valuation of product software from the point of view of the producer or original vendor of the software. It is also possible to approach this from the viewpoint of the buyer and include the value of the software set by the retailer, but that would involve some additional valuation steps that are not discussed here. It is always important to consider commercial profits and any prospects of growth for the product, as well as investment risks that could apply to the product's development.

The cost approach can be used for valuing product software in a manner similar to that described previously, by summing all the costs associated with re-creating the product software. As discussed in the application software section of this chapter, this would include the salary and benefits for programmers, as well as other associated development costs. Unfortunately, if the cost approach is used alone, the value derived does not consider some of the more important factors that apply to valuation of what would be proprietary and thus licensable product software, including the profits that come from its sale and growth potential. Neither does the value derived include the investment risks that are inherent in predicting future market needs and demand. Using the cost approach requires an accurate estimate of future unit sales in order to estimate a cost per unit, so it is often difficult to apply the cost approach early in the development of product software. Thus, many prefer to use the cost approach in conjunction with the income approach or the market approach discussed earlier.

Other Methods and Simple Examples

Other valuation methods that may be useful to value computer software include the income approach, which allows the incorporation of profits, growth potential, and investment risk into the final value. Other valuation methods can incorporate relief from royalty and discounted rate of return from potential licensing profits if the software is to be licensed.

Cost Approach Example as Applied to Application Software
Summary of the steps:

1. Estimate the number of hours it would take to recreate the software.
2. Determine the weighted average software development cost per hour.
3. Calculate the value of the software to a buyer, based on these trial and cost estimates.

Examples of each step are provided in the tables that follow.

The calculated replacement cost of $1,761,750 has not been adjusted for tax effects. These effects should be taken into account when accounting for a deduction related to both the tax benefit of the cost of labor and the amortization of a purchased software asset.

Table 12.1 Estimate the Number of Hours It Would Take to Recreate the Software

Modules	Lines of code	Lines of code per hour	Hours to recreate
Module 1	120,000	30	4,000
Module 2	160,000	40	4,000
Module 3	176,750	35	5,050
Total	456,750		13,050

Table 12.2 Determine the Weighted Average Software Development Cost Per Hour

Function	Number of people	Hourly rate
Project manager	1	$200
Systems analyst	2	$175
Technical writer	1	$150
Programmers	4	$125
Support	2	$75
Total/weighted average	10	$135

Table 12.3 Calculate the Value of the Software to a Buyer

Number of hours to re-create	13,050
Times: hourly rate	$135
Replacement cost	$1,761,750*

*When a calculated replacement cost needs to be adjusted for tax effects, such as when accounting for a deduction related to both the tax benefit of the cost of labor and the amortization of a purchased software asset, the tax effects can be taken into account, as shown here in an alternative tax application to the preceding example:

A simple example of a tax application applied to the preceding example is as follows:

Replacement cost	$1,761,750
Less: Taxes (40%)	($704,700)
After-tax value before amortization tax benefit	$1,057,050
Amortization tax benefit	$400,000
Fair market value of subject software	$1,457,050

Market Approach as Applied to Application Software

Summary of the steps:

1. Identify comparable software products.
2. Determine pricing for comparable software package(s).
3. Compute the value of the subject software by applying comparable pricing to the projected use of the subject software.

Examples of each step are provided in the tables that follow.

Table 12.4 Identify Comparable Software Products

Comparable software [list key aspects]	Base features	Software scalability (XML)	Interfacing	Activity-based management	Opportunity-based routing
Subject software	×	×	×	×	×
Comp #1	×		×		×
Comp #2	×	×	×	×	×
Comp #3	×	×	×		
Comp #4	×	×	×		

Table 12.5 Determine Pricing for Comparable Software Package(s)*

Type of Fee	Comp #2 Pricing
Initial costs and other up-front fees, such as installation costs	$50,000
Seat fees [licensing fees]: Back office users	$1,000/back office user/year
Field users	$300/field user/year
Maintenance	30% of seat fees

*Table 12.5 shows package number 2 (shown in Table 12.4 as Comp #2) because it is the most similar to the asset being valued.

Table 12.6 Compute the Value of the Subject Software by Applying Comparable Pricing to the Projected Use of the Subject Software

Type of Fee	Comp #2 Pricing	Number of Users	Total
Initial costs and other up-front fees, such as installation costs	$50,000	N/A	$50,000
Seat fees [licensing fees]:			
Back office users	$1,000/ back office user/year	5	$1,000 × 5 = $5,000 $5,000 ÷ .20 = $25,000
Field users:	$300/field user/year	100	$300 × 100 = $30,000 $30,000 ÷ .20 = $150,000
Maintenance	30% of seat fees	N/A	($25,000 + $150,000) × 30% = $52,500
Total			$277,500

CHAPTER 13

VALUATION OF NONCOMMERCIALIZED TECHNOLOGY: UNDERSTANDING INTELLECTUAL PROPERTY RIGHTS AND VALUE CONTRIBUTION

by

Carmen Eggleston

with an introduction by Weston Anson

Introduction

In this chapter, Carmen Eggleston provides a unique view of a uniquely challenging valuation environment: the valuation of noncommercialized technology. In valuing these particular intangible assets, the question becomes: How do you value an unproven, nonspecific asset that has only possible value when there is no certainty that any value will ever accrue? Where such uncertainty reigns, how is valuation possible? Will the traditional methods of valuation, such as the income, cost, or market approach, adequately establish reasonable value for an uncertain future?

With noncommercialized technology—whether chemical, software, or mechanical—the usual methods of valuation typically cannot be applied. One cannot use the market approach—how does one define market comparable transactions for technology that has not yet been propagated? The income approach is equally difficult because there is no absolute certainty that the noncommercialized technology will ever generate any income. Finally, the cost approach is usually not adequate to assess the technology, because the cost approach looks only at historical investments—it does not establish future potential value.

This chapter attacks this conundrum in a number of ways and illustrates two unique but proven techniques for valuation: decision tree/probability tree analysis and the Monte Carlo technique. Each of these is based on statistical and analytical approaches to valuation in complex situations fraught with uncertainty. Each technique looks at multiple possible scenarios and then assesses the likelihood or probability that a range of scenarios will come to pass. In essence, the weighted average value of those future probable scenarios becomes the value conclusion for the noncommercialized technology.

These two approaches are particularly useful with multistage technologies, such as pharmaceuticals. They are also useful when attempting to value a fully developed technology that has not yet been brought to market, to assess the likelihood of whether the market can or might support a product launch for a fully developed technology and therefore generate sufficient value.

Probability analyses like these are widely used in venture capital situations to assess the likelihood of whether an investment (not necessarily in technology) will pay off in the future. As applied to technology, this chapter takes us through four examples of the application of the decision tree and Monte Carlo analyses.

Valuing Noncommercialized Technology

The first step in any intellectual property (Intellectual Property) valuation is to obtain an understanding of the specific Intellectual Property rights that are being valued and where the rights are protected. In addition, it is equally important to understand how the Intellectual Property contributes value to the business. This value usually can be placed into one of four general categories:

- **Exclusivity value:** An Intellectual Property asset allows for an exclusive market, premium product pricing, increased market share in an existing market, enhanced customer satisfaction, or reduced manufacturing costs.
- **Defensive value, or freedom to operate:** The Intellectual Property asset contributes to an Intellectual Property arsenal by discouraging lawsuits by rivals or providing the ability to compete in a market where there is extensive protected technology.
- **Trading value:** The value is realized by entering into licenses or by sale.
- **Option value:** There are opportunities to develop and protect future Intellectual Property assets.

It is also important to remember that even though a technology can be superior to other existing technologies, there is no guarantee that the technology will be successful in the marketplace and derive a high value. There are numerous examples of how the best technology did not win the product race. For example, the Betamax format was generally thought to be the superior technology for making video recordings, but the VHS format became the industry standard. Another example is WordPerfect and Microsoft Word word-processing software. Many in the industry thought that WordPerfect was the superior product; however, sales of Microsoft Word have made it the dominant word-processing software in the market.

Finally, it may be important to determine whether the Intellectual Property asset is more valuable on a standalone basis or as part of a larger group of assets. Unlike most tangible assets, Intellectual Property assets often need to be packaged with other assets to maximize value. This packaging can take place horizontally, based on the type of Intellectual Property (i.e., all trademarks and logos), or vertically by product or business lines. It is important to understand the purpose of the valuation before considering whether to value the Intellectual Property asset on a standalone basis or as part of a large bundle of assets.

Specialized Approaches to Noncommercialized Technology

Technology that has not yet been commercialized presents a unique challenge to valuation. The application of the traditional income, asset, and market approaches to valuation of noncommercialized Intellectual Property can be difficult because of the uncertainty regarding whether the technology will be developed successfully, the amount of capital needed to finalize the development, and the market acceptance of the developed product. The traditional approaches can be limiting because they do not account for the multiple outcomes. For situations such as these, advanced valuation techniques, such as decision tree and Monte Carlo analyses, may be more appropriate ways of valuing products and processes in development. This is especially true when the owner of the noncommercialized technology is a company with limited funds that may not have sufficient capital to complete the technology's commercialization. Under this scenario, value will be realized only if a buyer or investor decides to risk the upfront expenditure of the necessary research and development funds for a chance to commercialize the technology in the future.

Decision Tree Analysis

In general, decision trees, sometimes referred to as *probability trees*, are useful tools that aid in determining the probability of the outcomes of various courses of action. They provide a highly effective structure from which different alternatives, along with the outcome of each alternative, can be examined. In addition, a decision tree creates a picture of the risks and rewards associated with each possible course of action, which makes the tree both visually and conceptually appealing. When applying decision tree analysis to Intellectual Property valuations, the traditional discounted cash flow method is used, and then expanded on with a decision tree analysis. The best way to illustrate this method is through examples.

Example 1

A noncommercialized pharmaceutical product is in the preclinical stage. In order to value the technology, it is necessary to evaluate the additional stages the product will go through in the process of getting FDA approval and the multiple possible outcomes.

A decision tree analysis can be used to determine the value associated with each of the multiple outcomes. First, the estimated development costs are calculated by separating the product's development cycle into the remaining stages of development: phase I, phase II, phase III, BLA filing, and product launch/approval. Each stage is assigned a probability that the company will incur those costs. Estimating and assigning realistic probabilities for reaching and completing each of the stages is the essence of the decision tree valuation method. Then, the discounted cash flow (DCF) model or net present value (NPV) model is used to determine the discounted operating income from the launch of the product. This amount is multiplied by the expected probability of having a commercial product.

The final value of the expected profitability of the product less the estimated development costs is the weighted average probability of the various outcomes. See Figure 13.1.

Discounted operating income from successful product launch							$ 100,000
× FDA approval probability							2%
Adjusted operating income							2,000
Less: estimated development costs							(1,655)
Estimated fair market value on indication							$345

| Clinical trials | | | BLA filling | Product launch approval | Total Costs through end stage | Probability of incurring costs | Costs incurred |
Phase I	Phase II	Phase III					
$500					$500	56%	$280
$500	$1,000				$1,500	27%	$405
$500	$1,000	$2,000			$3,500	8%	$280
$500	$1,000	$2,000	$3,000		$6,500	6%	$390
$500	$1,000	$2,000	$3,000	$3,500	$10,000	3%	$300
					TOTAL	100%	$1,655

Figure 13.1 Example 1 Illustrated.

Example 2

A software development company has as its major asset application software in the final stage of development. Although there is an existing customer base, it is not sufficient to cover the company's operating expenses. Therefore, the valuation needs to consider the potential for completion of the product and the expansion of the customer base.

A DCF valuation method can be used to determine the company's value under three different scenarios: highly successful, moderately successful, and unsuccessful. A probability of occurrence is estimated for each scenario. The probabilities are then applied to the respective DCF value derived under the three scenarios to determine the weighted DCF valuation for each scenario. The value of the company is the weighted average DCF of the three scenarios. See Figure 13.2.

Although the appeal of this method is that it allows for multiple potential outcomes, its problem lies in the difficulty in determining the appropriate probabilities to assign to the different outcomes. This is particularly true when considering new, unique technologies for which there is no established track record. Even when historic information is available for similar projects, it is difficult to use historic information and make correlations to predict success and failure probabilities. In addition, sometimes the sheer volume of potential outcomes can make the analysis unmanageable.

Scenario	Description	Unweighted DCF valuation	Probability	Weighted DCF valuation
1	Continued investment in business for a limited time horizon. Sales are not successful and profitability is not realized. Business is discontinued.	($1,500,000)	45%	($675,000)
2	Company is moderately successful in selling its product. There are financial resources to weather product development and product launch.	$1,000,000	40%	$400,000
3	Company experiences robust sales growth.	$4,000,000	15%	$600,000
		TOTAL	100%	$325,000

Figure 13.2 Example 2 Illustrated.

Monte Carlo Analysis

Monte Carlo techniques have long been used with engineering and science applications. Recently, they have gained widespread use with business applications to evaluate how possible future outcomes can affect a decision in the present. Monte Carlo analysis was named after Monte Carlo, Monaco, where the casinos contain games of chance (i.e., games that exhibit random behavior). This random behavior is similar to how a Monte Carlo analysis selects random input values to determine a range of possible outcomes.

Monte Carlo analysis is an analytical method that simulates a real-life system in order to analyze the effects of varying inputs and outputs. Traditional DCF models have limitations associated with the imprecise treatment of risk and the lack of information they provide (i.e., the analysis is based on single-value estimates of variables that drive projected revenues and costs). Monte Carlo analysis, on the other hand, works well with Intellectual Property valuations that contain numerous what-if scenarios and unknowns related to the future development of a technology. It is used to consider the intrinsic uncertainty in the underlying earnings potential of Intellectual Property assets. Monte Carlo is especially useful when the impact of multiple scenarios and unknowns would not be properly captured in a static spreadsheet calculation, such as a traditional DCF model or a decision tree analysis.

For noncommercialized Intellectual Property assets, the unknown variables can include (but are not limited to) the capital investment necessary to develop a technology successfully, the length of time until a technology would be ready to market, the size of the potential markets, potential product or licensing revenues, and the appropriate discount rate. A Monte Carlo analysis allows a user to assign acceptable ranges and probabilities to each of the key variables. The Monte Carlo analysis then runs a simulation that calculates various scenarios of the DCF model by randomly picking values from the probability distributions for each of the key variables and then incorporates the variables that it picks in each randomly generated scenario. The result of the analysis is a distribution of the present values of the many possible future outcomes. This is in contrast to the single-value answer that the traditional DCF method provides.

However, the uncertainty inherent in the single-answer DCF method is not solved by the application of Monte Carlo analysis. Instead, Monte Carlo analysis is a tool that is used in an attempt to identify and characterize future outcomes and interpret the present value of all possible outcomes. The range of potential outcomes provides guidance on the value of the overall opportunity to finalize development of the Intellectual Property asset. The following example provides an illustration of applying Monte Carlo analysis to Intellectual Property valuation.

Example 1

In this example, a DCF/NPV model is created based on a five-year forecast. Certain variables—such as year 1 revenue; annual growth rate; cost of goods sold (COGs); selling, general, and administrative (SG&A) and research and development (R&D) expenses; and discount rate—are entered into the model, and an NPV is calculated based on the inputs. It is important to note that COGS and SG&A and R&D are estimated as a percentage of revenue in order to keep the model simple.

Under the Monte Carlo analysis, a distribution type and a range of values are selected for each of the input variables. In addition, the number of time trials or iterations is chosen in order to determine how many different outcomes are to be tested and calculated. For example, if 500 time trials are selected, the NPV model is calculated 500 times, but each time a different combination of input variables, within the specified ranges, is used to determine 500 different outcomes. For the example shown in Figure 13.3, 1,000 trials were selected. See Figure 13.4 for the assumptions and ranges of each of the key input variables.

Based on calculating the NPV over 1,000 iterations while varying the input variables for each iteration, the mean NPV is $13,985,952.

Conclusion

Traditional valuation methods are not always adequate to perform reliable valuations on emerging and noncommercialized technologies. This can be caused by the inability of traditional methods to consider adequately the multiple outcomes that are possible with new technologies that have not yet been commercialized or proved in the marketplace. decision tree analysis and Monte Carlo analysis allow for consideration of multiple outcomes and may be the best valuation methodologies in certain situations. Decision tree analysis assigns varying probabilities to the various possible outcomes; Monte Carlo recalculates and runs a simulation a specified number of times while changing the key input variables to determine a range of possible outcomes.

Inputs

Year 1 revenue	$10,000,000
Growth rate	10%
COGS (% of revenue)	35%
SG&A & R&D (% of revenue)	30%
Discount rate	15%

Model

	Year 1	Year 2	Year 3	Year 4	Year 5
Revenues	$10,000,000	$11,000,000	$12,100,000	$13,310,000	$14,641,000
COGS	$3,500,000	$3,850,000	$4,235,000	$4,658,500	$5,124,350
SG&A & R&D	$3,000,000	$3,300,000	$3,630,000	$3,993,000	$4,392,300
Operating profits	$3,500,000	$3,850,000	$4,235,000	$4,658,500	$5,124,350
Present value factor	0.8696	0.7561	0.6575	0.5718	0.4972
PV of operating profits	$3,043,478	$2,911,153	$2,784,581	$2,662,512	$2,547,708

NPV	$13,950,433

Figure 13.3 DCF/NPV Model.

Assumption: Year 1 Revenue

Normal distribution with parameters:
    Mean   10,000,000
    Standard deviation   1,000,000

Selected range is from −Infinity to +Infinity

Year 1 Revenue

7,000,000   8,500,000   10,000,000 11,500,000 13,000,000

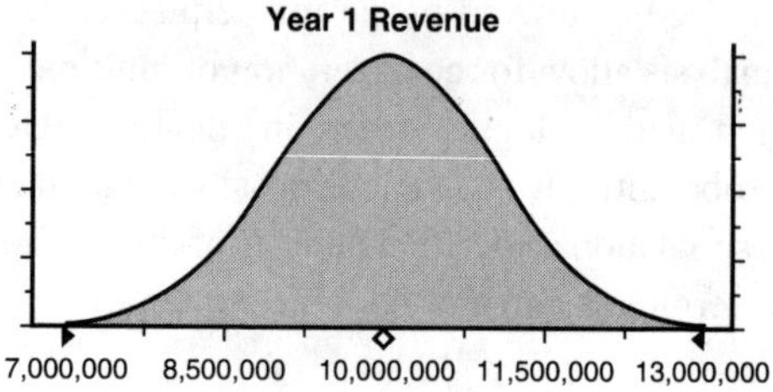

Assumption: Growth Rate

Uniform distribution with parameters:
    Minimum   5%
    Maximum   15%

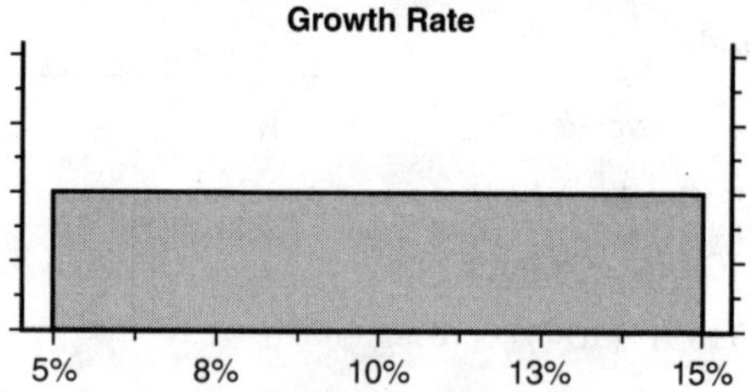

Growth Rate

5%   8%   10%   13%   15%

Assumption: COGS
(Percentage of Revenue)
Triangular distribution with parameters:
    Minimum   30%
    Likeliest   35%
    Maximum   40%

Selected range is from 30 to 40%

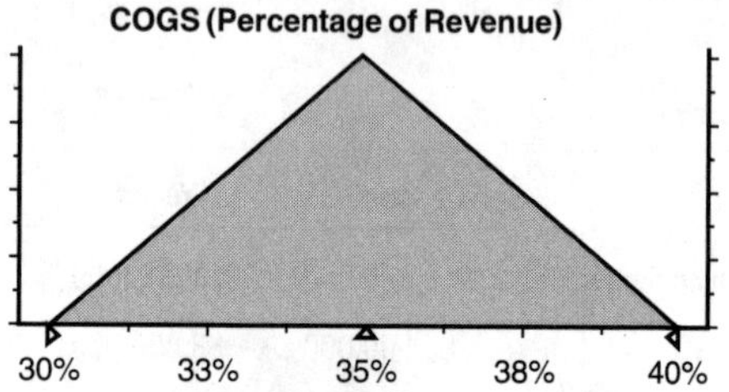

COGS (Percentage of Revenue)

30%   33%   35%   38%   40%

Assumption: SG&A and R&D
(Percentage of Revenue)
Triangular distribution with parameters:
    Minimum   25%
    Likeliest   30%
    Maximum   35%

Selected range is from 25 to 35%

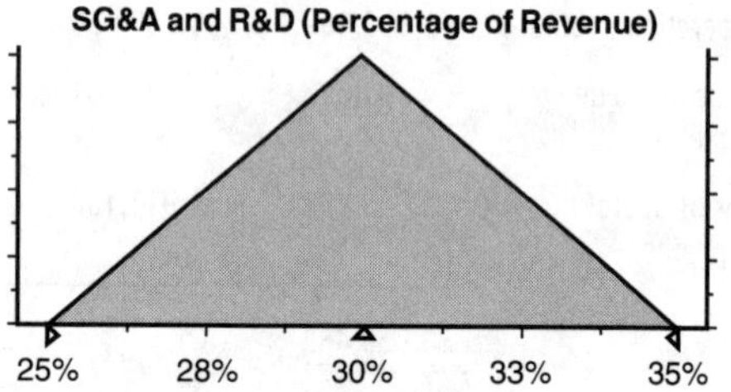

SG&A and R&D (Percentage of Revenue)

25%   28%   30%   33%   35%

Assumption: Discount Rate

Normal distribution with parameters:
    Mean   15%
    Standard deviation   2%

Selected range is from −Infinity to +Infinity

Discount Rate

10%   13%   15%   17%   19%

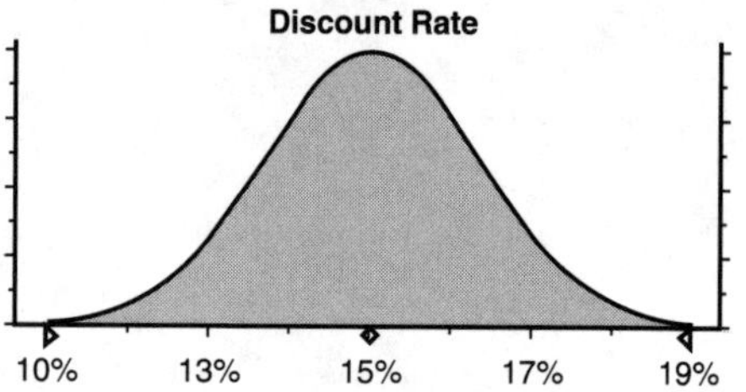

Figure 13.4   Monte Carlo Assumptions.

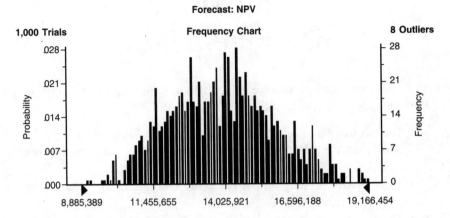

Figure 13.5 Monte Carlo Analysis Output.

Display range is from $8,885,389 to $19,166,454.
Entire range is from $8,677,340 to $23,124,933.
After 1,000 trials, the standard error of the mean is 62,684.
Mean: $13,985,952
Median: $13,949,059

CHAPTER 14

OTHER INTANGIBLE ASSETS

The very title "Other Intangible Assets" tells us something about the difficulties of covering this particular subject:

- The fact that the so-called other intangbile assets do not conveniently fall into one standard definition or another means that they are difficult to deal with.
- "Other assets" usually do not fall easily into one of the valuation approaches or categories.
- The market for these assets is more difficult to identify and often more difficult to quantify.
- Finally, these other assets, by implication, are often unique and, therefore, may have little value outside their current context. As a consequence, while these other intangible assets may have value within a company, in a disposal or liquidation scenario value they may be smaller or, in some cases, nonexistent.

Once again, context of the valuation is all important, particularly in this area.

It is not possible to provide a list of all of the other intangible assets. By the very definition of these assets, such a list could not be completed. Every company has unique intangible assets of some sort. Some are important; some have true market value and some do not. Similarly, some of the other assets are easy to define, but many are not. Some are, therefore, easy to quantify, and others are impossible to quantify. The short list in this chapter is intended simply as a sampling of what other assets might comprise. It is not meant to be exhaustive, but simply to open the reader's imagination to the possibilities. The reader should also see the discussion and list of other assets in Parts I and II in this primer and, in particular, refer to the list of assets and the groupings or bundles described in Chapter 2.

The Valuation of Unique Assets Included in Other Intangibles

Often times, other intangibles are grouped together because they are unusual and often unique, sometimes designed for one particular company (although there can be other users and purchasers). Because the list of these assets is different for each company, it is impossible to generalize how to value other intangible assets. Valuation of these assets is always done on a case-by-case basis. In assignments for our clients, individual assets are valued on their own merits. Therefore, valuation on a case-by-case basis is the rule that we have adopted. However, there are some general rules for valuation of other intangible assets:

- Because these assets tend to be unique to a company, it is unlikely that there is an active marketplace of comparable assets, so the market approach to valuation is not available—or is highly problematic at best.
- Income approaches, such as relief from royalty, can be used in some cases, such as valuing franchise rights. However, often a royalty rate cannot be established for a unique asset, such as shelf facings in retail stores. Income levels can, however, be established for some of these other assets, as we discuss later.
- In most cases, a cost or replacement approach to valuation is best. These approaches reflect the highest degree of reality and provide valuations either on the basis of what the Intellectual Property owner has spent to develop the property or on the basis of what he or she would have to spend to replace the property.
- Resale markets for these assets are thin, highly illiquid, and extremely volatile.
- There is a much wider range of uncertainty of value, and in our estimation the value of these assets should always be stated as a range of value.

In addition, we believe that two values should always be calculated for these assets: The first should be an in-place or going-concern value, and the second should be a liquidation or disposal value.

There are, however, a few areas with relatively stable valuation components and relatively stable marketplaces against which the assets can be valued. These include the following:

- Databases that have an open and liquid market
- Franchise rights that have a less liquid but nonetheless active market
- Concession rights (e.g., airport food catering) that have definable values
- Other supply and distribution contracts to which a defined value or income stream can be assigned

Case Studies

Because most of the standard valuation rules are out of consideration in this area, and because valuation is usually done on a case-by-case and company-by-company basis, the best way to illustrate valuation of these assets is through two case studies. These are actual companies whose names have been removed in order to maintain confidentiality. In the first case, a client asked us to value all of the intangible assets connected with its vehicle rental businesses. In the second case, a global health and beauty care company asked us to value the assets of a company it had acquired in North America that sells professional hair care products.

■ Case Study 1

Table 14.1 describes the primary intellectual assets of Company A. In addition to the trademarks in North America and overseas, which were valued using an appropriate relief-from-royalty method, the franchise rights, reservation systems, etc., required their own individual valuations. The franchise rights have substantial value because approximately one quarter of the company's outlets were operated by franchisees, and these franchisees generate substantial income and can be used as a future growth lever. The international franchise rights are even more valuable because there are large and growing franchise operations in overseas markets, particularly in Europe but also in Japan, and emerging markets in Latin America. As a result, current income and future growth potential are substantial. For both these franchise rights assets, we used two approaches:

- An income approach based on looking at current and future revenues from franchisees
- A market approach based on the sale of franchise groups from one company to another

Table 14.1 Company A: Vehicle Rental

Asset description	Primary methodology	Secondary methodology
Trademarks (North America)	Relief from royalty	Market
Franchisee rights (North America)	Income	Market
Trademarks (international)	Relief from royalty	Market
Franchisee rights (international)	Income	Market
Reservation system	Market approach	Cost
Airport concession rights	Market approach	Cost
Mailing list and consumer database	Market approach	Cost

The other key assets controlled by the company were its reservation system, airport concession rights, mailing lists, and consumer databases. The concession rights consist of coveted long-term leases within all major airports across America and the world. These airport counter rights, as well as concession rights for parking areas, are valuable not just to car rental companies but to a number of other parking operators and service suppliers to airport travelers. However, because of the specialized nature of these rights, there are only a handful of possible acquirers, coming from the vehicle rental business and related travel businesses. We found that a market approach to valuing some of these rights, based on some recent transactions, was appropriate. As a back-up methodology, we used the cost approach.

Mailing lists and customer databases that the company controlled had substantial value, because of their excellent record-keeping on millions of frequent renters and leisure travelers. That substantial information in the databases would have market value whether the company was a going concern or in a liquidation scenario. Here, we were able to depend on market comparables, because databases and mailing lists are a relatively freely traded commodity; we backed up that value conclusion with a cost analysis. Finally, the reservation system was valued using a market analysis based on a sale of a similar reservations systems within a few years previous, again backed up by a cost analysis.

Values are outlined in Table 14.2. Note the substantial variation in value from going concern to liquidation. This enormous fluctuation in value was caused, of course, by the deep discounts engendered in a liquidation, but it is also important to know that we had to make the assumption that this might be a fire-sale liquidation—in other words, the sale of the assets in as short a time period as possible. On balance, we believe that the liquidation scenario would have yielded roughly between 20 and 25% of going-concern value, given that a 90- to 180-day period would have been available to identify suitable purchasers. ■

Table 14.2 Company A: Intellectual Property Valuation Summary

Description	Going Concern Value (in millions)	Liquidation Value (in millions)
Trademark (North America)	$268.9	$60.5
Franchisee rights (North America)	38.2	8.6
Trademark (international)	56.6	10.2
Franchisee rights (international)	44.0	7.9
Truck license	9.4	1.4
Reservation system (global)	38.5	5.8
Airport concession rights	17.9	0
Mailing list and database	5.8	2.9
Total Value	$479.3	$97.3
Add: Potential tax benefits	75.8	15.4
Adjusted Value	$555.1	$112.7

■ Case Study 2

Our second case study involves an even more obscure group of assets that typify what could be included under the heading "other intangible assets." We were hired by a multinational health and beauty care company in Europe to value the intangible assets of a company it had recently acquired in North America. Besides the traditional assets, we were asked to engage in a separate assignment to identify and then value other intangible assets that were not categorized as trademarks, patents, know-how, customer lists, etc. We engaged in comprehensive research and identified several groups of potential value, focusing specifically on the following:

- Promotional programs
- Education programs
- Presentation and retail display assets
- Website assets

These were selected based on the four key tests established by the client in a tax-related environment:

- The asset should be identifiable and have a meaningful impact on the business.
- The asset should have a long or indeterminate lifespan.
- The asset should have the ability to be regularly revalued.
- The asset could be geographically divided so that it could be uniquely valued in the North American market.

The context of the acquisition was not under the terms of a merger, acquisition, or other financial environment. Rather, the valuation was done in connection with transfer pricing issues in both the U.S. and Europe. In determining the value for these assets, we looked at several methodologies—both traditional and non-traditional—including, of course, the income market and cost approaches. In this particular case, given the uniqueness of the assets we felt that a cost-related model would have to be used (see the preceding discussion of unique assets and cost-based valuations). Considering all of the information on hand and the other methods available, we determined that a replacement value approach provided the most accurate indication of value. The assets valued were as follows:

Promotional Programs

Contained within the promotional bundle were club membership programs, privilege programs, business-builder programs, and customer affinity programs. All of these programs were based on awarding points to the salons themselves, their sales personnel, and distributors of the product. In addition, there was a consumer points award royalty program. These points are redeemable for free products or product discounts, or for co-op advertising in the case of retailers. The costs associated with the program were identified and analyzed, including the cost of managing these awards programs, local and national co-op advertising, and promotional and PR activities, such as newsletters, mailings, customer list administration, personnel, and so on. This particular asset has real value: by providing these benefits and programs, the acquired company was able to build an absolute leadership position and a strong customer loyalty base in salon-based hair care products; as a result it was able to maintain its position in the industry as a supplier of quality hair care products. Distributors, salons, and consumers show a great deal of loyalty to the product family.

Educational Programs

The educational programs included materials, classes, special events, trade-shows, etc., all geared toward the further education of salon professionals and salon managers and the introduction of new products and styling trends. The costs of these programs are substantial and are critically important to the success of the company. Costs include production, educational materials, traveling shows, support for the development of the classes, conference fees, show space, and so on. Also included are fees for guest stylists, entertainers at these events, and independent teaching contractors who conduct the classes. By holding these educational programs and events, the company uses an educational strategy that further promotes its existing lines and introduces its new lines. The company represents itself as current with industry trends, creates a positive perception, and reinforces its reputation. Substantial benefits and goodwill are generated from these assets. Again, we measured value by assessing the costs that would be involved in duplicating the programs to an equally established level.

Product Presentation Assets

In earlier days, these assets might be described as *shelf facings* or *slotting allowances*. Today, the salon and supply-store shelf faces in displays are critically important. They vary in size from store to store. The company maintains displays in 60,000 salons and more than 200 beauty supply distributors. These costs are substantial and typically run in the eight figures on an annual basis. Product facings and shelf space are vital to the marketing assets of a beauty or health care company. Again, in this case, a cost can be specifically identified and quantified, so we used a cost-based replacement value to arrive at a going-concern value.

Internet Assets

This final group of assets includes traditional domain names, website designs, etc. The valuation of these assets is covered in detail in Chapter 10. ■

Table 14.3 HABA Company: Intangible Asset Values

Asset	Value (millions)
Promotional	$15.3
Education	13.4
Product presentation	22.4
Internet	1.0
	TOTAL $52.1

PART V

Valuation in Different Contexts

> **Context**
> 1. The parts of a discourse that surround a word or passage and can throw light on its meaning.
> 2. The interrelated conditions in which something exists or occurs.

Introduction

For the last 20 years, as intellectual property has grown in importance to all companies, valuation professionals have wrestled with the issue of the variations in values for trademarks, patents, other intellectual property, and the licenses attached thereto. The underlying reason that intellectual property value changes over time depends on the holder of the property, the intended end use, and, most importantly, the business or litigation environment. Recognizing the context in which the valuation is taking place is critical to the process—thought of in another way, intellectual property value is *context specific*. Unlike an apartment building, a tractor, or 10,000 dozen t-shirts, value can change quickly for trademarks and their licenses, as well as for other intellectual property.

If the word *context* can be defined as the situation, environment, conditions, or other external or internal determinants of value, then context affects every business activity, not just valuation. In this section, we have structured a discussion of context so that it falls into six broad areas:

- Licensing and licenses
- Mergers, financial deals, and SEC reporting
- Bankruptcy, reorganization, and securitization
- Tax and transfer pricing
- Donations
- Litigation

Chapter 15 begins our discussion by reviewing value and valuation in a licensing environment and of a license agreement. It is important to understand that although a license is in fact a piece of intellectual property, *the act of licensing is a specific context*—and the licensing context is one of the most complex, complicated, energized, and unpredictable environments into which one can place one's intellectual property. The very act of entering into a licensing negotiation changes the value not only of the license that will come out of the negotiation but also the value of the underlying intellectual property itself. Therefore, we have chosen to treat licensing and licenses in Part V, emphasizing context, as opposed to giving a straightforward treatment as a specific asset, as was done in Part IV.

Mergers, acquisitions, financial deals, and SEC reporting are all intertwined. The driver of industrialized business deals is the merger, acquisition, or other business combination. As these combinations have become more transnational and more complex, the rules of engagement have changed. Specifically, the rules of valuation for intellectual property have been substantially modified over the last decade. Most recently, the Sarbanes–Oxley Corporate Governance Initiative has had a major impact, and this, in combination with the new SEC regulations in sections 141/142 and 144, has dramatically changed the way intellectual property is accounted for and valued in a merger or other business combination.

Bankruptcy is a world unto itself and one that increasingly affects intellectual property. Fortunately or unfortunately, the growth in corporate bankruptcies has increased the focus on and scrutiny of the treatment of intangible assets and intellectual property. Whether a company is going through voluntary or involuntary bankruptcy, reorganization, or liquidation, the context of value will change.

Chapters 18 and 19 deal with tax related issues. Chapter 18 specifically deals with the process of intercompany exchanges of assets, known as *transfer pricing*, and the rules and regulations set by most governments today, typified by Section 482 of the IRS Code. That chapter also briefly discusses intellectual property holding companies. Chapter 19 covers donations of intellectual property. The topic of donations has much currency today because the IRS is increasingly scrutinizing donations of technologies to tax-free institutions.

Finally, Chapter 20 deals with the litigation environment. Scott Davidson of Canada has contributed to an outstanding chapter on some but not all of the issues regarding litigation, since this is perhaps the most complex context in which one can place a value on intellectual property.

Realistic and accurate valuation is crucial in the context of all financially driven situations. In order to value these assets accurately, one must address two core issues:

- Identify the underlying cause (e.g., litigation, Chapter 11, merger, etc.) that precipitated the need to value and sell the assets.
- Identify the basic premise of the valuation (e.g., liquidation or going-concern value).

The practical issue then becomes establishing current market value of the intangible assets, given the specific deal basis or business conditions, whether it is a merger, liquidation, orderly disposal, or reorganization.

Our team has worked over the last decade to understand how, why, and when the market value of a trademark or piece of intellectual property changes. Based on empirical research and hundreds of valuation studies, it is clear that Intellectual Property valuation is truly context specific, wherein the underlying business conditions of the company and other economic factors (many that do not weigh directly on the intellectual property) determine market value. In other words, context is the basis of true value for most intellectual assets.

The CONSOR® Context Continuum (CCC) has been developed for use in understanding intellectual property values in financially distressed companies. The four primary contexts in which Intellectual Property valuation is performed are

- Going concern
- Reorganization
- Orderly disposal
- Liquidation

The CCC is a graph of value curves that illustrates relative value for a piece of intellectual property, measured along two dimensions:

- The vertical scale establishes the conditions under which the asset is being valued.
- The horizontal scale measures time in monthly increments.
- As the graph illustrates, Intellectual Property value is a direct function of the specific context of the valuation environment with relation to time.
- In addition to these four value curves, two others could be considered, and we look forward to graphing them when we have enough empirical data; those two curves are as follows:

In the first case, the working title for the curve is *company in play*. This describes the value of the intangible assets in a context in which the corporate owner is involved in an acquisition, merger, stock buy-back, unfriendly takeover, or other corporate combination. In this case, our experience indicates that typically the value of the intangible assets are driven upward as the bidding for all the company's assets increases in pitch. In other words, the more attractive a company is as an acquisition candidate, the more likely the value of its intangible assets will increase.

The second curve is the *litigation curve*. It is perhaps the most difficult curve to map. It really is two curves: The first, which describes the value of Intellectual Property in a successful litigation, can be imagined as an upside-down bell curve where a piece of Intellectual Property in litigation loses substantial value at the beginning of the process and during court proceedings; when it is successful in its litigation, value pops back up. The second curve, for unsuccessful litigation, would look quite different, with an initial decline in value at the beginning of litigation, a flattening in mid-case, and then a decline upon losing the litigation. This curve would closely resemble the orderly disposal curve, at least in general form.

On the next page we graph the four curves with a brief explanation of each of the contexts.

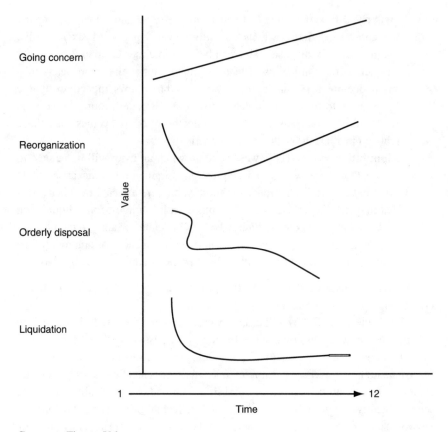

Context + Time = Value

Going-concern value: Addresses the true market value of intellectual property operating in an environment free from financial or litigation constraints. As the previous discussion indicates, going-concern value is typically the highest and most stable of the group. The straight line illustrates the existence of a mature Intellectual Property portfolio realizing steady growth over time.

Reorganization value: Involves a company in the process of repositioning itself in the competitive marketplace, either for financial or competitive purposes—either under the protection of Chapter 11 or self-imposed. As a company divests itself of underperforming business segments and attempts to secure additional funding, we initially witness a sharp decline in the value of the Intellectual Property portfolio. As time goes on and the reorganization plan is approved and implemented, the intellectual property will begin to experience a gradual increase in value, eventually reaching that of its prepetition status.

Orderly disposal value: Derived from the expectation that a company has chosen to wind down its operations over a period of six to twelve months. Orderly disposal value can be used in either Chapter 7 or merger and acquisition situations. The decision to shutter the doors leads to a sharp decline in value in the short term but allows the company the opportunity to market the assets actively to a broader group of investors, which ultimately leads to higher intellectual property values than those realized in a last ditch "fire sale" scenario.

Liquidation value: The lowest price at which an asset will be pegged to ensure that there will be an acquisition. Liquidation value arises most often in Chapter 7 situations, and these values are affected by other assets that may be available in the marketplace. In its simplest form, liquidation value is that price below which we can, with some certainty, guarantee the price will not fall. It is important to note that with each passing month in a liquidation, the value of the intellectual property can decrease by 5–10%.

We have focused here on intellectual property assets and how their value can change in different environments.

The chapters that follow will discuss various contexts for Intellectual Property valuation and how values also can be affected by the passage of time or the change in environment. Our focus in Part V is on valuing these assets in a business or legal environment; however, Part V is not intended to address legal issues of ownership, salability, transferability of licenses, and so on. Instead, we are dealing here with the practicality of putting market values on intellectual property in an economic environment such as a bankruptcy, merger, or tax environment. The underlying key to valuing intellectual property in any situation is recognizing two crucial concepts: First, valuation is highly dependent on the context in which it is being performed; second, valuation is also dependent on the time in which the valuation takes place, even in the same environment.

In other words, a technology in a going-concern environment can have different values today than it will have five years from now, depending on different conditions and value determinants, such as the competitive environment, declining size of the market, the rise of new technologies, etc. Keeping these two key value determinants in mind will help the reader better understand the valuation process— hopefully aiding in the process down the road and, finally, maximizing value of the intellectual property in any given situation.

CHAPTER 15

LICENSING AND LICENSES

This chapter covers a topic that can affect virtually every piece of intellectual property at one time or another. It is a topic that cuts across all contexts, business environments, and transactions involving intellectual property and intangible assets: the licensing of Intellectual Property assets to unrelated third parties, for use on a broad range of products and services, both domestically and in overseas markets.

There are various forms of intellectual property licensing. For example, *trademark licensing* includes the use of characters, entertainment properties, sports figures, celebrities and the estates of celebrities, and corporate-held trademarks and brands. *Patent and technology licensing* can include everything from the very simplest mechanical device licensed to an overseas company to the most complex genetically engineered plant and animal patent. This kind of licensing also covers the range of licensing using trade secrets, technology, and technical know-how. As another example, *copyright licensing* can include granting the right to use literary or artistic material; paintings, photos or other images; interpretive works, designs, and intellectual concepts. *Software licensing* also has multiple levels, from the shrinkwrap software we have all purchased at our local technology retailer, to midlevel software licensed to small, medium, and large companies, to large operating systems that can cost upwards of $100M when designed, customized, and installed for very large corporations.

How, then, do we cover this broad topic? The short answer is we cannot in a single chapter. In each of the earlier chapters on software, copyrights, trademarks, etc., we address, at least tangentially, the topic of licensing for those respective types of intellectual property. Here, we will focus on the licensing industry that is most likely to affect readers of this primer, trademark licensing, beginning with the simple question, how large is this industry? It is difficult to assess, because transfer of Intellectual Property rights in the form of license agreements is not typically publicly acknowledged, nor are the revenue data available for public consumption. Through extensive research and interviews with personnel from major technology licensing associations and the department of commerce, it was determined that limited technology licensing information is publicly available. The 2003 annual report on technology transfer, published by the U.S. Department of Commerce, estimates total income from technology licensing at $127 billion. Emmett Murtha, Fairfield Resources International, estimated $150 billion for patent and technology licensing in 2004.

Licensing can be done with many types of Intellectual Property, from copyrights to patents to software, and has a broad range of applications. In this chapter we try to condense the topic of licensing and licenses into four general areas:

- First, we will look at a definition of licensing and an historical overview of trademark licensing in the United States.
- Second, we will look at types of licenses and key differentiating points in licensing.
- We will then move to the valuation of licenses and licensing agreements, examining some of the clauses and key elements of value that can be built into a license agreement.
- Finally, we will take a brief look at licensing royalty rates.

The chapter concludes with a look at other issues that affect licensing, from bankruptcy to mergers, from taxes to the potential pitfalls of a licensing program.

Definition of Licensing

Licensing is the granting to others the right to use intellectual property, be it a patent, trademark, name, title, design, symbol, character, or personality image, in association with a particular product or service, for a given period of time, in a specific geographic territory. Why do people enter into licensing arrangements? Licensees hope that through the use of licensed properties they can create a greater market or more demand for their products or services. Licensors see licensing as an opportunity to gain not only royalty income but also additional exposure for their properties (which can be particularly significant if the licensors themselves are using their properties in connection with goods or services they are selling).

People sometimes confuse licensing and franchising. Until the early 1960s, licensing and franchising were seen as synonymous because both involved "licensing" (i.e., the granting of the use of a name or trademark in exchange for the payment of a fee). But these two concepts can be distinguished. In franchising, there is an additional aspect to the relationship, namely, the franchisee's operating system is prescribed by the franchisor. The ability to distinguish between licensing and franchising became important in the 1960s, because individual states and the federal government began to monitor and regulate franchising. Licensing, on the other hand, remains unregulated. Many old-line franchisors still, nevertheless, refer to themselves as licensors, and the major soft drink bottlers are still referred to as licensees.

A Historical Overview

Much has been written about the genesis and development of licensing. It is important to remember that licensing is neither a new phenomenon nor an overnight one. The concept of licensing has been around for hundreds of years. As recently as 25 years ago, however, licensing had only a minor impact in the marketplace.

The earliest examples of licensing date back to the Middle Ages, when the Popes granted *warrants* or licenses to local entrepreneurs to collect taxes and forward a royalty percentage to Rome. We then move forward to the early 1700s when two ladies of the British nobility lent their names to a line of facial cosmetics in return for a royalty on sales. Subsequent milestones in licensing's history have included the following:

> 1913: Teddy Roosevelt lends his name to the "Teddy" bear in return for a royalty that supported his efforts to establish a network of national parks.
>
> 1918: Raggedy Ann rears her stuffed head, followed two years later by Raggedy Andy.
>
> 1928: Walt Disney introduces Mickey Mouse to America.
>
> 1929: Buck Rogers appears and becomes an early licensing success. The first morning that Buck's licensed rocket pistol goes on sale at Macy's in the early 1930s, all 20,000 pistols on hand are sold out before noon.
>
> 1930: The Lone Ranger hi-ho's into America's consciousness.
>
> 1932: Herman Kamen establishes Disney's licensing program and Disney's acknowledged leadership in the industry.
>
> 1930s: Six million licensed Shirley Temple dolls are sold.
>
> 1940s: Hopalong Cassidy and Tom Mix gallop into our lives on the backs of palominos bought from royalties on toys, premiums, and endorsements.
>
> 1950s: Zorro slashes his way into the limelight.
>
> 1955: Disney builds the first complete family of licensees around a TV character, Davy Crockett.
>
> 1960s: Batman mania takes over.

Not until the 1970s did we witness the emergence of licensing as a major industry. The success scored by sport and entertainment properties such as Star Trek, Snoopy, the Fonz, Star Wars, and NFL team emblems, to name just a few, awoke corporate boardrooms everywhere to licensing's potential.

In the 1980s, licensing took on a new respectability—it became a science. As Greg Battersby was the first to report, in the January 1983 issue of *The Merchandising Reporter*, a character named Strawberry Shortcake was literally "born to be licensed." And it did not stop there. Licensees no longer focused on just the property. They began to want to know the licensor's marketing program and the property's expected exposure. It no longer was enough for the licensor simply to have a cute property.

Growth was steady in the 1980s and early 1990s. Since then, sales growth has stagnated. Reliable research and industry data exist concerning the size and growth of the licensing industry over the years. Based on the estimates of *The Licensing Letter* and EPM Communications, North America retail sales of licensed products in 2003 were $107.4 billion.

Table 15.1 Geographic Retail Sales of Licensed Merchandise

	2003 (in billions)	1998 (in billions)
North America	$70.8	$71.1
Europe	24.2	25.4
Japan	8.0	11.5
A/NZ	1.8	1.5
Other	<u>2.7</u>	<u>7.7</u>
Total	$107.4	$111.7

Table 15.1 illustrates how licensed sales have stagnated in the last five years. Why is this? The reasons are multiple:

- Consolidation of retailers and reduced retail space
- The number of licensing programs has increased rapidly, with some resultant confusion among consumers.
- The time period during which licensed products are sold has shortened noticeably, particularly for entertainment products. (Ten years ago, a licensed product connected with a movie would be on the shelf for six months; today it is lucky to be on the shelf for six weeks.)
- Many former licensors have decided to do their own manufacturing, thus eliminating the licensee. This can be seen in designer programs, such as Ralph Lauren or Donna Karan, and in corporate branded licensing programs where companies begin to acquire their licensees.

The various categories of licensing have changed in importance. A decade ago, character and entertainment merchandising was by far the largest category, followed by sports. Today, trademark and brand licensing is the largest category, followed by entertainment and character merchandise, and sports licensing has experienced a decade of decline.

Types of Licenses
Licenses can be granted for a wide range of intellectual property, including the following:

- Copyrights
- Software
- Trademarks
- Characters
- Patents
- Technology
- Databases

- Domain names
- Other intangible assets
- Art and imagery
- Franchise systems
- Hybrids of trademark and technology

Regardless of the type of intellectual property being licensed, in virtually all cases a royalty is charged and a fee of some type is established. Aside from the issues of compensation for the use of the intellectual property, fee structures are a useful way to manage and control licensees. In general, when looking at compensation for in-licensing agreements, one can broadly divide the compensation system or licensing agreement into two subtypes:

- A fully paid-up license
- Running royalties or other fees being charged on a regular basis

In the first case, a fully paid-up license is one for which the licensee pays the licensor a single, lump-sum payment at the beginning of the license agreement. (In some cases, this lump sum can be divided into two or three fixed payments spread over a period of one or more years.) The fully paid-up license is found almost exclusively outside the area of trademark and character licensing. It is used most often in patent and technology licensing, where the licensor essentially "sells" the license to its licensee in return for a single, lump-sum payment. Typically, a fully paid-up license will be attached to a patent license that will run for the remaining term of the patent.

On the other hand, the more typical arrangement for most intellectual property is a license agreement that calls for continuous payment or running royalties. The phrase *running royalties* can refer to an actual percentage royalty, a fixed quarterly payment, a fee per unit produced, and so on. There are multiple ways to establish royalty rates. Table 15.2 lists 10 different methods to establish running royalties or on-going payment structures.

Table 15.2 Alternative Fee Structures

1.	Percentage royalty rate on sales
2.	Per unit royalty rate on sales
3.	Quarterly fixed fees
4.	An annual cap on percentage or per unit fees
5.	Royalties declining with volume
6.	Royalties declining over time
7.	Royalties based on components of value
8.	Royalties based on percentage utilization within a product
9.	Royalties based on profits or margins
10.	Royalties on product cost

The next consideration in valuing of license revolves around the issue of exclusivity versus nonexclusivity. As its name implies, exclusivity is simply the concept of granting to a single licensee the exclusive use of the intellectual property based on some fixed parameter. Fixed parameters can include one or more of the following:

- Geographic exclusivity
- Product line exclusivity
- Distribution or retail channel exclusivity
- Price point or price range exclusivity
- Term or time exclusivity
- Design or specific art exclusivity, etc.

The benefits of exclusivity versus nonexclusivity are obvious. Exclusivity provides to the licensee a halo of protection for its products or services in that area of exclusivity. For example, one licensee may be granted exclusive use to make tempered steel using a smelting technology in the U.S., whereas another licensee may be granted the use of the same technology in Canada or Mexico or another overseas market. In another example, a licensee may be granted the use of a trademark on products to be sold through a mass-market retail channel, whereas a second licensee may be granted use of the same trademark for distribution of products by direct mail or via department stores.

In general, there is one other area that defines the type of license with which one is dealing. That area is the issue of time and renewals. In general, licenses break into two different types: those that have very well defined and limited time frames and those that do not. In the former case, most typically found in higher volume, more visible license agreements, a license will run for a fixed period of time that can range from one to ten years. That same licensee may or may not have an opportunity to negotiate renewals to its license agreement. In other words, this type of license agreement has a fixed term and a predetermined ending point. The second type of license is one that is sometimes incorrectly called the perpetual license. In this format, a licensee most typically will have a one-year agreement, which is renewed automatically (unless some calamitous event takes place). In other words, the licensee has the surety of an on-going relationship with its licensor that essentially lasts for as long as the licensee wishes.

Consider one final point on types of licenses: Typically, people think of licensing as monolithic and consisting essentially of one type of license. This is particularly true in dealing with trademark, entertainment, copyright, and character assets. In fact, maximizing value from these assets can be done by using a number of different licensing approaches, some of which are listed here:

> **Merchandise licensing:** Also known as *trinkets and trash*, merchandise licensing is best typified by Heinz pickle kitchen magnets, Coca-Cola mirrors, or Anheuser-Busch keychains. It best serves to promote awareness of a trademark or brand.

Brand extensions: These are licenses granted for use on products or services closely related to the licensor's own product or brand. Examples include Corvette automotive performance accessories and IBM-branded PC accessories.

Ingredient licensing: These are used as an endorsement form of licensing. Who can argue with the success of the Intel Inside ingredient licensing program? NutraSweet successfully built its name on an ingredient-licensing program.

Promotional licensing: Promotions and tie-ins via license have become more popular. Typical examples are short-term licenses taken by fast-food companies, such as Burger King and McDonald's, in conjunction with a movie or other entertainment property.

Hybrid licensing: These licenses most typically combine a patent or technology that has limited life with a trademark or brand that has an unlimited life. IBM was an early proponent of the hybrid licensing approach.

In addition to these forms of licensing, there are also licenses for use exclusively on the Internet and retail exclusive licensing deals, in which a licensor gives exclusive product rights to a single retailer, such as Callaway Golf with Nordstrom. There are also event licensing tie-ins connected with the Olympics, Super Bowl, World Cup, etc. As well, there are endorsement agreements, co-branding licenses, and venue-specific licenses. In some ways, the most important format, especially for technology, is *cross-licensing*. In cross-licensing, two companies hold complementary technologies, and each grants the other use of its own technology in return for the other's. Essentially, this is a swap of technology enabling both companies to compete better in specific markets.

Valuation

The process of valuing license agreements is often made overly complex and mysterious. This section attempts to simplify the valuation process, identifying the four key elements that go into establishing the value of a license agreement. Although modifications of these four elements exist, they basically break into the following core areas:

- Fixed royalty income
- Other contractural income
- Potential upside income
- Other elements of value

Fixed Royalty Income

Most licenses (although far from all of them) include a predictable fixed income component. This means that in each year or time period of the licensor, perhaps quarterly, the licensee is committed contractually to giving the licensor a predetermined amount of income. Although this income is typically in the form of cash or other legal tender, in some cases, the income can also be paid in the form of supplies, services, materials, or other goods that the licensee can give the licensor.

Let us focus on the most typical example, in which a licensee has a three-year agreement with the licensor that calls for total guaranteed payments of $150,000: $50,000 at the beginning of each of three years. This fixed, guaranteed income is the first and primary element of calculating the value of a license agreement. Assuming that the licensee is fiscally responsible, one can calculate the present value of this fixed component by applying the simple net present value calculation:

$$\text{income} \times \text{time} \times \text{discount rate}$$

This gives today's value of this guaranteed income.

Other Contractual Income

Many license agreements call for additional forms of revenue or income to the licensor. This usually takes the form of guaranteed marketing or advertising payments. Often, one finds that in large licensing programs—such as those run by Polo/Ralph Lauren, Disney, or large sports organizations—annual payments are expressed either as a fixed amount or as a percentage of gross revenue to be paid to the licensor for use in advertising. This so-called *advertising pool payment* is combined with other licensee payments into a pool of funds, which is managed and spent by the licensor on advertising and other marketing efforts.

In addition to these annual guaranteed funds, there can be other fees in technology and trademark licenses. These fees can include annual payment for design assistance, for technical know-how, for training of personnel, for site inspection or management, for formulas and blending instructions, and so on. Because any one of these elements is unique to an individual license agreement, the most common rule of valuation is to apply the same net present value calculation as was applied to the fixed or guaranteed royalty income described previously.

Potential Upside Income

Licenses typically contain guarantees from the licensee that are, at least in theory, less than the actual total payments that will be made each year. In other words, the minimum annual payment by the licensee represents only a portion of the expected royalty income that the licensee will generate in any given year.

Let us use the same example that we used earlier: A licensee paying $50,000 at the beginning of each year actually expects to generate total royalties in any given year of $150,000. Therefore, this additional potential upside element of value would be the sum of $100,000 per year over three years, at an appropriate discount. This seems simple and straightforward, but there is an important part of this calculation that takes a great deal of subjective judgment—the sensitivity analysis in advance, to determine the probability that these upside payments will be made. Although at the beginning of a license the licensee certainly intends to be giving a total of $150,000 each year to its licensor, in establishing value for this element of the license agreement the valuation expert must be keenly aware of market forces and engage in a rigorous sensitivity analysis.

Other Elements of Value

Other elements of value represent nonmonetary (and occasionally monetary) value that the licensee brings to the licensor. Some of these elements of value are easy to quantify, others are not. Examples are as follows:

- Entry into new channels of distribution or establishment of relationships with new retailers or distributors
- Expansion of the number of items or SKUs found under the licensor's trademark or technology in the marketplace
- Appeal to new customers: commercial, industrial, and/or consumers
- In the consumer realm of licensing, penetration of new demographics either based on age or income or geography or ethnic diversity
- Establishment of new product lines and product line extensions

Accurately combining these elements of value of a license agreement is the most difficult part of the process. These elements are indeed most open to subjective analysis. In fact, these elements of value will be context specific. For example, the licensor may value highly a licensee's ability to sell its products through Wal-Mart and may in fact want that licensee to be the lead into Wal-Mart. Thus, that element of value has perhaps greater value even than the fixed income called for in the license agreement.

How does one combine these elements of value? In simplest terms, the process is shown in Table 15.3.

Table 15.3 Valuing Licenses

	NPV (eg)	Probability (eg)	
Fixed royalty income	$1,000	100%	$1,000
Other fixed income	200	100%	200
Upside potential (additional royalty payments)	2,000	50%	1,000
Other elements of value	400	25%	100
Total Value			$2,300

Key Clauses of Value in Licenses

Some other very important areas should be addressed in a license agreement. Because the negotiation of a license agreement is highly complex, multiple books and articles have been written on the subject.[1] Below, we provide an overview of key clauses, terms, and conditions that, I believe, are most important in a negotiation. Although not exhaustive, they can be used as a partial checklist.

1. Preagreement considerations
   - Category research, market research
   - Prenegotiation due diligence (financial, etc.)
2. Grant of license: Core considerations
   - Exclusive or nonexclusive
   - Limitations to the grant
3. Goods to be licensed
   - Description and definition
   - Complementary goods being licensed
4. Territory
   - One country only or multiple territories
   - Geographic options
5. Term/timing
   - Length of contract
   - Marketing schedule
6. Renewals, options, and extensions
   - Renewal options
   - Additional product options
7. Fees, financial terms, and conditions
   - Initial fee
   - Royalty rates
8. Advertising, promotion, and marketing
   - Contributions to advertising
   - Approval of marketing plans
9. Approval process
   - Steps of process
   - How are submissions to be made
10. Controls and monitoring
    - Financial
    - Product
11. Quality assurance
    - Product standards
    - Packaging

---

[1] See *les Nouvelles,* Negotiating Complex License Agreements, September, 2003.

12. Ownership of trade dress and designs
    - Trademark notices
    - Derivative works from artwork and designs of licensor
13. Warranties/indemnifications
    - Licensees: Product quality
    - Licensor: Trademark ownership
14. Insurance
    - Product liability
    - Advertising liability
15. Confidentiality
    - Requirements
    - Publicity
16. Termination rights
    - Causes
    - Cures
17. Dispute resolution
    - Choice of law
    - Jurisdiction and venue
18. Assignability and subcontracting
    - Sublicensing
    - Contract manufacturing
19. Miscellaneous
    - Notices
    - Standard agreement provisions

Licensing Royalty Rates

When working with clients on license agreements, the question most often heard—and one that is most difficult to answer—is: "What is the right royalty rate?" The second question that we hear most often, and that is even more difficult to answer, is: "What is an average royalty rate?" There is no such thing as an average royalty rate. There are royalty rates that are more prevalent for a given product or more prevalent for a given geography or channel of distribution. There is, however, no single right answer. Instead, a range of royalty rates is appropriate in any given situation. As an illustration of this, Table 15.4 shows ranges of royalty rates for various types of technology.

A number of sources track royalty rates for trademark licensing. Among the best of those are the Grimes & Battersby royalty rate study, the annual LIMA study, and, most importantly, the well respected annual study put out through *The Licensing Letter* by EPM Communications of New York City. For many years, publisher Ira Mayer, editor Marty Brockstein, and their team have worked diligently with the trademark licensing industry to establish royalty rates on a product category basis. Table 15.5 summarizes their findings.

Table 15.4 Technology Royalty Rates

Industry	Range
Aerospace	2–15%
Chemical	1–10%
Health care equipment	5–10%
Electronics	3–12%
Medical equipment	3–5%
Software	5–15%
Semiconductors	1–12%
Pharmaceuticals	8–20%
Diagnostics	2–5%

Table 15.5 Trademark Average Royalty and Range of Royalties by Product Category, 2002–2003

Product Category	Average Royalty ('03)	Average Royalty ('02)	Range
Accessories	8.9%	8.6%	5–13%
Apparel	8.8%	7.1%	5–14%
Domestics	7.3%	5.0%	3–12%
Electronics	5.0%	6.5%	2.5–9%
Food/beverages	5.7%	6.9%	4–8%
Footwear	10.0%	5.3%	7–12%
Furniture/home furnishings	7.0%	6.6%	2.5–14%
Gifts/novelties	8.3%	8.7%	5–15%
Health/beauty	7.4%	8.7%	5–12%
Housewares	7.0%	6.6%	3–14%
Infant products	N/A	N/A	N/A
Music/video	7.0%	N/A	3–10%
Publishing	10.6%	10.2%	5–18%
Sporting goods	8.8%	N/A	7–15%
Stationery/paper	10.0%	7.8%	5–15%
Toys/games	8.4%	9.3%	3–12%
Videogames/software	4.2%	8.2%	3–6%
Overall average	8.4%	8.3%	2.5–18%

Note: Individual royalties may fall out of ranges; these are ranges of reported averages.
N/A = Not enough responses for meaningful number.
Source: *The Licensing Letter* © Copyright 2003 EPM Communications, Inc.

One of the most important things to note in Tables 15.4 and 15.5 is that royalty rate ranges are quite large for any given product category. For example, the range of royalty rates for electronic products can be as low as 3% or as much as 15%. Why is this? Why do we find this phenomenon so often and in so many industries, technologies, and product categories? The answer is that royalty rates, like other elements of a license agreement, are context specific and time critical. In other words, a royalty rate that may have been appropriate for a given trademark or technology two years ago may indeed be worth only half as much today. Alternatively, in a trademark licensing program, a royalty rate for a new licensing program may be substantially lower at the beginning than it will be three years later.

Finally, some general trends can be observed for royalty rates:

- Trademark rates are stabilizing in the range of 6.5 to 8.5%.
- Any increases in royalty rate seem to be behind us; there has been stability in the average royalty rates for the last three or four years.
- Technology royalty rates continue to vary substantially from licensor to licensor, from technology to technology, and from industry to industry.
- The negotiating of royalty rates is increasingly sophisticated, with licensors and licensees using more creative thinking to establish royalty rates. (See Table 15.2.)

Other Licensing Issues

Licensing and licensing assets, like many other intangible assets, have value that is very sensitive to change and context or time. We cannot overstress the contextual element in valuation. In the case study that follows you will find an excellent example of how the value of licenses changes because of context.

What are these contextual issues spoken of so frequently in this chapter? The four primary ones, we believe, are litigation, merger and acquisition, bankruptcy and reorganization, and changing market conditions. Each of these is dealt with in other chapters, but a brief review is useful here:

- In *litigation* over a license agreement, one can always expect a decline in the value.
- When licensee or licensor goes through a *bankruptcy or reorganization,* one can almost always expect a decline in value for the license agreement.
- In a *merger or acquisition* scenario, however, often the license agreements become more valuable to the acquiring party than they were to the original party.
- In the event of *changing market conditions,* one can only say that the specific condition will determine any change in value. Two simple recent examples illustrate this. In one case, the value of a Maratha Stewart license declined immediately after her indictment on criminal charges. In the other

case, the value of licenses using the logos and emblems of the New York City Police Department and Fire Department increased rapidly after September 11, 2001.

To recap, caution and contextual analysis are very important; equally important is a sensitivity analysis of dependent, nonguaranteed payments for potential incremental royalties. The case study that follows illustrates two things. First, that context does change the value of assets. Second, that the value of licenses and licensing assets can be accurately established.

■ Case Study

In 2000, we were asked by the owners of the World Cup licensing and merchandising rights to value these assets in preparation for a secured bond offering. In this case, Swiss company ISL/ISMM was going to take the future income from licensing and merchandising for the two World Cups in 2002 and 2006 and package them as security for the issuance of a bond in excess of $100M. To begin, we looked at the licensing rights and income streams to be received over the next six years and projected both quarterly income and a discount factor attached to that quarterly income. Using a 12% discount factor, the resulting valuation calculation shown in Table 15.6 illustrates that the value of the rights as of September, 2000, was $120M.

However, before the bond offering could be placed in the market, ISL/ISMM went into bankruptcy. The company was eventually dissolved and its assets sold. As a result, the uncertainty surrounding these rights and the disruption in marketing the licensing program substantially reduced the value of the rights. We observed a drop in value from more than $100M to something in the range of $50M as a result of the bankruptcy. As a consequence, FIFA decided to take back all of its merchandising rights and to manage the process itself. Table 15.7 illustrates the value of various licensing programs. Because of the confidential nature of each organization's revenues, we have modified the data somewhat to avoid client conflicts. Table 15.7 values the licensing program of World Cup compared to other sports organizations. The final three columns show the adjustments we made for different product categories and for different time intervals in order to arrive at the final column, which is an adjusted value based on a four-year revenue pattern. ■

Table 15.6 World Cup 2002 and 2006 Licensing Rights Valuation as of September 30, 2000 (thousands of CHF)

Period	Projected Licensing Revenue			Present Value of Projected Licensing Revenue		
Pre 4Q00	CHF	8,894	1.0000	CHF	8,894	
4Q00		8,350	0.9859		8,233	0.1250
1Q01		6,308	0.9584		6,046	0.3750
2Q01		11,200	0.9316		10,434	0.6250
3Q01		2,114	0.9056		1,914	0.8750
4Q01		21,808	0.8803		19,198	1.1250
1Q02		2,114	0.8557		1,809	1.3750
2Q02		36,355	0.8318		30,240	1.6250
3Q02		2,700	0.8086		2,183	1.8750
4Q02		–	0.7860		–	2.1250
1Q03		–	0.7640		–	2.3750
2Q03		–	0.7427		–	2.6250
3Q03		–	0.7219		–	2.8750
4Q03		–	0.7018		–	3.1250
1Q04		–	0.6822		–	3.3750
2Q04		4,688	0.6631		3,109	3.6250
3Q04		1,057	0.6446		681	3.8750
4Q04		4,688	0.6266		2,937	4.1250
1Q05		2,114	0.6091		1,288	4.3750
2Q05		24,000	0.5921		14,209	4.6250
3Q05		2,114	0.5755		1,217	4.8750
4Q05		26,114	0.5594		14,609	5.1250
1Q06		2,114	0.5438		1,150	5.3750
2Q06		27,568	0.5286		14,573	5.6250
3Q06		–	0.5139		–	5.8750
4Q06		24,750	0.4995		12,363	6.1250

* – Mid Period Convention

Present Value

CHF	119,566

Relevant Assumptions

Discount Rate	12.0%

Table 15.7 World Cup 2002 and 2006: Comparable Licensing Program Revenue

Event/Association	Territories (Primary)	Estimated Royalty Rate (Average)	Annual Licensing Revenue (Millions of U.S. $)	Adjusted for Product Categories (0.75)	Adjustments for Occurrence Interval* (Event Specific)	Adjusted Comparable Revenue (4-Year Period)
National Football League	USA	10%	$150.0	$112.5	2.4	$270.0
National Basketball Association	USA and Canada	10%	$70.0	$52.5	3.2	$168.0
National Hockey League	USA and Canada	10%	$50.0	$37.5	3.2	$120.0
Major League Baseball	USA and Canada	10%	$120.0	$90.0	2.8	$252.0
NASCAR	USA	12%	$60.0	$45.0	3.2	$144.0
NCAA	USA	10%	$23.2	$17.4	3.7	$63.9
Olympics (summer and winter)	Global	12%	$54.0	$40.5	1.5	$60.8
World Cup Skiing	International	8%	$52.0	$39.0	2.0	$78.0
Forecasted World Cup 2002 revenue**						$55,427,222
Forecasted World Cup 2006 revenue**						$66,666,667
Comparable property revenue range					$60,800,000 to $270,000,000	

*Occurrence interval adjustments take into consideration the event's seasonality, its selling period, and whether multiple playoff or championship events occur during the four-year period.
**Converted at 1.8 Swiss francs per U.S. dollar.

CHAPTER 16

BUSINESS TRANSACTIONS, THE SEC, AND FASB SECTIONS 141–142

Once again, we focus on context. In this case, the context is one that affects most publicly traded business transactions today. Greater scrutiny from the SEC and more stringent regulations from the Financial Accounting Standards Board (FASB) are now in place. These new regulations and increased scrutiny are a result of the very heavy merger and acquisition (M&A) activity in the 1980s and 1990s. During that period and until 2001, mergers and acquisitions often used the *pooling method* of accounting, by which nothing had to be valued or depreciated. In other words, one company could buy another's assets, put them together, and bury any excess goodwill or overpayment in the books of the combined company. The resultant opacity of corporate financial statements has been a primary reason why the regulations have been redone. And, of course, the corporate scandals of the late 1990s and the beginning of this century brought about the Sarbanes–Oxley Act.

In the broadest definition, business transactions include sales, acquisitions, mergers, spin-offs, licensing, joint ventures, and other business deals that involve the transferring of title from one corporate entity to another. In this environment, the valuation process is driven by business issues, as well as national and international tax and accounting regulations. The accounting standards boards in the United States, the United Kingdom, and elsewhere have issued new accounting rules for mergers, acquisitions, and business transactions. In the United States, the most important of these are known as sections 141, 142, 144, and 147. We will deal briefly with each of these complex new regulations.

The area of intellectual property valuation in mergers and acquisitions will experience great changes in the next decade. The scope, detail, definition of asset classes, due diligence, frequency of valuations, and federal and international scrutiny will all increase. Major impact on an acquiring company's earnings when it acquires another company is possible. The context we are dealing with here is pre- and post-M&A due diligence, as prescribed by the new FASB regulations.

After years of study, hearings, private input, and public testimony, FASB released these new regulations in 2001. Sections 141 and 142 primarily speak to valuation, and they require that all business combinations must use the purchase method of accounting and *must* value *all* intangibles in a purchase price allocation (PPA) report. This PPA must be done in all cases. Section 144 covers the so-called *impairment tests,* which state that if the value of an intangible asset has been impaired or reduced in value and the company chooses to dispose of it, 144 sets standards for disposal value.

The paragraphs that follow describe each section.

FASB Section 141

Section 141 addresses the issue of "business combinations" and how a merger or acquisition is to be accounted for. In simplest terms, it eliminates the old pooling of interest method and specifically requires that the companies use the so-called *purchase accounting method* when accounting for a merger or other business combination.

The underlying reason for this change was that similar business combinations were being accounted for using different accounting methods, depending on the company. Some used the pooling of interest method and some used the purchase method. This, of course, resulted in differing valuations and impacts on financial statements. In FASB 141, intangible assets are recognized as assets apart from goodwill, if

1. The asset arises from either a contract or other legal rights.
2. That asset can be separated from the entity itself and can be sold or otherwise exchanged.

With this new purchase method of accounting and the requirement for a PPA report, tangible assets and liabilities are still identified and evaluated at their fair value. Any excess of the purchase price over the fair value of these tangible assets becomes the total intangible asset value. This intangible value is separated and identified by type (e.g., trademark, copyright, workforce, software). Those intangible assets that cannot be identified become the company's goodwill and are recorded as such. The list that follows identifies intangible assets that meet the criteria for recognition as assets apart from goodwill.

1. Marketing-Related Intangible Assets
   - Trademarks, tradenames
   - Service marks, collective marks, certification marks
   - Trade dress
   - Newspaper mastheads
   - Internet domain names
   - Noncompetition agreements
2. Customer-Related Intangible Assets
   - Customer lists
   - Order or production backlog
   - Customer contracts and related customer relationships
   - Noncontractual customer relationships
3. Artistic-Related Intangible Assets
   - Plays, operas, ballets
   - Books, magazines, newspapers, other literary works
   - Musical works, such as compositions, song lyrics, advertising jingles

- Pictures, photographs
- Video and audiovisual material, including motion pictures, music videos, television programs
4. Contract-Based Intangible Assets
   - Licensing, royalty, standstill agreements
   - Advertising, construction, management, service, or supply contracts
   - Lease agreements
   - Construction permits
   - Franchise agreements
   - Operation and broadcast rights
   - Use rights, such as drilling, water, air, mineral, timber cutting, and route authorities
   - Servicing contracts, such as mortgage-servicing contracts
   - Employment contracts
5. Technology-Based Intangible Assets
   - Patented technology
   - Computer software and mask works
   - Unpatented technology
   - Databases, including title plants
   - Trade secrets, such as secret formulas, processes, recipes

FASB Section 142

In 2001, when FASB released its new regulations, these regulations radically affected the generally accepted accounting principles (GAAP) for business combinations. Section 141 specifically deals with "business combinations"; 142 deals with "goodwill and other intangible assets." Section 142 addresses the capitalization, valuation, and amortization of acquired intangible assets, including goodwill in a business combination. Most importantly, this section introduces new standard accounting provisions for the remaining useful life (RUL) of intangible assets and the amortizing of those assets; it also addresses impairment or reduction in value of acquired intangible assets *including goodwill*. In addition, this section requires regular periodic valuation and analysis of these assets, done on the business-unit level so that the greatest amount of detail can be shown. The thrust of 142 will likely cause corporations to make periodic adjustments to their financial statements whenever reductions in value of their intangible assets occur.

Section 142 requires that any intangible asset with a finite useful life must be valued, capitalized, and amortized; those intangibles with indefinite useful lives are not amortized. The RUL of an intangible is the "period in which the asset is expected to continue to contribute directly to the future cash flow of that entity." Further, the business unit is supposed to assess periodically whether the RUL of its various intangible assets has changed. If so, the amortization schedule must change. Finally, those intangible assets that are determined to have indefinite useful lives (e.g., some trademarks) are not amortized. However, that same business entity must annually reevaluate the intangible asset that is not being amortized, to determine whether any circumstances have changed to make the intangible asset have a specific RUL and, therefore, put on an annual amortization schedule.

Section 144 and the Impairment Provisions

One of the most important changes from the old rules is that companies are required to do periodic testing of value impairment for individual intangible assets as well as goodwill. Section 144 specifically provides guidance about how to test for impairment for intangible assets that are listed separately on the books. The regulations state, "An intangible asset not subject to amortization shall be tested for impairment annually or more frequently if events or changes in circumstances indicate that the assets might be impaired. The impairment test shall consist of a fair value of the intangible asset with the amount being carried on the company's books. If the carrying amount of the intangible asset should exceed its fair value, impairment shall be recognized in an amount equal to the excess value." In addition, goodwill shall be tested for impairment annually at a level defined as the reporting unit or business unit.

Sections 144 and 147 describes how to account for the disposal of the long-lived and overvalued intangible assets. They cover the sale of these underperforming assets and provides specific accounting guidance. If, however, an underperforming asset is sold as a "loss or impairment," then that impairment must be changed against earnings per share. As a direct consequence of these new regulations in mergers and acquisitions, overvalued intangible assets are often sold or spun off at the time of the business transaction.

Implications of the New Regulations

What does all this mean? What are some of the practical issues affecting value and valuations in mergers and acquisitions? The answer is more detail, more complexity, and, at the same time, more transparency and more frequent reviews. This is a very complex topic, and not everyone understands these new regulations yet. Here are some comments on the process and on the major issues and elements of the process:

- Sections 141 and 142 affect all business combinations. Although they eliminate goodwill amortization, they do require amortization of intangibles with determinable lives. Therefore, substantial additional valuation activity will take place on an annual basis, resulting in amortization or depreciation of specific intangible assets. The result is that the basic nature of acquisition valuation and accounting has changed, both at the time of purchase and for the future of the surviving company.

- Intangible assets are now a key part of the M&A equation. In general, lower purchase prices with less excess goodwill should result in the long term, because companies can no longer hide goodwill in their books as they could with the old regulations.
- What does this mean for valuation of acquisition targets? Companies with identifiable intangibles may be attractive acquisition targets if the acquisition price is reasonable. However, those same attractive targets may reduce the earnings of the new company after the merger. So, there are both earnings accretion issues and earnings dilution issues.
- The valuation process is more critical now than ever before, both in premerger due diligence and in the analysis for PPA process. In the preacquisition due diligence, a company should value intangible assets before acquisition to identify any potential excess amortization or any excess goodwill issues. The identification, separation, and valuation of these intangibles is a special skill, and the FASB regulations call for "fair value" (as opposed to fair market value) in establishing individual values. FASB is still determining what a fair value is, and this is a hot topic: Are we using a standalone value versus in-use value as definition of fair value?
- Intangible asset valuation methodologies under FASB are somewhat affected. The usual cost, market, or income valuation approaches, of course, are accepted, as is relief from royalty. One of the most important changes in valuation is that assets must be valued asset by asset or business unit by business unit. Currently, FASB calls for the valuation to be a *standalone value* versus an in-use value (in other words, a theoretical value should the asset be standing by itself). What is clear on a qualitative level is that the Intellectual Property valuation expert must understand how the SEC and the FASB think. For example, what does the SEC think is reasonable? What does FASB think an in-use value should be?
- The key trade-off is between certainty and uncertainly: certainty but low earnings per share now, by identifying and valuing as many intangibles as possible, and the uncertainty of possibly much lower earnings in the future should scrutiny identify substantial impairment in goodwill. In the latter case, the lower value would have to be deducted from earnings per share.
- Valuation under the impairment rule is the most complex part of 141 and 142. The test must be done annually and the intangibles valued at the business-unit level. (For this reason, fewer business units are better.) Intangible assets with finite lives only have to be valued once during their RUL. However, goodwill and indefinite life intangibles must be valued annually.

- If the fair value of the goodwill declines, that loss is charged to earnings. In simplest terms, the impairment test is really a two-step process: First, compare the fair value of goodwill or an indefinite-lived intangible to the value at which it is being carried on the company's books; and then determine whether that fair value is less than its carrying value.

If there is impairment, that amount of impairment is charged against the company's earnings.

■ Case Study: Purchase Price Allocation for Company X

As you can see in Table 16.1, Company X has a number of intangible assets, including software, trademarks, workforce, and customer relations. Table 16.1 shows that the purchase price of Company X is $1.25B and that there are cash and other tangible assets of $150M. Therefore, $1.05B must be allocated among the intangible assets and/or goodwill. After the intangibles are valued, their value totals $900M, so $200M of goodwill exists. ■

■ Case Studies

There are a number of ways to value these intangible assets. We have included examples of three different assets using three different approaches. Table 16.2

Table 16.1 Case Study of Company X: Purchase Price Allocation

I.   Purchase price of Company X = $1.25B

II. Assets	Methodology	Value (in Millions)	Subtotal (in Millions)
Cash		$50	
Net tangible	Replacement	$100	
Software	Replacement/cost	$50	$150
Trademark	RFR	$275	
Technology	RFR	$125	
Workforce	Valuation calculation	$250	
Licenses	Valuation calculation	$100	
Customer relations	Valuation calculation	$100	
	Total intangibles		900
			900
Total assets			$1,050
III. Goodwill			$200
	Overall total		$1,250

Table 16.2 Software Valuation by the Replacement Cost Method

Application	Active Lines of Code	Lines of Code/ Function Point	# of Function Points	Total Hours	Fully Burdened Salary/ Hour	Implied Value of Software
Software categories:						
Business	1,500,000	75	20,000	500,000	$50	$25,000
Operations	1,125,000	75	15,000	375,000	$50	$18,750
				Fair market value of software		$43,750

analyzes a software valuation using the replacement cost method. Table 16.3 values customer relations with and an income/excess return method. Table 16.4 values communication licenses by using market comparables. These next three tables are not intended to tie into Table 16.1; rather, they are intended as independent case studies and should be viewed that way. There are some general rules in methodologies:

Methodology	**Type of asset**
Market comparables	Licenses, certifications
Relief from royalty	Trademarks or established technology
Cost/replacement	Software and operating systems
Excess earnings or profit split	Workforce, order backlogs, customer relations, etc.

Conclusion

What do we gain from this chapter?

First, valuation and accounting for business combinations is much more complex today than it was before 2001. Second, the FASB regulations are very specific in their treatment of business combinations and the valuation of intangible assets. In many ways, these regulations make the valuation process more complex—and in some ways artificial, because fair value as defined by the FASB rules is *not* necessarily market value. The context of 141 and 142 can and will change the values that a company might otherwise attribute to its intangible assets.

Some closing thoughts on issues and dangers of this M&A valuation and PPA process: The biggest issue is subjective in-house identification and valuation of intangible assets versus objective outside valuation. A company that chooses to go with in-house valuation will certainly find greater scrutiny by the authorities. The temptation is for a company to go in-house and try for the no-amortization

Table 16.3 Customer Relationship Valuation by the Excess Return/Income Method

Year	Total Pretax Revenues Attributable to Existing Customers	EBIT Margin	EBIT Attributable to Existing Customers	After-Tax Earnings	After-Tax Fair Return on Net Tangible Assets	After-Tax Fair Return on Other Intangibles	Total After-Tax Excess Return	Present Value Factor	Present Value of After-Tax Excess Return
1	$500	12.20%	$61.00	$42.70	$9.00	$12.00	$21.70	0.931	$20.20
2	450	13.80%	62.10	43.47	8.25	10.50	24.72	0.846	20.91
3	350	15.60%	54.60	38.22	7.00	8.00	23.22	0.769	17.86
4	250	16.30%	40.75	28.53	5.00	5.50	18.03	0.700	12.62
5	100	16.30%	16.30	11.41	3.00	4.00	4.41	0.636	2.80

Fair value of customers relationships $74.39

Table 16.4 Spectrum License Valuation for Company X, by Market Comparable Method

Country	Year of License Agreement	Spectrum Allocation	Population	Payments (U.S. $)	Bandwidth (paired MHz)	Price/ MHz/Head of Population
Austria	2000	GSM 1800: 2 × 22.2MHz	8,500	$200,000	22.2	1.06
Netherlands	2000	GSM 1800: 2 × 17.4MHz	16,500	$300,000	17.4	1.04
Netherlands	1999	GSM 1800: 2 × 14.7MHz	16,500	$150,000	14.7	0.62
Germany	2000	GSM 1800: 5.0MHz	81,000	$250,000	5	0.62
Czech Republic	1999	GSM 1800: 5.4MHz	32,000	$110,000	5.4	0.64

Relevant price/MHz/head of population	0.87
Average MHz	7.2
Company X market population	5,000
Fair market value	$31,320

strategy. The very fact that there is no amortization as a result of the purchase price allocation will certainly raise a red flag with the authorities. On the other hand, now that CFOs and CEOs must personally sign these reports, valuations are now more cautious, given the potential personal liability. Finally, the deals at greatest risk of scrutiny, as well as having a potential impact on a company's earnings, are those with the greatest amount of goodwill and those with the highest amount of goodwill proportionate to the company's capitalization.

CHAPTER 17

BANKRUPTCY, REORGANIZATION, AND SECURITIZATION

Throughout this primer, we often refer to the importance of context and time in establishing real value for intellectual property. In no other situation is time as critical as it is in a bankruptcy or reorganization—and no other context is as fluid, fraught with potential change, and with such a depressive effect on the value of intellectual property. The term *valuation in a bankruptcy environment* can really mean one of many things. It can be a valuation in a reorganization of a company, orderly disposal of assets, liquidation of assets, securitization of those Intellectual Property assets for continuing funds, or partial sell-off of the assets. Each of these scenarios can lead to the development of different values. The reader would do well to refer back to the introductory pages of Part V, which includes graphs of the value of Intellectual Property assets under the four bankruptcy scenarios.

During the last decade, we have worked on valuations for a number of companies that found themselves going through reorganization. In Table 17.1, we look at companies whose going-concern values and liquidation values were established. The five different companies come from five distinctively different businesses, ranging from high-tech fiber optic assets through photography and chemical technology to fast food and comic books, with a stop on the way to take a look at TWA Airlines. Table 17.1 is clear in its conclusions. On average, liquidation value runs less than 15% of going-concern value.

A word of caution: These particular examples are extreme; nonetheless, they serve to illustrate the point that the value of a company's Intellectual Property in a going-concern environment is so substantially different from a disposal or liquidation environment as to be almost unbelievable.

The accelerating pace of bankruptcies, both Chapter 7 and Chapter 11, is alarming to us all from a business point of view. However, from an Intellectual Property point of view, it raises bigger and brighter red flags. In bankruptcy, who owns the licenses and the intellectual property controlled by the company going bankrupt? Can those licenses be sold? Can the intellectual property be licensed into other areas or sold? These issues are still being debated in the courts, and answers vary depending on the district and the case.

This primer looks at how to value and monetize intellectual property, information technology, and other intangible assets in a bankruptcy environment. It is not intended to deal with the legal issues of ownership, salability, provenance, and so on. Instead, it deals with the practicalities of valuing and selling intellectual property in the economic environment created by bankruptcy or reorganization.

Table 17.1 Going-Concern Value versus Disposal/Liquidation

Case	Going-concern value ($)	Disposal or liquidation value ($)	Proportion of value
Polaroid	400M+	60M	15.0%
Boston Market	210M	31M	14.7%
TWA	800M	50M	6.3%
Marvel	1.0B	223M	23.2%
Amherst Fiber Optics	5.0+M	<250K	5.0%
Average			12.8%

Questions that Need to Be Answered

The reality of the current economic environment means that the legal issues surrounding the sale of Intellectual Property assets out of bankruptcy will arise more frequently. In other words, there will be more bankruptcies involving intangibles. At the start of the process of valuing and selling a company's intellectual property and intangible assets, two sets of questions must be asked.

The first has to do with the value and ownership of the intellectual property:

- Does the intellectual property maintain its value when a company is in bankruptcy?
- Who owns and controls that value?
- Do the licenses have value?
- Who controls the destiny of those licenses?

The second set of questions deals with the practicality of the valuation and disposal process:

- What sort of liquidation discount is experienced when a patent, a trademark, a copyright, or a software license is sold in an orderly disposal?
- How are these assets valued in a liquidation scenario?
- Is there a formula to establish the descending value of these assets in liquidation?
- How can these assets be marketed and disposed of in the most cost-effective and time-effective manner?

The two most interesting questions to be addressed in a bankruptcy situation are the following:

- How does one treat trademark assets, since trademarks are specifically excluded from the definition of Intellectual Property under bankruptcy law?

- What happens to trademarks and technology licenses in a bankruptcy or reorganization?

As to the latter, the code prohibits assignment of intellectual property licenses without the consent of the nondebtor party, regardless of whether the license agreement has a bankruptcy clause. Naturally, a debtor with critical Intellectual Property license agreements that was prevented from assuming those agreements would have a much more difficult time reorganizing and emerging from bankruptcy. In addition, if that same debtor was going to use the assignment of valuable license agreements as a basis to reorganize, prohibiting that assignment would defeat the ability to reorganize.

There are no hard and fast rules. However, here are some important thoughts:

- The license can be allowed to pass through the bankruptcy proceedings without assumption, but this depends on the ruling of the bankruptcy court and cannot always be depended on.
- When writing the license agreement, the licensor can add a bankruptcy clause that specifically states that if the licensor files for bankruptcy, the licensee or trustee has the absolute right to assume the license and to continue to use the Intellectual Property.
- One can preempt problems by making the license an exclusive license. Under a non-exclusive license, the licensee has a right but not an obligation, whereas under an exclusive license, the licensor can be considered to have transferred implied title in a nonexecutory sale. Executory contracts are subject to bankruptcy approval, but nonexecutory sales would not be subject to assumption or rejection under the bankruptcy code.

As to the second issue regarding trademarks and the treatment of trademark licenses under bankruptcy, the law is even muddier, because (after much lobbying from very big trademark interests such as Disney and the movie studios) trademarks were specifically excluded from the last overhaul of the bankruptcy code. However, one piece of advice we give our clients if there is any hint of bankruptcy or reorganization on the horizon is to sign a *hybrid license*. By this we mean a license written for both trademarks and technology of some sort, ranging from software to technical advice to trade secrets, processes, etc. In doing this, one has transformed what would normally be a trademark license not subject to bankruptcy protection into a license containing technology that would be specifically under the realm of the bankruptcy code. However, this brings its own dangers, and one must be certain that protections are written into the contract—the most important one being to ensure that it is an exclusive contract.

This discussion of key questions is complex and based heavily on law. Because this is not intended as a legal primer, the issues and details of bankruptcy law are not addressed here. However, it is important to know that two sets of laws collide at the intersection of a company's bankruptcy:

- The bankruptcy code and laws
- The intellectual property code and PTO regulations

Often, these two sets of rules and regulations are at odds. Therefore, trademarks in bankruptcy are most often dealt with on a case-by-case basis. A final piece of advice: Get two good lawyers—one who knows bankruptcy and one who knows Intellectual Property licensing.

Comparative Examples of Value

When Warnaco sought protection in the courts, this action affected multiple pieces of intellectual property, including the Warner's brand, the Calvin Klein licenses held by Warnaco, and the Speedo brand. In addition, Warnaco had software and operating systems that had value and could have been sold if the company were to be liquidated. In a different case, when Montgomery Ward elected to shut its doors, it had a great deal of intellectual property and intangible assets to be sold. We valued and sold the trademark, brand names, shrinkwrap software, operating systems, and software licenses owned and controlled by Montgomery Ward. Each bankruptcy is different, and each company has different types of intellectual property. Table 17.2 compares six companies and their full range of Intellectual Property and intangible assets.

Identifying the Portfolio of Intellectual Property

When the harsh realities of bankruptcy or liquidation descend on an enterprise, where can the lenders or ultimate stakeholders look to maximize cash or other value beyond the obvious bricks-and-mortar, inventory, FFE&I, and real estate assets? Increasingly, the answer is to the intellectual capital. However, within the context of a bankruptcy or reorganization, those assets and their valuation and sale are often treated as an afterthought. Although obtaining accurate market-based values in these situations is important, the value and disposition of assets for creditors are often made on a basis that is less than well informed.

Accurate valuation of intellectual property and other intangible assets is crucial not only in bankruptcy situations, but in the context of mergers and acquisitions, off–balance sheet financing, tax planning, and internal-asset allocation. To address the need for accurate valuations of intangibles and intellectual property in bankruptcy or liquidation and disposition situations, it is necessary to address two core issues:

- Identify the underlying cause (e.g., Chapter 11 or merger) that precipitated the need to value and sell the assets
- Identify the basic premise of the valuation (e.g., going-concern or liquidation value)

The core objective is to establish the then-current market value of the intangible assets, given the conditions and valuation goals.

Table 17.2 Intellectual Property and Intangible Assets in Bankruptcy: Summary Case Studies

Relative value ranking[1]	Company	(A) TMs and brands	(B) IT and databases	(C) Patents and technology	(D) Internet	(E) Other
A plus B + C	Warnaco	Warners, Speedo, CK licenses	Complex operating systems	Manufacturing technology	Domain names and website	N/A C + B
D, A, E	Borden Chemical	Corporate brand and subbrands	Manufacturing systems	Multiple and proprietary	Modest	Chemical processes
B A + D	Montgomery Ward	Montgomery Ward, Ship N Shore, and 100+TMs	Operating platforms, mailing lists	None	Online store	Mail order system
B, C, D, E	Exodus	Corporate identity	Massive systems	Multiple BMPs[2]	Complex assets	Hosting processes
C + D B	beenz.com	Corporate TM	International databases	Proprietary technology and BMP	Online sweepstakes service	Other BMPs
E + C A, D, B	Mosler	Corporate name	Security IT and software	Multiple patents	Modest	UL certifications

[1] The rankings for each company reflect relative value within that company, in a bankruptcy or liquidation scenario (e.g., Montgomery Ward will realize most value from B assets, IT, and databases).

[2] BMP = business method patent. A BMP provides protection for intellectual concepts and systems sufficiently unique to earn patent protection. The 1-Click ordering system of Amazon.com is a BMP.

The intellectual capital of the enterprise should be viewed as a portfolio of intangible assets. These include the obvious patents, trademarks, copyrights, brand names, logos, and other elements frequently lumped into the category of goodwill and seldom valued individually. In addition, proprietary methodologies, best practices, application-specific software, operating systems, enterprise information infrastructures, and the tools to operate and support the information needs of a 21st-century business comprise the intangible-asset bundles that contribute directly to return on equity and free cash flow. Their value, in terms of cash equivalence, is complex in composition and depends heavily on the context in which they are evaluated.

The Valuation Process

The steps for valuing intangibles in a bankruptcy or reorganization follow much the same pattern as when intellectual property is valued in a merger and acquisition environment. The first is to identify all the intangibles involved (see Chapters 2 and 3). The second is to separate those intangibles from the tangible assets so that a separate valuation can be established. The next step is to identify incremental value within the family of intangibles, looking for additional financial security and financial leverage.

The goal is to maximize the value for the creditors and the bankruptcy estate by identifying all intangibles and their potential uses that have market value. This gives the court, creditors, or corporation a solid basis for a total asset valuation and allocation.

At this point, we all understand that the context in which an intangible asset is valued is important. We have reviewed the Context Continuum value charts. There is another graphic way of illustrating the high degree of uncertainty in intellectual property valuation, based on context. In the second edition of the Smith and Parr book, *Valuation of Intellectual Property and Intangible Assets*, the authors discuss asset characteristics. In Chapter 12, they include a chart titled "Business Asset Characteristics," as shown in Figure 17.1. The most striking aspect is that as an asset type goes from left to right on their chart, it becomes less liquid and more volatile in value. Put another way, cash assets do not have a variation in value, whether or not they are in bankruptcy. As we move to the right, we see that tangible assets, such as buildings, also have a relatively small variation in value. Finally, on the right-hand side of the chart, intangible assets have the greatest variation in value. This chart illustrates graphically the effect of uncertainty on groups of intangible assets—and there is no more uncertain situation than bankruptcy.

Whether calculating a value of the assets based on replacement value, auction value, liquidation value, or traditional market value, account must be given to the environment for disposal. Because of bankruptcy or reorganization, the valuation is *context specific*, meaning that some discount from normal market value will be

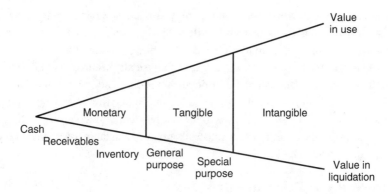

Figure 17.1   Business Asset Characteristics.

needed. It must be remembered, too, that intellectual property and intangible assets are wasting assets—as time goes by, their value declines relatively quickly. Finally, in a liquidation scenario, the "willing buyer/willing seller" premise of value is modified to account for the distressed environment in which the assets will be sold.

Therefore, one should take an approach to valuation during bankruptcy that from typical, going-concern market value, a liquidation discount will be applied. That discount can be as little as 30% and as much as 90% and, in some cases, possibly even more. As each month passes, the value of the Intellectual Property or intangible asset can decrease by 5–10% (databases, mailing lists, and technical know-how will degrade more quickly than trademarks and brand assets).

Therefore, the final thought in bankruptcy valuation is this: Going-concern value less liquidation discount, less a further discount for competitive bankrupt asset offerings, is a realistic and attainable market value.

The Marketing and Sales Process

The central issue of selling or liquidating intangible assets in bankruptcy is to find the most effective way to maximize value. Whether in the context of acquisition or merger, IPO, private sale, foreclosure, reorganization, or bankruptcy, how do these intangible assets, the intellectual capital of the company, become converted to real cash? To answer this question, one must look at the elements and the process of monetization, and then to the mechanics of the process in its implementation.

Viewed with a jaundiced eye, the assets need to be analyzed as if they were merchandise. That is, they must be prepared for sale, described with collateral material, and packaged as if they were inventory, fixtures, or other tangible assets being sold in the ordinary course of bankruptcy, which, in fact, they are. Further, because the assets are intangible, they need to be collected in their electronic or graphic form and secured off site by the outsource provider, since the old operating environment in which they were deployed is unstable and going away. The remaining people in the organization will be disappearing, and a knowledge transfer must be accomplished to a safe haven of stability and continuity.

As part of the process, the assets must be physically secured, including source code libraries and technical and user documentation, in addition to the contracts, licenses, certifications, patents, trademarks, and other filings and registrations. Although many of these originals will remain resident with counsel for the company, an inventory of all relevant materials related to salable assets must be collected and organized.

■ Case Study 1: Polaroid

To illustrate the marketing and sales process, we have included two case studies. In the first, Polaroid Corporation, we were asked to put together a contingency plan to dispose of the assets. Under one contingency, we were asked to look at liquidation, and on the other hand at an orderly disposal. At the same time, we were asked to establish going-concern value for a legacy company. We will focus here on the first two valuation premises. Tables 17.3, 17.4, and 17.5 summarize the project very simply. Table 17.3 lays out what we were asked to do, Table 17.4 lists the assets of value, and Table 17.5 summarizes the values.

The Polaroid case had a happy ending: An investor was found for a legacy company, and the intangible assets were used as securitization for a $50M–60M asset-based loan. ■

Table 17.3 Polaroid: The Project

Assist Polaroid in maximizing the value of its intellectual property and other intangible assets via:

Valuation of the assets

Identification of target markets, economic conditions

Suggestion of monetization alternatives

Recommendation of an asset disposition or securitization plan

---

Table 17.4 Polaroid Corporation: Bankruptcy/Reorganization

Key assets	
Technology	Marketing
• 800+ patents	• Core Polaroid brand
• 52 clusters	• Subbrands
• 500+ patent applications	• Trademark licenses
• 30,000+ chemicals	• Photo archive
• Patent licenses	

Table 17.5 Polaroid Net Asset Values

	Liquidation	Orderly disposal
Total technology asset value	$15.2M–19.5M	$36.5M–43.0M
Total brand asset value	$30.8M–45.2M	$67.0M–78.0M
Net value (after all hard costs)	$46.0M–65.0M	$103.5M–112.1M

■ Case Study 2: Amherst Fiber Optics

In the second case, Amherst Fiber Optics, the situation was quite different. Amherst was a subsidiary of TVC, a company in Chapter 11 reorganization.

In order to come up with an adequate plan of reorganization and emerge from bankruptcy, the parent company discovered that there was a great deal of unlocked value in the Amherst Fiber Optics assets—but this was value of a unique sort. In this case, Amherst stood to recover a $20+M tax refund from the federal government for its investments in R&D. However, there was an important key constraint: The assets had to be sold on or before December 31, 2002, in order to earn the tax credit. In this environment, we were given less than 90 days to identify, assemble, market, sell, and close the transaction. Therefore, assets that might have brought a few million dollars in a liquidation scenario were reduced to an absolute fire-sale context.

Table 17.6 outlines the assets for sale, and Table 17.7 shows the result of the project. Although we had only a few weeks to sell and close the assets (and, as a consequence, received less than $700K in cash for the assets) the process was a

Table 17.6 Amherst Fiber Optics: Liquidation/Asset Sale

Company	TVC
Context	Liquidation of subsidiary
Cause	Massive potential tax benefit
Components	Eight independent patent bundles Fiber optics after-market Repair/maintenance
Valuation approach	Components of value Liquidation value

Table 17.7 Monetization of Amherst Fiber Optics

Trademark and technology assets

- Identify all Intellectual Property in each bundle

- Inventory patent applications and registrations

- Collate related trade secrets, designs, assemblers, etc.

- Benchmark valuation
  - Liquidation context
  - End-use dependent

- Market the assets/close transactions

- Results:
  - $400–700,000 cash sale
  - $20+ million tax refund

great success because all assets were sold, transferred, and money exchanged before December 31, 2002. As a result, the client received a tax refund in excess of $20M, enabling the parent company to proceed with its reorganization plan.

Conclusion

The legal issues regarding intellectual property in bankruptcy are complex. Nonetheless, in the midst of the radical change wrought by liquidation, bankruptcy, or sale, intellectual property and intangible assets should be looked to first, not last. The company or its trustees should begin the process of monetization in parallel with tangible asset reviews of merchandise, inventories, real estate, and FFE&I.

This brief overview of intangible assets and intellectual property in reorganization and bankruptcy stresses accurate values and orderly disposition. This chapter is only a summary of a subject that is complex and increasingly important. However, five specific observations should be restated:

- The increasing importance to a corporation of intangible assets
- The increasing recognition by bankruptcy, tax, and other courts of both the importance and the value of intellectual capital
- Similar recognition by creditors of the importance and value of these assets
- The awareness that intangible assets and intellectual property can be valued accurately
- The realization of Intellectual Property disposal or liquidation values in the tens of millions of dollars

Finally, there are the legal issues regarding Intellectual Property ownership and rights in bankruptcy. Whether it is primary ownership of the trademark, patent, copyright, a fully paid-up license, or a series of product-specific licenses, ownership and disposal are and will be issues in bankruptcy. This is not an analysis of the legal issues. Rather, it puts forth the business issues. However, all professionals involved with intellectual property in a bankruptcy environment must be cautioned that substantial uncertainty remains as to ownership and disposal powers over shrinkwrap licenses, trademark licenses, patent and technology agreements, and so on. These issues likely will be worked out on a case-by-case basis as the number and range of bankruptcies get more complex.

CHAPTER 18

TAX ISSUES: TRANSFER PRICING, ROYALTY RATES, AND INTELLECTUAL PROPERTY HOLDING COMPANIES

by

Weston Anson and Chaitali Ahya

Transfer pricing is the practice by which the price or fee for use of an asset is established for transfer from one affiliated company to another. In a simple example, two companies merge operations and the larger of the companies has technology, trademarks, or other intangibles that the newly acquired company would like to use. In that case, an arm's length royalty rate would have to be established for use of the intellectual property, and/or a fixed price would have to be negotiated for outright transfer of the asset from the parent to the subsidiary. Therefore, transfer pricing is the process encouraged by tax authorities of setting appropriate and market-based values and royalty rates for use and acquisition of intangible assets. Most major governments have stated fairly similar regulations for appropriate transfer pricing, consistently referring to market-based methods to establish the royalty rate or transfer price. (See Table 18.4.)

The problem, of course, is the fact that what is a fair transfer price to one country's tax authorities may not appear to be fair to another country's. For example, the IRS would like to see subsidiaries of U.S. companies paying very high royalty rates to the U.S. companies for the use of intellectual property, because this would obviously engender income to the American parent company and, as a result, tax revenue. At the same time, overseas governments would like to see the royalty rate paid to the American parent company minimized; again, because that would reduce the amount of outflows paid by the overseas subsidiary in royalty rates, thus retaining more income in its own country and generating more tax revenue for that country.

There are three intertwined tax topics here:

- First, what methods of transfer pricing are acceptable in the United States and key overseas markets?
- Second, how does one value an asset or set market-based royalty rates for what are essentially in-house license agreements among affiliates?
- Third, what is an Intellectual Property holding company, and what is its role in this transfer pricing environment?

The goal in any transfer pricing valuation project should be approximately as follows: to ensure that the sale price or royalty rates for use or transfer of a piece of intellectual property between related or affiliated companies reflects market conditions, so that the tax authorities in each of the countries see the transparency of the process and believe that the pricing truly reflects what would represent an arm's length transaction between two unrelated third parties.

These are difficult topics to describe in the abstract (anyone who has tried to read through the IRS or Inland Revenue regulations on the topic of transfer pricing will know just how difficult it is to write cogently about such an abstract project). The quickest way to illustrate the issues of Intellectual Property valuation in a tax environment is to rely on a case study. The case study that follows is based on a project for two companies, one European based and one U.S. based, in similar service industries. In the acquisition, the European company had a famous name and logo, and the American company had a famous name and logo; the European company had sophisticated systems and technical know-how, and the U.S. company had sophisticated systems and technical know-how. Our task was to establish fair market pricing for the use of these four groups of assets by the two companies. What follows is a description of how that process proceeded. At the end of the case study is a brief write-up on the role and function of Intellectual Property holding companies.

Overview of the Project

The demand for commercial/industrial services in areas ranging from waste disposal and maintenance to temporary staffing has increased dramatically over the last decade. With this expansion has come a new focus on higher-quality service and on global marketing and recognition. Opportunities to secure new contracts are influenced by the reputation of a company. As a consequence, the importance and value of trademarks and marketing intangibles have increased dramatically.

Company B provides commercial/industrial services to major corporations, government agencies, and a wide range of industrial and commercial customers. Their trademark and logo are well established in the United States. In addition, they are recognized for their technical expertise and their training programs in commercial/industrial services.

Company A, a large, publicly traded multinational based in Europe, acquired Company B in early 2002. Company B has subsidiaries in more than 85 countries and provides a wide range of commercial and industrial services.

We began the process by reviewing the data and the proposed license agreement between the two. Both trademarks and technical know-how were being transferred from Company A to Company B, whereas only technical know-how was being transferred from Company B to Company A. At the same time, the trademarks of Company A were being licensed to its subsidiaries and affiliates. Our goal was to establish appropriate royalty rates and fee structures for these transfers. (In addition, Company B had placed its intellectual property in an Intellectual Property holding company, which licenses Company B's intellectual property to both Company A and to Company B's operating subsidiaries. See figure on following page.)

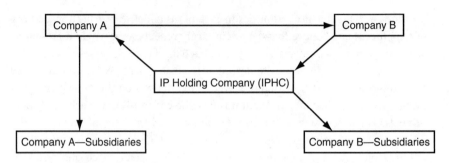

Table 18.1 Each Company's Contribution of Trademark Assets

Company A	Company B
Logo	Logo
Trademark registrations	Trademark registrations
Copyrights	Copyrights
Trade dress	Trade dress
Corporate name	

We reviewed the trademark assets of Company A, as well as the bundle of intellectual property controlled by Company B and the proposed use of its logo by all subsidiaries of both companies. Royalty rates established were for the trademark assets listed in Table 18.1.

In addition to these trademark assets, the license agreement between these companies covered transfer of technical know-how between companies. The know-how being transferred from Company B to Company A consisted of two components:

- Company B's training programs and HR management
- Three sophisticated IT systems

The transfer of know-how from Company A to Company B included transfer of

- Training and HR management
- Financial and treasury systems

Transfer Pricing Methodologies

Tax authorities around the globe continue to increase enforcement of transfer pricing issues and, therefore, compliance requirements on taxpayers. Arm's length consideration for intangible asset transfers must be commensurate with the income attributable to the intangible, as required by the 1986 Tax Reform Act and subsequent revisions and additions. IRS Section 482 generally considers three methods for intangible asset transfer pricing valuation: transaction based, cost based, and profit based.

Transaction-Based Methods

Transaction-based methods provide that intercompany fees are determined by reference to terms between uncontrolled entities. The key to successful utilization of these methods is the ability to satisfy the criteria for a "comparable" transaction. Transaction-based methods include the following:

- Comparable uncontrolled transaction (CUT) method
- Comparable uncontrolled price (CUP) method

In the CUT method, a reasonable basis for determining a royalty rate is royalty rates in similar licensing situations. Based on investigation of the industry, review of the intellectual property being valued, and market transactions, a royalty rate that is appropriate for the intangible assets is estimated.

Profit-Based Methods

Profit-based methods look to a taxpayer's relative contribution of profit by its intangibles to the combined entity and provide that intercompany fees or royalty rates may be allocated based on this relative profitability. Profit-based methods include the following:

- Comparable profits method (CPM)
- Profit split (PS) method
- Taxable net margin method (TNMM)
- Relative profit (RP) method
- Resale method (RSM)

Cost-Sharing Methods

A company may demonstrate the arm's length nature of intercompany charges by the execution of a cost-sharing agreement with subsidiaries and their controlled entities. A cost-sharing arrangement is defined as an agreement to share the costs of development of one or more intangibles in proportion to the share of anticipated benefits from the parties' use.

IRS rules generally require that a participant in a qualified cost-sharing arrangement must reasonably anticipate benefits from the use of intangibles. In addition, to qualify for a cost-sharing arrangement, certain formal requirements must be satisfied related to accounting, documentation, and reporting. Separate consideration (the buy-in payment) is required for preexisting intangible property made available to the arrangement.

Royalty Rates for Trademark Assets

Having completed a thorough background analysis, we moved to the next step in establishing marketplace royalty rates: analyzing select comparable transactions. Our initial goal was to identify transactions that involved trademarks, which were as similar as possible to those of Companies A and B. Based on our experience, we established ten specific criteria:

1. That the licenses involve commercial services
2. That the comparable trademarks operate and license in both the United States and international markets
3. That the comparable trademarks be moderately well known in more than one major market or country
4. That the comparable trademarks be represented by meaningful companies with substantial financial resources
5. That the license agreements cover products or services for customers that are comparable
6. That the license agreements have multiyear terms
7. That the license agreements be renewable or extensible
8. That the license agreements be exclusive for a given product or service to a given licensee in a given country
9. That the comparable transactions cover commercial/industrial service-based trademarks that can be used in more than one service sector
10. That no patents or technology be included

These criteria were used to screen contractual terms and conditions. Most importantly, use of these criteria meant that the comparables did not include any deals where technical know-how or patents were included.

A final step in our analysis was to benchmark and compare those comparables against Company A and B. We looked at all comparable transactions and quartiles, as shown in Table 18.2.

Cost-Sharing Arrangement for Technical Know-How

The other part of the assignment was to determine an appropriate fee structure for the transfer of the IT and technical know-how between the two companies, because exchange of technical know-how was flowing both ways. After collecting and analyzing all information, we determined that a cost-sharing arrangement was the most applicable transfer pricing method in this case. Rights to the preexisting intangible property could be purchased through a buy-in payment. However, development expenses on both sides were at a similar level, so there was no imbalance in each party's contribution, and no buy-in payment was deemed necessary.

- Both companies had well developed and equivalently valuable HR and training programs.

Table 18.2 Summary of Royalty Rate Ranges

Statistical function	Range
1st quartile	1.4–3.0%
2nd quartile	1.0–1.4%
3rd quartile	0.75–1.0%
4th quartile	0.5–0.75%
Minimum	0.5%
Maximum	3.0%
Median	1.0%

Table 18.3 Each Company's Contribution of Know-How

Company A	Company B
HR management	HR management
Training programs	Training programs
IT: Risk management system	Financial systems
IT: Client management system	Treasury systems
IT: Global intranet	

- Specialized IT services were developed in three general areas by Company A, which incurred costs equal to the financial and treasury systems that were developed by Company B. All these systems were to be used across the entire group.
- We therefore concluded that the costs and efforts of Company A for training and to develop IT systems, and of Company B for training and to develop financial and treasury services and systems, were approximately equal, so no buy-in payment by either party was necessary.
- Based on the benefits ratio standards laid out in Section 482 of the IRS regulations, we established a benefits and utilization ratio between the two parties using one of gross revenues as a basis, and a benefits ratio of 75:25 weighted for Company B was most appropriate. The cost-sharing arrangement reviewed annually, using a benefits ratio calculation based on gross revenues generated by each entity.

- A key benefit of using a cost-sharing arrangement is that as intangibles, know-how, and best practices are developed in the future, they will be developed based on this pool of ownership that already exists.

Conclusions

We determined that CUT was the best method to use for the trademark assets and that the cost-sharing arrangement would be most appropriate for transfer of know-how. We established a royalty range for the use of Company A's trademark and logo by Company B, and a royalty rate for use of Company A's trademark assets by its subsidiaries.

Finally, for the transfer of the technical know-how we used the cost-sharing method, per IRS regulations, and determined a benefits ratio to share the benefits derived from the use of the intangibles developed by both the entities. Because both the companies spent equal amounts to develop these intangibles, no buy-in payment was deemed necessary. Our recommendation was to move forward with a cost-sharing arrangement between the two companies with the benefits ratio calculated annually. Recommended charges were as follows:

- Looking at marketplace transactions, the full range of market comparables for similar trademarks and logos runs between 0.5 and 3.0%, applied as a percentage of net wholesale sales.
- Given the strengths of the trademarks and brand name of Company A and the associated intangibles being provided to subsidiaries, the most likely range of royalty rates for use of these trademark assets would be between 1.4 and 1.75%.
- Because Company A subsidiaries and affiliates typically provide their own advertising and promotional funding, an advertising allowance or rebate can be given, thus lowering the effective net range of royalty rates for their name and trademarks to 0.9–1.25%.
- We also analyzed appropriate royalty rates for Company B. Based on its new image, low profile, and lack of awareness in the U.S. market, appropriate royalty rates should be at or near the lower end of the range, or 0.5–0.75%.

Intellectual Property Holding Companies

The growing importance of intellectual property for tax planning purposes is clear. When management is looking at its Intellectual Property portfolio, it should think of the interplay of four factors:

- Where to hold the trademarks, patents, or other intellectual property
- Whether and how to license the use of intellectual property on an intercompany basis
- What to charge and how to structure that license agreement
- To what state or offshore location to direct the royalty payments

Table 18.4 Global Transfer Pricing Trends

	Possible valuation methods	Preferred method	Level of activity
Europe:			
U.K.	CUT, CPM	Comparables	High
France	CUT, CPM, PS, CS	CPM	Increasing
Germany	CUT, CPM	CUT	Increasing
Spain	CUT, RSM, S, CS, TNMM	Best method	Increasing
Americas:			
United States	CUT, CPM	Best method	High
Canada	CUT, CPM	Comparables	Increasing
Mexico	CUP	Comparables	High
Asia/Pacific:			
Australia	CUP, RR, CP, PS, CPM	Comparable transaction	Increasing
Japan	CUP, RP, CP, other	CUP, RP, CP	High

All of these factors have an impact on a company's tax liabilities. By managing them correctly, an intellectual property owner can minimize state and federal taxes. By using the right state or offshore domicile, the intellectual property, and the right mechanisms to ensure arm's length royalty rates and licensing terms, a company can substantially decrease state taxes.

The Intellectual Property Holding Company (IPHC)

An intellectual property owner can minimize taxes by selecting the best state or overseas domicile and intercompany licensing mechanisms. The general concept is to move a company's portfolio of intellectual property (trademarks, copyrights, patents, even unpatented technology) to a venue with low or no state income taxes on passive income. Income that otherwise would be taxable by the IRS or the state in which a company conducts its business operations can be converted into nontaxable passive income in another jurisdiction, with a corresponding tax deduction in its home state.

To effect this arrangement, a number of technical requirements must be met. Broadly, they are as follows:

The parent must establish a new company in Delaware[1] (or another low-tax domicile state or country, such as Bermuda or the Bahamas). It should be a holding company without any active operations within, for example, Delaware. Its sole function should be to own and manage the intellectual property transferred to it and to hold title to the trademarks, patents, or other intellectual property, administer them, and manage the royalty income received.

Fair market royalty rates must be established. An outside licensing consulting firm or other professional should be retained to establish what royalty rates will be paid from the operating company to the IPHC. These royalty rates must be based on market comparables and must be able to withstand the test of fairness if challenged.

The fair market value of the intellectual property must be estimated, using an outside third party to establish that value. Thus, one establishes the value of the intellectual property as a contribution to the IPHC.

The company must transfer its intellectual property to the new company, receiving in return stock in the new IPHC. It is important that the company make the intellectual property the only asset of the investment-holding IPHC.

The IPHC, as licensor, and the parent and its operating subsidiaries, as licensees, must draft, sign, and implement license agreements, requiring payment of fair-market royalty rates to the IPHC for use of the intellectual property. These agreements should be constructed as if they were established with true third parties.

Finally, the company must ensure that the license agreements are monitored and managed on an ongoing basis. It is important to ensure that they be enforced and that royalty rates be paid promptly, as they would be in any third-party transaction. Thus, by treating the intercompany licensing and royalty rates as arm's length, the legal status of the IPHC is not endangered.

Benefits, Management, and Support

As briefly summarized in the preceding section, substantial tax benefits can result from following these logical steps and establishing a holding company in Delaware or another low-tax state to receive royalties from operating companies.

There are other benefits, of course, including streamlined management of intellectual property. The monies received by the IPHC can be borrowed by the parent or one of the other operating companies. Again, any interest paid to the IPHC is not taxed. It is imperative that tax counsel be consulted on any transaction like this.

---

[1] As would be expected, other states do not like the Delaware holding company, and some have started a counterattack. For example, in 1991 Ohio passed legislation barring Ohio operating companies from deducting such payments to Delaware holding companies. In 2002, New Jersey announced it would disallow or reduce intercompany payments as it saw fit.

CHAPTER 19

VALUING FOR CHARITABLE DONATION

by

David C. Drews

with an introduction by Weston Anson

Introduction

Part V of this primer focuses on context as it affects value. In this chapter, David C. Drews, who is well known in the area of valuation of technology for donations, deals with what is perhaps the most context-driven form of valuation: valuation of technology for donation to a nonprofit organization. In general, this form of valuation is done purely because of the context. Unlike many other contextual value situations, the context *itself* becomes the valuation objective. In other words, without the donation scenario, the technology would be unlikely to command much value. The exception would be an unused piece of technology that a corporation could possibly sell to a competitor but refuses to do so for competitive reasons.

The system of donation of technology enables a company to extract value from underutilized or unusable technology. It is a tool for a corporation to increase its overall return on investment of the R&D or technology development function, by donating the technology and receiving a tax benefit equivalent to the donor corporation's tax rate. In other words, if the corporation has a 35% federal income tax rate, then for every $1M of value that it donates to a nonprofit research organization or university, it generates value of $350K in tax benefits. This tax benefit is as real a benefit as cash received from a sale to a third party.

However, valuation for donations has come under increasing examination by the IRS and is now being scrutinized on a regular basis. In fact, many of the donation valuation projects done in the late 1990s and at the beginning of this century are now being challenged by the IRS. As a consequence, a note of caution to those considering donations: Ensure that the value is truly a market value, to the best standards of valuation professionals.

This chapter describes the process and methodology of valuing technology for donations. It looks at all the standard methodologies and also describes the technology factor approach and the 25% rule of thumb.

Valuing for Charitable Donation

Corporate managers understand that a vital part of every successful technology-oriented company is a significant investment in research and the development of patented technology. Patents allow a company to exploit its inventions for a period of time (currently 20 years from the initial filing date), while giving that company the right to prevent others from practicing the technology. This can provide a competitive advantage that increases the likelihood of growing revenues and increased profits.

As a company searches for new products or improvements on existing product lines, some of the ideas that are generated and the initial research are never carried through to the commercial stage. Frequently, even though the underlying product or process has been patented, the project is abandoned or otherwise idles, and the company's resources are redirected elsewhere.

Orphan Technology

It is an unfortunate fact of corporate life that there are not enough resources available to commercialize all the ideas that the Research Department may generate. Although the projects that a company chooses to commercialize are typically thought to be the best bets for achieving the required return on investment, there is also a way to derive benefits from the company's so-called orphan technologies. Many companies donate their orphan technology to a variety of nonprofit recipients and reap significant benefits.

These abandoned research projects are typically referred to as *orphan technology*. More specifically, they are patents that are awarded by the U.S. Patent and Trademark Office, but the corresponding technology is never fully deployed for commercial use. To get an idea of the magnitude of this phenomenon, BTG International, a technology transfer consultancy, claims that the typical U.S. company ignores more than 35% of its patents. When considering the number of issued patents and technology-oriented companies in the U.S., it is obvious that a large quantity of assets is being underutilized in our nation's economy.

The number of orphan technologies at any one time will vary, as a result of new investment decisions, abandonments, and expirations. Often the decision to forgo commercialization of a patented technology is tied to merger and acquisition activity; a company will be acquired for a specific set of assets, and any others are divested, shut down, or abandoned.

The value of these donated patents is often significant, and many large, globally known corporations are exploring this option for tax reasons. In 2002, the National Technology Transfer Center in Wheeling, West Virginia, received three related patents with an appraised value of $2.1M from Eaton Corporation. The patents encompass alloy valves for internal combustion engines.[1] Also, Boeing

[1] NTTC press release, April 2, 2002.

donated technology with applications in bone replacement and strengthening to the University of Pennsylvania in 2001.[2]

Donation

Everyone is familiar with the concept of donation and the benefits it brings: One donates something of value to a deserving organization and is then able to deduct the corresponding amount when calculating taxable income. The financial benefit to the donor is a function of the donor's tax rate. For example, if someone donates $100 to a charity and his or her tax rate is 28%, this action would generate tax savings of $28. The process works essentially the same for corporations as it does for individuals. There are limitations to its use, however. The company must rely on its tax experts in order to utilize this process effectively. Should the company elect to donate its technology, the following factors must be understood:

The company should be profitable and have tax liability. For any company, the main focus of its activity is the most efficient use of its resources. When considering the donation of patents, the primary benefit in most cases is the realization of tax benefits. However, if the company has no taxable income or if it can dismiss taxable income through the use of net loss carryforwards, donation is not a viable option. Without taxable income, the tax benefit associated with donation does not apply. The company can still donate the assets, but the financial benefits will not be available.

The company gives up all ownership of the technology. Sometimes companies are interested in donating only the applications of a particular patent that they have no interest in pursuing. At the same time, they want to hold on to the rights associated with applications that they do want to commercialize. This is a very risky strategy that should not be pursued. The most appropriate course of action is to donate all rights to the patented technology, including all possible applications. Every effort should be made to ensure that all rights associated with the patents are included in the donation.

The assignment of value for the donation must be objective. In order to meet IRS guidelines regarding the value of donated technology, an independent third party, recognized as an expert in intellectual property valuation, must be used to determine the value of the patents. Without a valid and objective valuation of the donated patents, the credibility of the tax deductions is called into question.

The timing of the independent valuation is also important. Depending on the technology involved, the valuation will likely become "stale" within three to six months. This is due to the dynamic marketplace in which most

---

[2] Boeing press release, October 15, 2001.

technologies compete, which may lead to obsolescence or changes in the competitive equation utilized to determine the value of the donated technology. Any delays in the donation process will most likely create the need for a second look at many of the inputs used to value the technology. For these reasons, it is best to have a recipient lined up before engaging the valuation expert. The cost of an update is relatively low, however, and may be mitigated entirely through an ongoing relationship with the intellectual property valuation expert.

The recipient must be a qualified nonprofit organization. The fit between the intended donation and the potential recipient must be considered. The donated patents must be relevant to the charter of the nonprofit organization to which they are donated. For example, if the patents are related to the automotive industry, the American Red Cross is probably not going to be interested in them. More importantly, the IRS will look less kindly on this donation if for some reason the Red Cross were to accept it. It is important that the recipient be an organization that is likely to continue the development of the technology, so that there is a better chance the technology may one day benefit society. Potential candidates for receiving donations include state, regional, and national technology transfer centers; think tanks; university research centers; and other nonprofit research organizations. The intellectual property firm relied on for the valuation can often help locate an enthusiastic recipient.

The patented technology must be viable. This is the most important element of the donation process. Patents that cover obsolete technology or products or processes that do not work well enough to be commercialized are not good choices for donation. Candidates for donation should cover products or processes that have not been commercialized because of a business decision, not because of fundamental flaws with the technology itself. This is the number one concern of the IRS in relation to the donations of intellectual property. In fact, it is probably a good idea to document the reasons for choosing not to pursue commercialization of the intellectual property before obtaining an independent verification of market value.

Alternatives to Donation

When considering a technology donation, one should review alternative strategies. Among these are sale, abandonment, and (in certain cases) depreciation. Selling the asset can potentially provide the largest benefit but is usually the most difficult and costly to implement. Of course, there is no guarantee of obtaining a favorable price. Also, unless it is a marquee technology in a highly competitive field, there may be a limited number of potential purchasers.

The benefit provided by abandonment is the removal of the ongoing administration costs of "warehousing" the assets. These fees can be significant. A detailed cost/benefit analysis should be undertaken in regard to any patent that is unlikely to be commercialized. Besides the removal of the maintenance fee obligations, no other benefits or additional revenue are forthcoming. Accordingly, this should be considered only as a last resort.

The final alternative discussed here is *depreciation*. Like donation, the benefit enjoyed via depreciation is in the form of a lower tax liability because the impact is a noncash charge against earnings. But there are problems with this strategy as well:

- First, in order to depreciate an asset, the asset must appear on the balance sheet. As a result, this option is only available for use with purchased technology. Purchased technology most likely has to be depreciated anyway, so flexibility in the management of the assets is undermined to some extent. In addition, it is important to understand that depreciation is tied to the original price paid for the assets and may ignore additional value above and beyond the initial purchase price allocation.
- Second, depreciation is unavailable for use with any technology developed in-house. Technology developed in-house frequently has value and may certainly be a candidate for donation, sale, or abandonment, but depreciation of the development costs is inapplicable.

Additional Benefits

Better resource management is another benefit. For example, if the Research Department can net the tax savings against its overall budget, those dollars can be directly assigned to ongoing research projects. This also provides an incentive to the scientists working in the labs to help identify potential donation candidates, because it can provide additional funding for their other projects.

The recipients of the donated technology also enjoy benefits. These include gaining additional technology in their Intellectual Property portfolio, most of which will likely complement their existing research efforts, and a potential source for technical consulting, equipment, or research resources. They may also gain the ability to generate revenue from commercializing the technology associated with the donated patents.

The cost to implement such a strategy is relatively low. Fees paid in relation to the independent valuation and transfer of assets are insignificant compared to the potential benefits. When considered in its appropriate context, any additional cost is typically recouped within the next few months as taxable income is calculated for that quarter. In addition, the transfer of ownership from the company to the recipient is simple and inexpensive. All that is required is the completion and filing of a form with the U.S. Patent and Trademark Office, along with a minimal filing fee.

■ Case Study

This simple case study illustrates how donation works under typical circumstances. Company A has developed and patented a new technology but finds that it does not meet its required internal rate of return for continued development and commercialization. The technology does, however, provide significant benefits in a field in which Company A does not compete (the Boeing donation mentioned earlier is an example).

Company A contacts an intellectual property management and valuation firm (B) to determine its options in regard to the patent. B explores the various options available to Company A in regard to the patent and ultimately agrees to help identify potential recipients for a donation. After confidentially speaking with several potential recipients to gauge interest and proper fit, B introduces Company A to Nonprofit C, a research department at a major university that is active in the relevant field.

After a detailed negotiation that stipulates the transfer of the ownership of the patent in detail and provides for additional resources to be utilized for patent registration maintenance and further research, Nonprofit C agrees to accept the donation from Company A. B then undertakes the independent valuation of the patent. Utilizing various valuation techniques, B determines that the fair market value of the patent is $2M.

Company A transfers the patent to Nonprofit C, which in turn provides Company A with a declaration stating that it has received a donation of property from Company A. Company A then claims the $2M donation on its tax return and deducts the $2M from its taxable income. Because the tax rate for Company A is 34%, the net benefit from this tax deduction is $680K.

Before it can conclude to its overall financial benefit, however, Company A must consider the additional expenses associated with the donation. These include the cash portion of the donation that Nonprofit C required for maintenance and additional research funding, the time and resources required to implement the donation and provide information to the valuation expert (legal and research personnel, among others), and the cost of the valuation analysis. In the case study, all of the expenses amount to $75K, which reduces the net financial benefit of the donation to $605K. See Table 19.1 for an overview. Additional benefits to Company A include an improved relationship with an important research entity and a positive public reaction in the surrounding community.

This case study illustrates the win–win outcome frequently associated with donation of patented technology. Company A obtains significant financial benefits from a technology that would likely have languished on the shelf otherwise. Nonprofit C acquires the rights to important technology in a field in which it has invested time and resources, along with additional research capabilities. ■

Table 19.1 Tax Benefit Calculation

Appraised patent value	$2,000,000
Corporate tax rate	34%
Tax deduction benefit	$680,000
Donation-related expenses/additional cash donation	$75,000
Net donation benefit	$605,000

Valuation Methodologies

There are many methods available for determining the value of donated technology, each having its appropriate applications. A brief overview of several is presented in this section. Of these, the technology factor, relief-from-royalty, and income approaches are used to isolate the value of the technology from the value of the business as a whole. However, it is important to be familiar with all of the available approaches in order to understand the effectiveness of any method that might be used.

Market Approach

Intangible assets can sometimes be valued by comparing the technology under consideration to purchase or license transactions involving similar assets that have occurred recently in similar markets.

The conditions of the market at the time of the transaction will influence the expected sale or license price for an intangible asset. When using this method, one must consider contributing factors, such as historical transactions and the participants' influences on them. With the market approach, data analysis is most critical. Empirical sales and license data must be selected, analyzed, and possibly adjusted before they can be applied to the valuation of the intangible asset. Then, this data must be analyzed in the context of

- The economic income generated by the transaction
- The risks associated with achieving that economic income
- The remaining useful life of the asset involved
- The transaction date
- The type of arrangement (exclusivity, lump sum, ongoing royalties, milestone payments, paid-up value, etc.)

Most intangible assets are not traded frequently enough to provide reliable information for a comparable market value. Moreover, when transactions are available, it is very difficult to get enough detail to be certain that you have all the elements that make for a good comparison.

Cost Approach

The cost approach to intangible asset valuation may involve two different analytical methods: the *reproduction cost method* and the *replacement cost method*. The reproduction cost method uses the current cost to construct an exact replica of the intangible asset being valued. The cost of the reproduction, however, does not consider the actual demand for the asset in the marketplace.

The replacement cost method, on the other hand, focuses on the cost to re-create the function or utility provided by the intangible asset. This replica may not appear exactly the same as the intangible asset being imitated.

This approach is useful for valuing intellectual properties when

- The flow of income or other economic benefits related to the asset cannot be reasonably or accurately quantified.
- The intangible asset is only a small part of a larger collection of assets.
- Another valuation approach is inappropriate or cannot be used.

For the most part, the cost approach might be an appropriate method to use when valuing technologies in the earliest stages of development, or when equivalent functional, noninfringing alternatives may be easily designed (e.g., software), because it reflects the cost a company could avoid by purchasing, rather than duplicating, a similar R&D effort.

Income Approach

The income approach is based on discounted cash flow theory and focuses on the income-producing capability of the property. The theory of this approach is that the value of an asset can be measured by the present value of the anticipated net economic benefits to be received over the asset's life. Whereas the market and cost approaches have particular applications in certain situations and with certain types of intangibles, the income approach is generally applicable to all situations and all types of intangible assets and intellectual properties.

The income approach is based on determining the future income or cash flow streams expected from the business (or business segment) under consideration. The income approach focuses on the main parameters that determine value, including the following elements:

- The expected size and duration of future income or cash flows
- The size and nature of the potential market, recent and expected future trends, etc.
- Factors affecting demand
- The risk factors associated with the generation of the income or cash flow stream, such as competitive actions, ability to attract customers, etc.

Technically, the valuation of free cash flows is recommended. This requires additional assumptions or estimates about annual depreciation amounts, specific capital expenditures for a given situation, and additional estimates for anticipated changes in working capital. All of these factors can vary greatly, depending on the owner or licensor of the technology.

In a typical time period, it can sometimes be reasonably assumed that capital expenditures will approximately equal depreciation and that changes in working capital required to finance changes in inventory requirements or an imbalance in receivables will have an insignificant impact on the valuation. If no historical or other precise data of this type exist for a technology, after-tax profit may be relied on as an acceptable surrogate for cash flow, with minor adjustments for additional investment in early years if necessary.

The most common error in performing intellectual property valuation is failing to differentiate between the business enterprise value and the value of the intellectual property that supports the business. When valuing intellectual property, it is critical to separate this value from the value of the business as a whole.

Technology Factor Approach

The technology factor approach is designed to avoid the common error described previously. It is a measure of the extent to which the profit derived from the practice of the technology is based solely on the technology itself. This factor, applied to the value of the ongoing business enterprise, determines the fair market value of the intellectual property. The technology factor is used extensively in the licensing community and in intellectual asset management.

In the technology factor approach, the present value of the business' ongoing cash flow is determined first by the income approach. Then, a maximum technology percentage for the industry is determined. This represents the maximum percentage of total business value that can be attributed primarily to technology, as opposed to value attributed to other assets, such as property, plant and equipment, or financial assets. It is therefore also the maximum possible technology factor. Referred to as the *technology factor upper limit,* this maximum percentage of technology value varies from industry to industry.

Next, various competitive and utility attributes that reflect the commercial strengths and weaknesses of the technology are reviewed from the points of view of both the buyer and the seller. These attributes are weighted and scored based on the circumstances specific to the valuation. The resulting calculation determines what portion of the maximum industry percentage is to be used for the present valuation. This results in the final technology factor, which reflects the technology's risk of further development cost and commercialization and its relative contribution to cash flow and fair market value. In this way, the approach separates the value of the technology from the value contributed by other assets of the business. The final value of the technology is calculated by multiplying the present value of the commercial cash flow by the technology factor.

Relief-from-Royalty Approach/25% Rule

In the relief-from-royalty approach, the value of an intangible asset is equal to the present value of the after-tax royalties that the technology owner is relieved from paying by virtue of owning the assets. This approach quantifies the royalties a licensee would be willing to pay for the use of the technology and is typically based on a percentage of revenues. It is a function of the rights being granted to the licensee and the royalty payments that would be necessary to acquire those rights.

The relief-from-royalty approach generally uses royalty rates that are market driven and applied to the projection of revenue as determined by the income approach. However, some practitioners also may apply the 25% rule, which has become a commonly cited guideline. The phrase *25% rule* and the idea behind it are widely recognized in the licensing community. It appears in many articles about valuation and has been cited in many court cases.[3]

The 25% rule assumes a royalty equal to 25% of the operating profits of the enterprise in which the licensed intellectual property is used. It is a simple rule of thumb based on equitably dividing the economic profits between the licensor and licensee, according to their relative contributions. It gives an approximate estimate of the value of intellectual property that would be paid in a reasonable arm's length negotiation.

Although it is known as the 25% rule, in practice experienced appraisers of intellectual property recognize that the percentage may vary from 10 to 50%, based on many factors that add to or detract from the contribution of the intellectual property. Some positive aspects of this approach make it popular and worth using:

- It gives a feeling of fairness. Because it is based on apportioning anticipated gain, it creates a basis for considering the respective contributions of the seller and the buyer.
- It is based directly on resulting benefits. The 25% rule focuses on the earnings-before-income-tax line in the income statement. This is an appropriate measure of the direct benefit of the subject license.

Conclusion

By utilizing the concept of donation in managing its patented research, a company can increase its return on investment in research and development. This is accomplished by donating the technology to an appropriate organization and taking the deduction when calculating taxable income. Understanding exactly what is being measured in a technology valuation can help to answer any questions that the

---

[3] *Valuation of Intellectual Property and Intangible Assets,* Gordon V. Smith and Russell L. Parr, 3rd Edition, John Wiley & Sons, 2000, pp.366–368.

tax authorities are likely to have regarding the value of donated assets. As long as the homework is done beforehand and an independent appraisal of the property from a reputable intellectual asset valuation expert has been obtained, the generation of the benefit and disposition of the assets are quick and easy.

This strategy will be effective as long as management fully considers the following:

- The company must have taxable income and tax liability.
- All ownership interest in the technology is relinquished.
- An independent appraisal from a recognized expert is required.
- The recipient must be a qualified nonprofit organization.
- The patented technology donated must be viable.

When one considers that more than 35% of the average company's intellectual property could be sitting idle, the positive impact on research and development assets that this strategy provides becomes readily apparent.

CHAPTER 20

VALUATION AND THE LITIGATION ENVIRONMENT

by

A. Scott Davidson

with an introduction by Weston Anson

Introduction

In this chapter, Scott Davidson does an excellent job of describing the process of valuing an intangible asset or a piece of intellectual property in a litigation environment. The chapter illustrates two broadly different ways to calculate value and to establish damages in litigation. The focus of the analysis is on technology, which is arguably the most complex piece of intellectual property, both in litigation and in establishing value.

In order to fill out the picture on litigation for other sorts of intellectual property, a few comments are in order on trademark and copyright litigation and on royalty rates in general. In trademark and copyright litigation, it is easier to find actual royalty rates. There are multiple resources, including

- Royalty rate databases
- Industry averages
- Public resources
- Proprietary databases
- Industry associations
- Specialized publications
- Royalty rate books (including "Royalty Rates" by Grimes and Battersby)

Additionally, average royalty rates for certain technologies are available, as Table 20.1 shows. Technology royalty rates tend to have much broader ranges and therefore a greater flexibility and openness to interpretation during litigation. Sources for technology royalty rates include industry associations, such as Licensing Executives Society (LES) and the American Intellectual Property Law Association (AIPLA); specialty magazines and publications, including *Licensing Economics Review*; proprietary databases, such as those controlled by AUS Consultants and Consor; and public documents that can be located through a company's 10-K and 10Q filings via Edgar or other search sources.

Before we turn the chapter over to Scott Davidson, it is useful to look at the rules and standards of negotiating a royalty rate in litigation. Because each situation is different, there will be different ground rules and contextual impacts. However, litigation courts often look at earlier standards and earlier rulings. One of the

Table 20.1 Technology Royalty Rates

Industry	Range
Aerospace	2–15%
Chemical	1–10%
Health care equipment	5–10%
Electronics	3–12%
Medical equipment	3–5%
Software	5–15%
Semiconductors	1–2%
Pharmaceuticals	8–20%
Diagnostics	2–5%

landmark rulings in licensing negotiations is the Georgia-Pacific case of 1970. Because of its landmark status, *Georgia-Pacific* is often referred to by other courts. In particular, the negotiating elements or rules that were established by *Georgia-Pacific* are often cited in other rulings. It is indeed a landmark case in licensing. In an attempt to establish clarity and set new standards, the court offered 15 factors to consider in setting royalty rates to be used in litigation.

Hypothetical Negotiations
15 Georgia-Pacific Factors[1]

1. The royalties received by the patentee for the licensing of the patent *in situ*, providing or tending to prove an established royalty
2. The rates paid by the licensee for the use of other patents comparable to the patent in the suit
3. The nature and scope of the license, as exclusive or nonexclusive, or as restricted or nonrestricted in terms of territory, or with respect to whom the manufactured product may be sold
4. The licensor's established policy and marketing program to maintain its patent monopoly by not licensing others to use the invention, or by granting licenses under special conditions designed to preserve that monopoly
5. The commercial relationship between the licensor and licensee, such as whether they are competitors in the same territory or in the same line of business, or whether they are inventor and promoter

---

[1] Thanks to Campos & Stratis, LLC.

6. The effect of selling the patent specialty in promoting sales of other products of the licensee, the existing value of the invention to the licensor as a generator of sales of these nonpatented items, and the extent of such derivative or convoyed sales

7. The duration of the patent and the terms of the license

8. The established profitability of the patented product, its commercial success, and its current popularity

9. The utility and advantages of the patent property over the old modes or devices (if any) that had been used for working out similar results

10. The nature of the patent invention, the character of the commercial embodiment of it as owned and produced by the licensor, and the benefits to those who have used the invention

11. The extent to which the infringer has made use of the invention and any evidence probative of the value of that use

12. The portion of profit of the selling price that may be customary in the particular business or in comparable businesses, to allow for the use of the invention or analogous inventions

13. The portion of the realizable profit that should be credited to the invention as distinguished from nonpatented elements, the manufacturing process, business risks, or significant features or improvements added by the infringer

14. The testimony of qualified experts

15. The amount that a licensor and a licensee would have agreed upon (at the time the infringement began) if both had been reasonably and voluntarily trying to reach an agreement; that is, the amount that a prudent licensee—who desires to obtain a license to manufacture and sell a particular article embodying the patent invention—would have been willing to pay as a royalty and yet be able to make a reasonable profit, and which amount would have been acceptable by a prudent patentor who was willing to grant a license

Finally, not to overcomplicate damages calculations, it is particularly true when complex calculations regarding royalties and damages are undertaken in litigation, a great amount of detail is offered and many assumptions are made—and too many assumptions mean a greater chance of error. Full calculation in accepting a litigation-based valuation is important, and thorough review of all calculations is a must.

Damages in Intellectual Property Disputes

A *damages award* focuses on the loss suffered by the plaintiff as a result of the infringing activities of the defendant. It is intended to return the plaintiff to the position it would have been in but for the defendant's actions.

For demonstrative purposes we often refer to damages in patent cases in this section, as is discussed, but the principles generally also apply in trademark/trade name and copyright cases.

Trademark and trade-name infringements can be more problematic than patent infringements insofar as it is often difficult to prove that damages were suffered specifically because of the infringement. Unlike in patent cases, where there is a monopoly on a characteristic of the product itself (as opposed to the name or mark it bears), the infringing use of the mark or name may not be essential to making a sale, so the plaintiff may have difficulty proving lost sales. Similarly, it is unusual to quantify trademark damages on the basis of a reasonable royalty.

Copyright infringement damages may reflect a calculation of the plaintiff's lost profits flowing from lost sales of the copyrighted material. Alternatively, copyright damages may be on the basis of a royalty that the plaintiff would have realized under a license to the defendant.

In all contexts, the damages depend heavily on how the plaintiff would have exploited the intellectual property. With long-established businesses, one can determine the most likely exploitation plan through examination of established strategy. However, in determining that operating reality, one must look not only to historical patterns but to business plans, strategic plans, budgets, mission and vision statements, and the like. With early-stage companies, such as technology companies, there will be a much greater reliance on "what if" scenarios. In trademark/trade-name infringements, factors including the novelty of the business will drive the importance of the mark/name to the plaintiff's business.

If a plaintiff habitually grants licenses and a "normal" royalty rate can be established, and if it has been established that this is how the right-holder would likely have exploited the specific property infringed, then the award will in all likelihood be calculated by applying the established royalty rate to the infringing sales. In this manner, the plaintiff is restored to where he or she would have been if the defendant had legally acquired a license.

If the intellectual property, particularly a patent, was exploited through manufacturing and distribution, the referee can divide the infringer's sales into those that the right-holder would have captured absent the infringement and those that the right-holder would not have captured. For the sales the plaintiff would have captured, the court will award lost profits. This might be as simple as multiplying the lost profits per sale *times* the number of sales diverted from the right-holder to the infringer. For those sales the plaintiff would not have captured, the court will award the right-holder a reasonable royalty on the sales. Finally, if the parties cannot establish either the lost profits or a normal licens-

ing policy, the default remedy is the reasonable royalty. This scheme is dia-
grammed in Table 20.2.

Lost Profits

A successful plaintiff is entitled to compensation for all lost profits resulting
from the infringing act. Damages are computed assuming that the infringer had not
entered the market at all. It is subject to the usual tort considerations of remoteness
and foreseeability.

Apportionment may be appropriate if it can be proved by the defendant that
the infringing item is separable from the product sold by the plaintiff or a separable part of it.

The difference or comparison noted here yields the starting point for a damage
calculation:

- The hypothetical experience of the plaintiff as it would have been but for
  the infringement *minus*
- The actual experience of the plaintiff, reflecting the negative consequences
  of the infringement

Table 20.2 Scheme for Damages

Damages	
"To restore the person who has sustained injury and loss to the condition in which he would have been had he not so sustained it"	
Use does not damage plaintiff	Determine reasonable royalty
Use damages plaintiff	Determine the operating reality of the plaintiff as it would have been but for the breach
If plaintiff habitually licenses at a given rate	Consider the following remedies in light of the plaintiff's operating reality at the relevant time. The choice remedy should be the more appropriate one: • Reasonable royalty • Lost profits
If plaintiff normally exploits through manufacture and sales ⟶	Same as above
If operating reality of plaintiff is ⟶ not definitive	Reasonable royalty

This comparison must be detailed so as to stratify or highlight component parts, including the following:

- Lost profits on sales that would have been captured by the plaintiff if the defendant hadn't infringed *plus*
- Lost profits in actual sales from price competition from the infringer *plus*
- Lost profits from higher production costs *plus*
- Lost profits from lost convoyed sales *plus*
- Lost profits from springboard damages and early-adopter advantages *plus*
- Losses of subsidiary companies *less*
- Mitigation

Lost Profits on Defendant's Sales that the Plaintiff Would Have Captured

The burden is on the plaintiff to prove that he or she would have captured sales made by the defendant in the absence of the infringement. The assessment depends on a balancing of many factors, including

- The presence of competing products in the marketplace
- The advantages of the patented products over competing products
- The advantages of the infringing product over the patented product
- The market position of the patentee
- The market position of the infringer
- The market share of the patentee before and after the infringing product entered the market
- The size of the market both before and after the infringing product entered the market
- The capacity of the patentee to produce additional products

This implies a detailed market analysis. It is relatively straightforward to show that there was market demand for the infringed products. However, other items require much more detailed and careful market analysis. For example, showing that the plaintiff would have captured the defendant's sales requires proving that the intellectual property has market power or that it could influence the market and draw sales to the item.

To capture these sales, the Intellectual Property owner must demonstrate how it would satisfy market demand. Alternatives include in-house production with existing or expanded capacity, outsourcing, joint venturing, and the like. The most appropriate basis will depend on the operating reality of the right-holder. Lost profits are, of course, a function of the method by which demand is satisfied.

After the lost sales have been quantified, cost must be determined in order to arrive at the lost profit. As a general principle over the short term, the variable cost or differential costing method is appropriate.

When costs are truly fixed and would have been incurred by the plaintiff in any event, it is usually inappropriate to deduct these costs in calculating damages. The applicability of certain opportunity- or economic-related costs will depend on the facts. There is no general rule.

One criticism of the differential method or variable cost method of determining damages is that the result is so different from what would be determined under a reasonable royalty method or the analytical or investment methods (discussed later). The primary difference between these latter methods and the variable cost basis is that the latter methods include significant absorption of fixed costs. They do not address the problem from a variable and fixed costing point of view but from a more holistic one.

Lost Profits due to Price Reductions

A successful plaintiff can also claim damages from price reductions forced by competition from the infringer. Courts in the U.S. have awarded damages where the effect of the competition was only to prevent the plaintiff from making price increases where sufficient proof of the effect has been offered.[2]

Lost Profits due to Higher Production Costs

Damages on account of increased costs caused by lower volumes resulting from the defendant's infringement are often a successful point of claim. These higher costs are often called a *loss of economies of scale*.

Other expenses may increase absolutely or relatively to meet the competition from the infringer and can be included in a damage claim. These include heavier advertising expenses, adding sales personnel, increased use of discounts, or investing more heavily in a distribution system to improve service.

Lost Profits from Lost Convoyed Sales

Convoyed sales are sales of goods that are normally or often sold with an allegedly infringing item but are not themselves covered by the intellectual property in question. To the extent that the loss of convoyed sales flows from the loss of the sales of the patented product, it is appropriate to quantify and claim both amounts.

Reasonable Royalties

Reasonable royalty calculations are generally made in three contexts in patent cases:

---

[2] See *Minnesota Mining and Manufacturing v. Johnson & Johnson Orthopaedics* 976 F.2d 1559; 24 USPQ2d 1321 (Fed Cir 1992) and *In re Mahurkar Patent Litigation* 831 F.Supp 1354; 28 USPQ2d 1801 (ND Ill. 1993), aff'd 71 F.3d 1573; 37 USPQ2d1138 (Fed Cir. 1995). Price reductions that are compensable include reductions upon the announcement of the introduction of a competing product: see *Brooktree v. Advanced Micro Devices Inc.* 977 F.2d 1555 at 1578-81, 24 USPQ2d 1401 at 1417-19 (Fed. Cir. 1992).

- Where the company normally exploits its intellectual property through licensing
- Where the company exploits its intellectual property itself, but the defendant has made sales that would not have been captured by the plaintiff in any case
- Where the parties have failed to prove either a "habitual" licensing fee or lost profits

The method to determine reasonable royalties has been given a number of formulations in different cases, a recent one is the *hypothetical negotiation*, in which a reasonable royalty rate is what the infringer would have had to pay if, instead of infringing, the infringer had come to be licensed under the patent.

It is possible that, in some cases, the price at which the right-holder acting reasonably would have licensed his intellectual property is higher than the maximum price that the infringer would have been willing, or perhaps able, to pay. The principle of restoration suggests that the court should act to restore the licensor to where he or she would have been absent the infringement, not to where the licensor would have been if he or she had licensed the infringer.

It would seem that the circumstances of each case push the judiciously acceptable royalty rate to one end of the scale or the other, depending on the court's perception of equity. For example, in the United States case of *Rite-Hite*, the court was faced with determining a reasonable royalty in a situation where there was no logical reason for the right-holder to agree to license the hypothetical licensee. The Court of Appeals for the Federal Circuit found that in this situation, it was appropriate to award a royalty of 50% of the *plaintiff's* normal profits for sales to retailers.

Historical Licenses

Strong, but not necessarily definitive, evidence of the market rate for a license exists if the plaintiff has an established history of negotiating licenses for products comparable to the one that has been infringed. The historical evidence, however, is only a guide, a starting point.

The Hypothetical Negotiated License

If the evidence of past licensing activity is not consistent with the evidence in the case before the court, or in the absence of previous licensing arrangements, the reasonable royalty is usually based on a hypothetical negotiated license between the two parties under the conditions described previously.[3] The court's or referee's

---

[3] Of course, previous licensing arrangements are still valuable evidence in finding this hypothetical royalty. Chisum §20.03 [p. 20–176] notes that in the United States, existing licenses provide, as a practical matter, a floor beneath which the judicially ascertained reasonable royalty is unlikely to fall.

role in this case is to weigh all the relevant evidence placed before it to determine the hypothetical royalty.

A list of factors that may be considered in determining the hypothetically negotiated royalty was given by the court in *Georgia-Pacific Corp v. United States Plywood Corp*:[4] These fifteen points are listed in this chapter's introduction.

The 15 *Georgia-Pacific* factors emphasize a reliance on profits and precedent to set a royalty. Notably, the hypothetical negotiation between a licensor and licensee is identified as only one of many factors to consider. Some U.S. courts have placed less emphasis on comparable licenses and more emphasis on the expected profits from the license and the marketplace as a whole.[5] Because there is no prescribed method to determine reasonable royalties, expert witnesses are crucially needed to guide the court through these considerations in a persuasive manner in the context of a given case.

The Sharing of Future Profits

Numerous methods exist to decide how to divide the profit flow between the licensee and licensor. We will briefly examine three: the so-called 25% royalty rule, the analytical approach, and a return-on-investment approach.

The 25% Royalty Rule

One framework for the split of estimated profits between the hypothetical licensee and licensor is the *25% royalty rule*. This rule seeks to split the profits in a fair manner so that each party could expect to benefit from the relationship proportionately to its investment and level of risk. The 25% royalty rule recognizes as a benchmark that in a "normal" technology licensing relationship—where the licensee bears the risks of investment in manufacturing and commercialization of the technology and the risks of competition from the marketplace and the licensor provides a strong technology package—the licensor should be entitled to 25% of the predicted "profits."[6] However, this 25% royalty rule is only a starting point. The profit split should then be adjusted up or down to reflect the exact circum-

---

[4] *Georgia-Pacific Corp v. United States Plywood Corp,* 318 F. Supp 116 (S.D.N.Y., 1970), mod'd & aff'd496 F.2d 295 (2d Cir., 1971).

[5] In *Honeywell v. Minolta,* factor (12) was restated as: "What the parties reasonably anticipated would be their profits or losses as a result of entering into a licensing agreement" and three new considerations were added: "The relative bargaining positions of [the plaintiff] and [the defendant]....The extent to which the infringement prevented [the plaintiff] from using or selling the invention...The market to be tapped. See Goldscheider, R., *Technology Management: Law, Tactics, Forms,* (1984) Clark Boardman Callaghan, §24.02. The *Honeywell v. Minolta* case (D.N.J. Jan. 28, 1992, Civil Nos. 87-4847, 88-1624) was settled: the details are from the jury instructions.

[6] It is sometimes suggested that the parties begin with an assumption that licenses are typically in a 25–33% range. See W.M. Lee, "Determining Reasonable Royalty", in J. Simon and W. Friedlander, eds., *The Law and Business of Licensing* (New York: Clark Boardman Callaghan, 1996), 2061 at 2067, who cite numerous earlier sources for this approach. Alternatively, the companies could begin with a typical split for their industry or look to an investment-based analysis to set a range in which to negotiate.

stances of the license, and it is not unreasonable for the ratio to be adjusted so far as to be reversed.

The Analytical Approach

The analytical approach is very similar to the investment approach, except that it does not take market values into account. Rather, it relies on historical accounting information.

The analytical approach to determining a reasonable royalty estimates royalties by subtracting the normal profit margin of a business from the expected profit margin to find the appropriate royalty rate.[7] In this approach, an absorption cost approach is used to deduct both variable costs and a portion of fixed costs from the infringer's net sales. The "normal" profit margin is that which would likely have been realized by the infringer if he or she had sold similar products without infringing the intellectual property. The remaining amount is then awarded to the rightholder as a "reasonable royalty."

This approach tries to split the profits between the plaintiff and the defendant while allowing the defendant to keep a normal level of profits. The practical problem is the determination of what "normal" profit margins are in the industry in question. As a first cut, it can be difficult to define precisely in what industry or market the infringement is taking place. Even within an industry, there is a wide discrepancy in profit margins, often by almost an order of magnitude. Furthermore, large companies with many product lines may well have large differences in profitability among individual products that relate only in the aggregate to the overall profitability of the company. The logic of this approach suggests that the court will need to apply the normal profitability of the individual profit line, not the profitability of the company.

Aside from this, the analytical approach has three potential pitfalls:

- It ignores the cost or contribution of all other complementary assets unique to the business of the infringer.
- It leads to erroneous results when the "normal" profits include the use of other intellectual properties. For example, suppose a company is found liable for infringing the trademark of a well-known soft drink. Finding the "normal" level of profit by looking at the profits of Coca-Cola, Pepsi, and Cadbury-Schweppes would be unfair to the plaintiff, because these companies all have established trademarks themselves. If these are used to find a normal profit level, the calculation will in effect assume that the infring-

---

[7] This was originally used upon appeal in *Georgia-Pacific Corp. v. U.S. Plywood-Champion Papers, Inc.* 446 F.2d 295, 170 USPQ 369 (2d Cir 1971) and has been used or referred to in a number of cases, including *Panduit supra, Tektronix Inc. v. U.S.* 552 F.2d 343, 193 USPQ 385 (Ct. Cl. 1977), *Paper Converting Machine v. Magna-Graphics* 745 F.2d 11, 223 USPQ 591 (Fed. Cir 1984), and *TWG Mfg. Co. v. Dura Corp* 789 F.2d 895 at 899 (Fed. Cir. 1986).

ing company, in the absence of the infringement, would have had legal access to a valuable trademark for its products.[8]

- It ignores the alternative licensees available in the marketplace.

The analytical method is different from the investment method. It is less comprehensive. However, when most comprehensively applied, a "normal profit margin" begins to look like economic profit, and that in turn begins to move toward investment return analysis.

Investment Return Analysis: The Economic Return from Intellectual Property

One approach to the estimation of reasonable royalties (or the negotiation of licenses in general) is to determine the royalty rates that will provide an investment-quality return on the hypothetical licensee's assets that are contributed to the licensing relationship and the licensee's profit from the license. Excess return resulting from the infringer's use of the intellectual property should be available to pay the reasonable royalty or as a measure of damages.

A thorough examination of this approach is beyond the scope of this discussion.[9] In short, however, under this approach, based on their respective market values and appropriate market rates of return for each, one calculates the level of income required to be generated to provide a market return to the infringer for the noninfringing assets deployed in the business. Those assets include working capital, fixed assets, and all applicable complementary intangible and intellectual property assets (the last, which will have higher market returns attributed to them than will working capital and fixed assets, can be valued by a business valuator).[10]

Any excess of the infringer's actual total income over that required to provide a market return to the noninfringing assets must necessarily pertain to the infringed-upon intellectual property. That excess income is therefore available to pay the royalty. The royalty rate can then be mechanically calculated, typically on a pretax, per unit sold basis.

Note how the preceding analysis has focused solely on the infringer. Given that the calculation is for damages and not profits to be disgorged, however, one must also consider the circumstances of the innovator/right-holder or plaintiff and assess the operating reality of the plaintiff.

---

[8] Recognizing these limitations, R.L. Parr, *Intellectual Property Infringement Damages: A Litigation Support Handbook* (Toronto: John Wiley & Sons, 1993), at 159–162, suggests that the "normal profit margin" be replaced by a "commodity product profit margin," where the commodity product margin should be derived from a product that 1) lacks intellectual property, 2) requires a similar amount of investment in complementary assets, and 3) is in the same (or a closely similar) industry to the infringing product.

[9] For a detailed discussion of this type of analysis, see G.V. Smith and R.L. Parr, *Valuation of Intellectual Property and Intangible Assets,* 2nd ed., (Toronto: John Wiley & Sons, 1994), Parr, *supra* note; and R.L. Parr, "Advanced Royalty Rates Determination Methods", in R. Parr and P. Sullivan, eds., *Technology Licensing* (Toronto: John Wiley & Sons, 1996).

[10] See Parr *supra* note at 110. Methods of more precisely evaluating this amount may be found in Smith and Parr, *supra* note.

The calculated royalty might be reasonable as a starting point. It might be a reasonable ending point if all of the complementary assets to manufacture the product were not owned by the plaintiff.

If, on the other hand, all the complementary assets were in place or accessible to the plaintiff, then the plaintiff's damages should increase by approximately the required rate of return on each of the complementary assets it was not otherwise able to put to use. For example, assume that the plaintiff was able to otherwise utilize its working capital. However, its fixed assets, identifiable intangibles, *plus* the intellectual property were all left idle as a result of the infringement. Then it would be reasonable to increase the damages by the required rate of return on those other assets. The royalty would also increase correspondingly.

An investment approach can produce a highly defensible assessment of the range of royalties that would be acceptable to a hypothetical licensee in a licensing negotiation.[11] However, it is silent as to the determination of the actual reasonable royalty within this range. This final assessment is made judgmentally by weighting all of the associated market- and company-specific factors that must also be considered under the two other approaches discussed previously.

Conclusions

The determination of damages in any intellectual property case can be difficult, particularly if the case is hotly contested between two parties willing to commit considerable resources to litigation. The assessment involves the argument of hypothetical negotiation, and damages arguments can involve complex market and financial analyses.

---

[11] It can also be used to determine a lower bound of acceptable royalties for the licensor. This is straightforward if the licensor's only income from the intellectual property is the royalties; however, it can be quite complicated and subjective if the intellectual property is exploited through a complicated combination of sales and licensing.

PART VI

Summary and Conclusions

Trends
1. The relatively constant movement of a variable throughout a period of time. The period may be short-term or long-term, depending upon whether the trend itself is short-term or long-term. For example, a rising market is taken to mean that prices of most stocks are in an upward trend.
2. A general direction in which something tends to move; "the shoreward tendency of the current"; "the trend of the stock market."
3. A general tendency to change (as of opinion); "not openly liberal but that is the trend of the book"; "a broad movement of the electorate to the right."

Introduction

In the last part of this book, we present our vision of the future, both for the practice of intellectual property valuation and for the underlying assets. The opinions and trends discussed here do not just represent our personal vision; they are based on a review of our colleagues' concerns, ideas, and prognostications. In the first four sections of this primer, we provided a survey of the "state of the nation" in Intellectual Property valuation. We reviewed different approaches and methodologies; we reported on preferences and issues in selecting methodologies; we provided a brief overview of various analytical tools and a condensed review of current contexts in which intellectual property can be valued.

The first four sections are generally fact-based and historical in nature, including definitions of current terms of the art, vocabulary, usage, a review of various methodologies, and, of course, case studies. In general, we have presented current and historical views of Intellectual Property valuation, and we have discussed at length today's various contexts of valuation.

This final section brings a change in perspective. Its focus shifts toward the future and identifies the main issues affecting both intellectual property valuation and intellectual property itself. These future trends involve legal issues, economic issues, and global harmonization issues.

The focus of the book changes from past to future, from reportage to prediction, from current facts to future speculations. This section also introduces a new concept—*intellectual capital*. We conclude this Intellectual Property valuation primer by looking at five companies familiar to all of us, whose intellectual capital asset base drives the value of the companies and their market capitalization.

Finally, we end this book as we began it, by talking about "Grandmother's chicken soup." It is useful to remember that everyone's grandmother knows how to make chicken soup and everyone knows what chicken soup tastes like, but no two people can agree precisely on the best recipe for chicken soup. Much like chicken soup, Intellectual Property value depends on using multiple good possible approaches to value—context and time being key determinants of best methodology and, ultimately, of value.

CHAPTER 21

REVIEW OF VALUATION TRENDS

The following examples show just how rapidly the value of intangible assets can change over a relatively short period of time:

- A generation ago, the two most important brand names in the United Kingdom brewing industry were Whitbread and its rival brand. The two held almost equivalent market shares. Today, the rival brand has nearly disappeared from view and the value of Whitbread has tripled.
- In technology, a decade ago, Commodore was a leader in personal computers, as well as being a top brand in the PC business. Today, the value of its technology brand and associated intangibles has declined from a high of $500M to zero.
- Another example of changing values can be found in the venerable Oldsmobile brand, which is more than 100 years old. At one time, the brand and its associated technological innovations were worth scores of millions of dollars. Today, its value has declined virtually to zero, because the brand will disappear from the market over the next model year.
- Two decades ago, Sony's Betamax format was worth more than a billion dollars. Now, it is gone from the consumer market.

Table 21.1 illustrates how quickly value can change.

Valuation is a movable feast. Much as Grandma's chicken soup changes from kitchen to kitchen, so does the value of an intangible asset change, depending on time and context. The two most important factors in valuing intellectual property or intangible assets are time and context: At what point in time are we valuing the asset? For what reason and in what context is it being valued?

Context can include any of the following:

- Merger and acquisition
- Property replacement
- Tax-based transfer
- Outright sale
- Bankruptcy or reorganization
- Corporate liquidation
- Intercompany transfer
- Litigation or arbitration
- Securitization or collateralization

Each of these can be reason to value.

Table 21.1 Value over Time

Value over Time: Brand Valhalla	
• Admiral TV	• Sanka
• Oldsmobile	• Fels Naphtha
• Chesterfield	• Montgomery Ward
• Commodore	• Cellophane
• Blatz Beer	• TWA

Another question is: What basis of value will we use? Value for tax purposes or for the SEC is far different from litigation value, for example. Among the multiple definitions of value for intangible assets are the following:

- Fair value
- Fair market value
- In-place value
- Tax value
- Liquidation value
- Deal value
- Securitization value
- Replacement value

There are six basic questions to ask oneself when considering a valuation project for a piece of Intellectual Property or an intangible asset:

1. What asset or bundle of assets is being valued?
2. Why is the bundle or asset being valued?
3. What definition of value is being used?
4. Are there legal, tax, financial, or other business implications or constraints that will affect the valuation?
5. What methodology are we using?
6. At what time and in what context are we valuing?

As the early chapters of this book showed, there are multiple valuation methodologies. The primary ones are the market approach, the cost approach, the income approach, and the relief-from-royalty approach. However, a brief review of Chapters 4 and 5 illustrates that there are multiple methodologies; in fact, we describe more than 25 of them. The impact on valuation trends is clear—more creativity in valuation methodologies will be seen. At the same time, however, there is an increasing level of professionalism in the practice of valuation.

Summarizing valuation trends is a disparate exercise. Trends differ, based on the type of intellectual property and on the context in which the valuation takes place. However, we can make brief observations applicable to various types of intangible assets and context, as follows:

- Goodwill, in the form of corporate identity, is increasingly important and increasing in value. One has only to look at how the market capitalizations of corporations with substantial goodwill are increasing.
- Trademark and brand valuation is growing in all segments of industry, from consumer goods to services and commercial/industrial products.
- The formal discipline involved in valuing intangible assets like trademarks has been in existence for less than a generation. During the last 20 years, professionalism and complexity of analysis have increased as the global role of Intellectual Property has expanded.
- Patent and technology valuation is also increasingly important and complex with the increase in the range and types of patents, from design patents to animal patents, plant patents, and business method patents. It is also important to note that the value of technology or a patent rises as it goes from very early-stage technology through patent application to fully mature and commercialized technology.
- The value of Internet assets has stabilized. Since the bursting of the dot-com bubble, prices for domain names have declined substantially, but they have shown signs of stabilization over the last two years. Those domain names that have a reasonable sense of place and appropriateness for the end user will maintain their value.
- The valuation of software is in a period of flux. As more companies are reorganized, acquired, or merged or go into bankruptcy, they are left with software assets to be disposed of. These assets can be application software/operating systems or product software/shrinkwrap. Affecting the valuation process (more than any other class of intangible assets) is the legal environment surrounding the ownership, transferability, and sale of these assets.
- The world of value for licenses and establishing royalty rates is maturing but also changing. For example, although there is stability in trademark licensing and royalty rates, there has been a decline in sales of products under trademark licensing, thus affecting value. In technology, licensing activities are increasing and royalty rates continue to explore the outer limits of value.
- An area with some of the greatest changes in valuation is the valuation of intangible assets during a merger, acquisition, or other business combination. The new FASB regulations under Sections 141, 142, and 147 establish new, different, and very specific rules about when and how often in-

tangible assets and goodwill must be valued. These changes will have a substantial impact on all future business combinations.

- In the area of bankruptcy and reorganization, the valuation of intangible assets has begun to dominate many key cases, ranging from Marvel Entertainment and Polaroid Corporation to companies like Warnaco, Budget Rent A Car, New World Pasta, and Amherst Fiber Optics. This is a result of the increasing importance to a company of its intangible assets and the increasing recognition by bankruptcy courts of the importance in value of the company's Intellectual Property.
- In the area of tax-related valuation projects, the greatest change being seen is a much greater realism and conservatism in the valuation process. Whether the valuation is being conducted for an Intellectual Property holding company, for donation purposes, or to establish intercompany transaction values, valuation professionals are being more cautious and realistic about establishing values in these tax-based environments.
- Finally, valuation of these assets for litigation purposes has expanded exponentially over the last decade. Not only are the values of intellectual property and intangible assets increasing, the damages being sought and won for misuse and misappropriation of these assets have increased. As a consequence, the valuation of intangible assets involved in litigation or arbitration is much more important now than ever before.

We have come full circle back to the overriding philosophy of intellectual property valuation: Context and time are the most important determinants of value. When these two elements are properly combined with the correct methodologies, valuation of any intangible asset can proceed with a high degree of certainty.

The Due Diligence Process

A cornerstone of that certainty, however, is the assumption that appropriate and extensive research and due diligence has been done on the asset being valued. To aid in that process, we offer a preliminary list of due diligence questions that should be reviewed on any Intellectual Property or intangible asset valuation.

Industry Overview

- General characteristics, including size, trends, and growth outlook
- Marketplace changes affecting industry, including social, economic, and technological changes
- Review of current and historical trends

Overall Strategic Plan

- Company's growth strategy as a whole

- Review of both short-term and long-term growth opportunities, including associated risks
- Discussion of capital expenditure plans, expected returns from new business initiatives
- Discussion of strategic threats to company's business
- Plans to support and enhance the company's house brands
- Cost reduction opportunities and plans
- Discussion of acquisitions made to date and future acquisitions contemplated
- Copies of feasibility and marketing studies

Competition

- Discussion of major competitors, including respective market share, products, strengths and weaknesses, expansion plans, and potential entrants
- Discussion of competition and relations to changing prices, market conditions
- Discussion of elements of competition and successful competitive strategy

Intellectual/Intangible Property

- Detailed patent registrations
- Complete detail of trademark registrations (including International Trademark Classification System breakout)
- Detailed marketing/advertising expenditures and extant prospective plans for exploitation of intangible and intellectual property
- Complete copies of executed licensing agreements, if any
- List of contemplated potential licensees, if any
- List of other Intellectual Property

Sales and Marketing

- Overview of marketing function: any basic differences from primary competition?
- Promotion strategy/budget licensing activities
- Description of advertising, trade show, and other marketing materials
- Any market research in existence on Springs trademarks and consumer awareness, trust, etc.

Distribution and Retail Relations

- Discussion of industry standards
- Review of channels employed: past, present, and future

- Retail operations
- Industry relationships: Who are your partners?

Historical Financial Information

- Income statements, balance sheets, and cash flow statements for each of the last five years, as well as quarterly statements for the last year and most recent interim period (each business segment); if any statements are prepared along brand lines, these will be most helpful to the valuation process
- Analysis of revenues, cost of sales, and gross profit by major product line/brand and other costs and expenses

Five-Year Financial Projections
(and Accompanying Assumptions)

- Projected income statements, balance sheets, and cash flow statements for the next five years with detailed assumptions related thereto, including:
  - –Revenue breakout (dollars and units, when applicable)
  - –Gross margin breakout
  - –Detail of operating and overhead expenses
  - –Capital requirements (maintenance versus expansion, if possible)
- Potential cost savings/synergies from restructuring, if applicable
- Components of selling, general, and administrative expenses
- Assumptions for effective tax rates, including estimates of deferred taxes

An ABA Section of Intellectual Property Law Survey of Valuation Trends

The ABA Section of Intellectual Property Law recently undertook a member survey to attempt to establish how, how often, when, and why members value intellectual property. Under the direction of Gordon Smith and Richard Realbuto, the Special Committee on Intellectual Property valuation organized, budgeted, and planned a survey of members. The survey was conducted among ABA IPL members only and was sent to both corporate members and noncorporate members. Roughly 85% of the respondents were noncorporate members, primarily from law firms; the other 15% were from corporations and valuation companies. The noncorporate members outsource more than 80% of their valuation projects and use both Intellectual Property valuation firms and accounting firms, with the majority of assignments outsourced to specialized Intellectual Property firms. On the corporate side, respondents tended to do much more of their valuation in-house. The respondents from both parts of the survey were well diversified as to industry and size of company; they were also well diversified in the qualifications of the respondents, including many with multiple graduate degrees. The Special Committee on Intellectual Property valuation was chaired by Donna Suchy and was responsible for this initial survey.

It must be stressed that the data we are summarizing here are preliminary, and more refinement, as well as a broader sampling of members, is needed, because many of the 25 questions had opportunity for multiple responses. One finds that there is some inconsistency in the total number of responses from one question to another. We review here just a few of the key questions, specifically those that focus on the types of intellectual property, why they are being valued, and how they are being valued.

Broadly, eight types of intellectual property were included in the survey:

- Patents
- Trade secrets
- Trademarks, domain names, and design patents
- Software
- Chip circuits
- Copyrights
- License agreements
- Nondisclosure agreements

The initial results validate many of the intuitive conclusions on which Intellectual Property valuation professionals agree. Some of those include the following:

- More than three-quarters of the responding corporate members have specialized intellectual property departments or Intellectual Property holding companies.
- Among corporate respondents, a roughly equal number of patents and trademarks are being valued, and those two categories account for the largest portion of assets being valued.
- Surprisingly, the next largest category of assets being valued is license agreements. (This may reflect the fact that respondents were confusing the actual valuation of a license agreement with the establishment of royalty rates or other pricing.)
- Among corporate respondents, more than half have dedicated Intellectual Property valuation departments.
- Because many respondents gave multiple answers, some may be confusing the market approach and the income approach; therefore, the responses regarding methodology may be skewed.
- In any case, approximately 40% of respondents stated that they use the market approach, and 30% use cost and income methodologies, as illustrated in the Figure 21.1.

In the next part of the survey, the purpose or context of the valuation was examined. Respondents were given eight reasons or rationales to choose from, as follows:

- Sale or purchase
- Tax

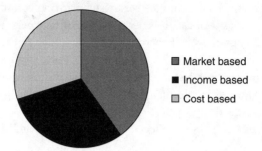

Figure 21.1 Intellectual Property valuation survey, corporate: What methods does your company use to value Intellectual Property?

- Transfer pricing
- Intellectual Property holding companies
- Litigation
- Licensing
- Financial reasons
- Other/Internal

Some of the key findings from this portion of the survey are rather surprising:

- The largest single reason given for valuation was tax-driven issues, with approximately 15% of all valuations being done for tax reasons.
- In addition, two other contexts, intercompany transfer pricing and Intellectual Property holding companies, when combined with tax-driven motivations, showed that more than 35% of all intellectual property valuations are, to a greater or lesser degree, driven by tax considerations.
- In examining methodology as it relates to context, there was an even split among the three primary methodologies of income, cost, and market.
- One of the more surprising findings was that less than 10% of all Intellectual Property valuations were done in support of a litigation environment.
- Equally surprising was that a relatively high proportion of valuations were done because of licensing considerations, with roughly 15% of all valuations done in a licensing context.
- Finance issues accounted for roughly 5% of contextual issues, with purchase price allocations/acquisitions accounting for another 5%.
- The largest single context among corporate users was for the sale or purchase of a piece of Intellectual Property, with roughly 20% of all the corporate valuations being done for that reason.

In sum, we have an initial statistical sampling of ABA Section of Intellectual Property Law members as to the number of valuations being performed, the type of intellectual property being valued, the methodology being used, and the context in which the valuations are taking place. Key points from the survey follow:

Table 21.2 Intellectual Property Valuation Survey: Corporate Groups Involved in Valuations

	Dedicated Intellectual Property	Internal Finance	Business Units	Outsiders
Litigation support	39	13	29	6
Financing issues	22	21	29	18
Set up Intellectual Property holding company	14	8	8	5
Management information	28	10	32	11
Tax-driven issues	62	58	41	42
Intercompany transfer	25	23	19	7
Joint venture	33	12	46	11
Licensing	65	16	60	15
Allocation of purchase price	23	28	22	14
Sale/purchase	84	37	98	38
	395	**226**	**384**	**167**

Among the three traditional valuation methods, there is a roughly equal split, with the market-based method preferred.

Among corporate respondents, more than half have dedicated Intellectual Property departments and more than three-quarters do their valuations in-house.

On the other hand, noncorporate members, such as law firms, farm out more than 80% of their valuation projects to Intellectual Property professionals.

Finally, the context of valuations is largely driven by tax considerations and by deal-making environments such as sale, purchase, or joint venture.

CHAPTER 22

INTELLECTUAL PROPERTY TRENDS: THE FUTURE IS NOW

The purpose of this primer has been to provide a practical, useful, and straight-forward guide to the identification and valuation of intellectual property and intangible assets. By its very nature as a basic book on the subject, we have focused on what has come before in the area of valuation and what exists today. Relatively little time has been spent (nor should it be spent in a primer) on predicting future trends and changes in the valuation, management, use, and protection of intellectual property.

This chapter concludes this primer by looking at the major trends that will affect intellectual property—without regard to whether those trends include an impact on value—from a business perspective. By its very nature, however, intellectual property implies a legal context, so we do touch on some of the broader legal trends that will affect intellectual property in the next five to ten years.

Although there are many short-term trends affecting intellectual property, such as temporary movements in royalty rates or expanding/contracting use of one operating system versus another, we believe there are five underlying trends that will affect intellectual property:

- We are entering a period of globalization and harmonization of the recognition and use of intellectual property; we are simultaneously going through a period of substantial change in how intellectual property is viewed and defined in the United States.
- Intellectual property will continue to be an increasingly important element of corporate value and capitalization, as well as a highly important tool in managing a corporation's future plans for expansion, acquisition, merger, etc. (See case study.)
- The family of intellectual property and intangible assets is growing, with an expansion in the number and type of intellectual properties being recognized, registered, protected, leveraged, and valued.
- The cost-effective managing, leveraging, and licensing of intellectual property will continue to grow in importance as a corporate tool and a generator of cash flow and value.
- The management, valuation, and value-extraction of intellectual property and intangible assets are becoming increasingly professional, mainstream, and sophisticated.

Each of these trends is substantial, and we will expand on each. However, let us first look at a new view of intellectual property and intangible assets—intellectual capital as part of a corporation's all-important balance sheet and capital structure.

Intellectual Capital: The Future Is Today

There are two types of intellectual capital: human assets and structural (or created) assets. The human assets are employees, their professional knowledge base, and their personal knowledge base. Structural assets include patents, copyrights, trademarks, software, systems, trade secrets, etc. If the intellectual asset cannot go home at night, then it is a structural asset. If the company can use it again and again without its wearing out (and it does not ask for a raise), then it is a structural asset. Structural intellectual capital assets should amplify human assets and make tangible assets, such as factories and pieces of equipment, more efficient. Human intellectual assets have sustaining value to many corporations. For example, where would Microsoft be without the driving force of Bill Gates? However, human assets are worthless if they cannot create enduring and evolving structural assets.

Intellectual and intangible assets represent the industrialized world's most undervalued group of assets. Trends that drive the need for their accurate identification and valuation include the following:

- Increasing globalization of the business community
- A need to maximize return from all assets, not just tangible ones
- Expanded global marketing
- Expanded global use of intellectual property, such as trademarks, brands, and patents
- Increasingly competitive corporate environment
- A rising tide of product parity—parity in quality, appearance, or function—so that an intangible asset may be able to differentiate a product
- Stagnant returns on fixed and tangible assets in many countries like France and Germany
- Increased use of licensing and leveraging of intangibles as a strategy to build value
- A growing awareness that protection of such assets is critically important

Beyond these, there are other corporate reasons that explain the growing emphasis on intellectual and intangible assets: pressures to maximize financial returns within companies and within business units, along with the realization that there is an underutilization of all corporate assets. As an example of the increased leverage and use of intangible assets, one only has to look at the explosive growth in the licensing of technologies, software, trademarks, and brands.

How can a company identify, inventory, and manage these assets? The collection process is perhaps one of the most difficult tasks. Some very large multinational companies have made a concerted effort to identify and manage their intellectual capital effectively. These companies have found that the most critical part of the process is, in many ways, the identification of the assets. One only has to look at Dow and Skandia for good examples of companies that have managed to develop techniques for identifying and managing these assets. Each takes a different approach, but both believe in working with *knowledge maps*. These so-called maps are actually indexes, flow charts, or databases that identify where the intangible or intellectual assets rest.

Whether one starts with an internal audit, uses external intellectual property consultants, or simply asks everyone to hand over their suggestions, the process is time consuming. The most effective way to inventory these assets is on a business-sector or business-unit basis. An alternative is to identify and categorize these assets on a subsidiary, affiliate, or even brand basis. Occasionally, companies use separate balance sheets, as Skandia does, that quantify on an annual basis the value of this portfolio. Once the audit is complete, the company must classify and evaluate the assets and make decisions about a knowledge strategy to protect, build, or abandon parts of the portfolio. The most important thing is to operate and evaluate many businesses in a functional manner, when knowledge is a chief resource and a chief result. Certainly many companies, like Microsoft, have intellectual or intangible assets that are far better security, both as collateral and from the stockholders' point of view, than any hard assets the corporation may own.

Why value these assets? Who really cares? How do you use the values once you have arrived at them? All are valid questions that need to be addressed. Intangible or intellectual assets affect every single part of this economy, whether a company is in the manufacturing business, a service company, or an entertainment or software company. Whether a company is top end–loaded with trademarks and brands or heavily dependent on technology and patents, the ability to manage and leverage these assets is important.

The concept of return on assets employed (ROAE) should perhaps be renamed return on *all* assets employed, or ROAAE. Too often and for too long, companies have focused on return on tangible assets only. If the CFO and CIO are going to be making logical recommendations to a competitive CEO as the basis for the right decisions, they must be looking at how to manage all assets based on their overall value. In addition, one can make strategic allocations of funds for expansion of these critical assets only if one knows the value base whence they come.

Beyond that, accurate valuations allow a company to perform a meaningful *triage process*. The act of triage sorts the intangible assets based on their importance to the company. Triage should be a part of the audit of intellectual assets, and companies should perform it at least as often as they apply it to the tangible asset base. A company can identify the key building blocks within its intellectual capital portfolio only if it can ascertain values on a consistent and logical basis. The overall corporate strategy must focus not only on tangible asset employment, but also on maximizing value from intangible assets.

Beyond internal usage, there is a need to establish value for external reasons. However, you can answer the question "Who cares?" very directly: Everyone who is involved in the corporation's well being cares—every stakeholder, every employee, every outside supplier. Specifically, the following stakeholders are critically concerned about the value of these assets:

- Bankers
- Shareholders
- Wall Street
- Suppliers
- Partners
- Employees

Once the identification process is essentially complete (although it is an organic process that will change every year), the move to the valuation process is critical. Using the example of IBM to illustrate the shifting tides of value, one only has to quote Tom Stewart from the editorial board of *Fortune*: "IBM after all was much richer in human capital when it had 406,000 employees than it is today with 150,000 employees. If physical attributes followed generally accepted accounting principles, fat would be counted among a body's assets."[1] In other words, human assets are far less important today than structural assets to IBM, and the company is far richer today even though it has 250,000 fewer employees.

How, then, does a company value its intellectual capital? Where does it start, and what issues must it address? Primary issues of valuation are as follows:

- The discipline to undertake the valuation process across all asset groups
- The need to have consistency in the method of valuation
- The need to select a methodology from among those available
- The need to decide whether to use market values, going-concern values, or liquidation values as the underlying principle of valuation

Managing intangible and intellectual assets on a rational basis is a new and difficult discipline beyond charted waters for many companies. The goal is to extract maximum benefits and maximum payoff. Managing these assets on a rational basis is like trying to herd cats.

The issues of managing for the payoff are relatively clearcut: Companies must avoid the postvaluation paralysis that many encounter, having gone through the process of identification and valuation. Often companies ask, "What do we do now?" The discipline to manage these assets effectively, with a clear strategy and an effective ongoing implementation plan, can be difficult for many companies. Many problems can potentially arise. Stepchild management, inattention, and management-by-committee are all manifestations of the "postvaluation paralysis syndrome."

---

[1]Thomas Stewart, 1999.

Leveraging these assets can pose a more difficult puzzle for management than working with tangible assets. Often the best internal opportunity for leverage is not necessarily the best choice, nor is value maximization necessarily the best internal approach. In some cases, top management cannot see the internal opportunities, cannot afford to pursue those leverage opportunities, or simply is averse to risk. In those cases, external leverage via licensing, joint venturing, or other approaches becomes appropriate. Often, external usage through third parties can add more value to the corporation.

Whenever possible, internal leverage is the preferred method of value maximization, if for no other reason than to satisfy the issue of improved control. Examples of internal leveraging of assets include the following:

- Brand extensions
- New product introductions
- New affiliate operations
- Reduced cost via commonality
- More cost/income- or cost/benefit-effective R&D
- Extension of markets and geographies

There are also many external opportunities to maximize value. The obvious ones are

- Cobranding
- Licensing
- Franchising
- Promotional tie-ins
- Joint ventures
- Corporate spin-offs
- Sale of the intangible assets

All these are forms of third-party commercialization and leveraging of a corporation's intellectual assets. Perhaps the best example of two corporations taking divergent paths in leveraging intellectual assets is shown in the strategies of Apple and IBM. Twenty years ago, the two companies were competitors with similar bundles of assets involving PC technologies. As we all know, today those assets controlled by IBM have prospered and are the basis for the great majority of all PCs.

Why? The answer is simple: More than 20 years ago, IBM made the decision to license its patents and technologies relating to PCs to all third parties that asked. At the same time, Apple decided to license to no one. As a result, today nearly 90% of PCs in America use the IBM operating platform and IBM intellectual assets. As a consequence, IBM's market position and the IBM Company have grown, while Apple lost market share. Apple's decision in 1996 to begin licensing other manufacturers to use its operating platform was too little, too late.

The Five Major Trends
Globalization and Harmonization

Unlike any other time in history, the industrialized nations are coming closer together in their identification, definition, recognition, registration, and management of intellectual property and intangible assets. This globalization and harmonization can be seen in very tangible ways: the European patent program, and now the community patent program, the Madrid protocol for registering trademarks globally, and TRIPS.[1] The effect of this period of harmonization and globalization is that the United States will continue to communize its treatment and law regarding intellectual property and will pull our systems and legal mechanisms more into line with Europe and other industrialized nations. Also, this period of change means we will continue to lose our unique and somewhat isolated identity and definition of intellectual property, in order to better align ourselves with mainstream thinking on intellectual property.

This globalization and harmonization also means a period of change in the United States in the treatment of intellectual property, its ownership, and registration. For example, the tradition in our country is to recognize the small entity against the large entity (this is best illustrated in our tradition of awarding patents to the person or company that was first to invent), as opposed to the rest of the world, which awards patents to the first to file. Recently, the Intellectual Property community in the United States has moved to the first-to-file methodology, and we believe it will, eventually, be ratified as law. Similarly, in trademarks, we have traditionally recognized the first use as opposed to the first registrant.

Increasing Importance of Intellectual Property in Corporate Value Structures

As American industry rapidly moves into a postindustrial intelligence- and information-based economy, the importance of tangible assets will continue to wane, while the importance and value of intellectual property (particularly in a company's balance sheet) will continue to increase. In the case study at the end of this chapter, we examine a handful of American companies that understand the relative importance of their intangible assets or intellectual capital to their overall value.

Expansion of the Range and Type of Intellectual Property and Intangible Assets

For decades, generations—even centuries—the basic definition of a patent or a trademark remained essentially unchanged. However, in this postindustrial information/technology age, our identification and definitions of these important

---

[1]TRIPS (trade-related aspects of Intellectual Property rights) was the World Trade Organization's trade-related treaty negotiated in 1986–1994 during the Uruguay Round that introduced intellectual property rules into a multilateral trading system for the first time.

value elements have been forced to expand. We have added new categories of patents and trademarks, new definitions of design, and new ways of protecting those designs, as well as multiple ways to identify intangible value elements for software and a variety of ways to register and protect those elements.

As an example, in the last generation we have added animal and plant patents to more traditional patent categorizations. The design patent, perilously close to the definition of a trademark, has come into popular use. Further, we have business method patents and computer-implemented inventions. In trademarks, we have new parameters. Now there are trademarks based on sounds, colors, and even smells. For software developers, protection can be sought as a patent, as a copyright, or even as trademark material.

The trend is clear—more and more diverse types of intellectual property and intangible assets are being identified, defined, and protected every day. This will not necessarily be a smooth process, however, as the battle over the protectability of business method patents continues; in Europe, authorities will not soon follow the American example of recognizing business method patents.

Developing and Leveraging Intellectual Property via Licensing and Similar Methodologies Will Grow as a Corporate Tool

Virtually every meaningful corporation in the United States is looking for ways to leverage, license, extend, expand, promote, and cultivate its intellectual property for two primary reasons. The first, of course, is to generate capital and cash flow, and the second is to establish competitive advantage. For example, in 1976 $18B worth of products were sold in retail under trademark licensing. In 1996, that number had grown to $72B, and in 2005, it is projected to be $110B. In technology licensing, the LES and other special organizations estimate that the volume and dollar value of technology licensing are growing at a rate two to three times that of our economy's GNP rate of growth.

How do we see demonstrable proof that this extension, leverage, licensing, etc., of intellectual property is growing? Four major American corporations serve to illustrate.

- In the first case, Louis Gerstner made it the stated goal of IBM to expand the influence, reach, and financial return of its intellectual property. The company's licensing revenues have quadrupled in the last few years.
- Lucent Technologies has formed a separate division, with its own president and CEO, to manage the intellectual property portfolio and maximize cash flow and value.
- Xerox Corporation has been a leader in establishing best practices in the global licensing of its technology and is beginning the process of leveraging its trademark assets.

- After years of disdainful ignorance of the potential from licensing and leveraging, Microsoft has jumped into the process with both feet—hiring a key executive from IBM, who revolutionized IBM's licensing and leveraging of intellectual property, and building an extraordinary staff of lawyers, financial experts, and business developers.

The Frequency and Importance of Intellectual Property Value Will Grow Logarithmically

This major trend may seem self-evident, but a brief examination of the underlying factors might be useful:

- There is a continuing shift from opportunistic management and valuation of intangible assets to strategic management of those same assets.
- Global management of these assets is increasing.
- Companies are looking to maximize the value of the entire bundle of intangible assets and rights.
- The valuation process itself is becoming more sophisticated and professional.
- There is a globalization and professionalization of Intellectual Property management techniques.

Intellectual property, intangible assets, and intellectual capital are increasingly critical in more business deals and combinations for multiple reasons:

- Establishing deal value
- Dealing with the FCC and other regulatory bodies
- Determining earnings-per-share and shareholder value
- Addressing and defending tax issues
- Leveraging competitive value

For example, the value of individual patents will increase, but at the same time, there will be greater uncertainty as litigation over these increasingly valuable assets becomes more intense. There will also be a value migration within the family of intangible assets and intellectual capital—there will be more future value in nonpatent areas, such as trade secrets, copyrights, trademarks, software, databases, and IT assets. What this means is that a major corporation has an imperative to put into place a multidisciplinary team of Intellectual Property managers, business development staff, legal experts, and licensing and valuation professionals.

■ Intellectual Property/Intangible Assets Drive Corporate Capitalization: A Case Study

In this case study, we look at a handful of companies and the relative importance of their intellectual capital and intangible assets to the overall capitalization of the company. In other words, we can identify the proportion of market value or stock price attributable specifically to a company's Intellectual Property and intangible assets. The old relationship between earnings per share and stock price is no longer the only factor driving market capitalization of most companies. A new measure is the value of a company's intangible assets and intellectual capital. Trademarks, patents, brand names, copyrights, software, and other intangibles comprise the primary bundle of underlying value for emerging U.S. companies, as well as for many mature companies. The most important relationships are those of the company's intangible assets and its overall market capitalization. In this section, we focus on that relationship.

A quick overview of several companies illustrates the relationship of intangible assets to market value. We will look at the total market value of several companies: Microsoft, Merck, Procter & Gamble, Amazon.com, and Arch Coal. Investors realize that important assets are not just bricks and mortar or conveyer belts and lathes, nor are they necessarily trailer trucks and air-conditioning systems. Substantial value in our newly emerging industrialized companies is found in the form of intangible assets. The relationship between the value of intangible assets, stock price, and market value is a key relationship. Figure 22.1 provides a snapshot of two companies in which there is a very high degree of intangible asset value. Both companies are well established and are recognized for their operational efficiencies and their intangible asset management: Microsoft and Merck.

In the case of Microsoft, the value of its intangible assets and intellectual property is more than 90%; for Merck it is 80% of the total capitalization. Yet, no one would suggest that the per-share price of Microsoft or Merck is out of line, given today's values for industrial companies.

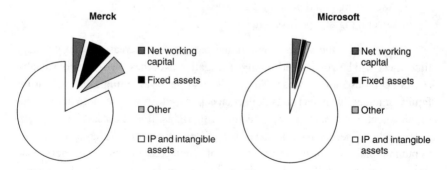

Figure 22.1 High degree of intangible value.

Figure 22.2 shows two other companies that are useful to analyze because of their use of intangible assets—and because of the way those intangible assets obviously drive the value of the stock in the marketplace. The first is Procter & Gamble. It is interesting to note that the total value of intangible assets at Procter

& Gamble approaches the 84% range. Yet, for years it has been viewed as a solid, extremely well managed consumer goods company based in the bedrock of American industry.

Amazon.com, the other company in Figure 22.2, may be seen as overly dependent on its intangible assets for value. Yet, at 93% of market capitalization, its proportion of intangible assets as a percentage of market capitalization is within range of Microsoft, Merck, and even Procter & Gamble.

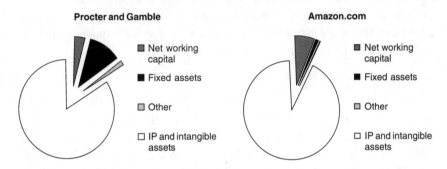

Figure 22.2 High degree of intangible value.

Finally, let's look at a company with a relatively low degree of intangible asset value, Arch Coal. (See Figure 22.3.) It is a commodity business with a commodity product, and the vast majority of its asset base is in fixed and semifixed assets. The total value of its intangibles is roughly 25% of the total capitalization. Arch Coal is as good an example as one can find of a solid, tangible asset–based business in an established industry. Its stock price reflects the fact that investors recognize this key element of Arch Coal.

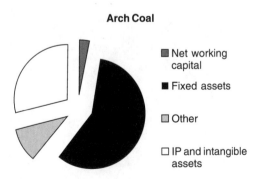

Figure 22.3 Low degree of intangible value.

One of the other causal reasons that intangible assets and intellectual property represent so much value can be found in what is known as *Tobins Q*, which states that the market value of assets and the replacement cost of assets are critical factors, and the highest values and highest market valuations tend to go to those companies that have a competitive advantage in the form of assets that are difficult to reproduce. In other words, the competitive advantage represented by patents, trademarks, brands, know-how, and technology reap the highest rewards in the marketplace.

Finally, there is the issue of reproducible assets versus competitive advantage. This means that competitors can reproduce tangible assets—anyone can build a toothpaste factory or an automobile factory or dig a gravel pit. However, intangible assets are the specialized resources and knowledge that permit a company to earn higher cash flows and market capitalizations. ■

Concluding Thoughts

Our thoughts, at the end of this primer, bring us back to those we expressed at the beginning: the identification and valuation of intellectual property and intangible assets is much like Grandmother's chicken soup. Most everyone's grandmother knows how to make chicken soup, but each and every recipe is different. We all know what chicken soup looks like, and we can all describe what it tastes like. The difficulty is in identifying and agreeing upon the common elements of taste—or value—within chicken soup.

And, so, as with Grandmother's chicken soup, we are dealing with a group of assets that are subject to interpretation, modification, and a broad range of potential valuation considerations. At first, the permutations and uncertainty seem enormous; upon reflection, however, given professionalism, experience, and a broad enough range of market information, intangible assets and intellectual property (much like chicken soup) can be broken down and evaluated in their component parts, and an accurate valuation of those component parts, or individual assets, can be done.

BIBLIOGRAPHY

Articles Published

Anson, Weston. "A Business Person's Perspective on Setting Marketplace Royalty Rates for Intangibles." *Tax Management Transfer Pricing Report*, September 6, 1995.

Anson, Weston. "A Licensing Retrospective and Glimpse into the Future." *The Merchandising Reporter*, June/July 1984.

Anson, Weston, and Daryl Martin. "Accurate Intellectual Property Valuation in Multiple Environments." *Intellectual Asset Management*, February/March 2004.

Anson, Weston. "Corporate Identity—Value and Valuation." *Corporate Reputation Review*, Spring 2000.

Anson, Weston. "Identifying Valuable Intellectual Property in Bankruptcy— Part 1." *American Bankruptcy Institute Journal*, May 2002.

Anson, Weston. "Identifying Valuable Intellectual Property in Bankruptcy— Part 2." *American Bankruptcy Institute Journal*, June 2002.

Anson, Weston. "Negotiating Complex Licensing Agreements." *Les Nouvelles*, September 2003.

Anson, Weston. "PC Brands: Where They Stack Up." *Brandweek*, December 1996.

Anson, Weston. "Snapshot Approach to Market Value for Trade Secrets." *Corporate Legal Times*, June 1995.

Anson, Weston and Mark Edwards. "The Basics of Licensing Trademarks." *Les Nouvelles*, Journal of the Licensing Executives Society, December 1996.

Anson, Weston. "The Impact of Intangible Assets under Section 141/142: What Investment Bankers Need to Understand," *The Daily Deal,* January 2002.

Anson, Weston. "The World's Tax Authorities Latch on to Rights." *Managing Intellectual Property*, June 1996.

Anson, Weston. "Using a Delaware Holding Company to Lower the Software Company's State Income Taxes." *Kutish Publications, Inc.*, 1992.

Anson, Weston. "Valuing and Monetizing Intellectual Property in Bankruptcy." *The Secured Lender*, May/June 2002.

Anson, Weston. "Valuing Intangible Assets." *Les Nouvelles*, Journal of the Licensing Executives Society, June 1996.

Block, Donna. "Brand Conscious." *The Daily Deal*, March 21, 2002.

Breese, Pierre. "Valuation of Technological Intangible Assets." *Licensing Executives Society.*

Damiano, Karen J., CPA/ABV. "Valuing Intangible Assets under SFAS 141." *Insights*, Winter 2002.

Hampton, Scott. "Hypothetical Negotiations—15 Georgia-Pacific Factors." Campos & Stratis, LLC.

Kerr, William O., and Gauri Prakash-Canjels. "Patent Damages and Royalty Awards: The Convergence of Economics and Law." *Les Nouvelles,* June 2003.

Khoury, Sam, and D. Scott Lukeman. "Valuation of BioPharm Intellectual Property: Focus on Research Tools and Platform Technology." *Les Nouvelles*, June 2002.

Khoury, Sam, Joe Daniele, and Paul Germeraad. "Selection and Application of Intellectual Property Valuation Methods in Portfolio Management and Value Extraction." *Les Nouvelles*, September 2001.

Lefton, Terry, and Weston Anson. "How Much Is Your Brand Worth?" *Brandweek*, January 29, 1996.

Neuenschwander, Charles R. "Is That Your Final Offer? Valuing Patent Licenses in Infringement Negotiation." *Les Nouvelles*, September 2002.

Ourusoff, Alexandra, Michael Ozanian, Paul B. Brown, and Jason Starr. "What's in a Name? What the World's Top Brands Are Worth." *Financial World,* September 1, 1992.

Reilly, Robert F. "Business Combination Purchase Price Allocation Procedures." *The CPA Journal.*

Reilly, Robert F., and Melvin Rodriguez. "Using Intercompany Transfer Price and Analysis in Bankruptcy Valuations—Part II." *ABI Journal*, March 2004.

Rodriguez, Melvin, and Aziz El-Tahch. "What You See Is Not What You Get: Cost Sharing Buy-in Payment Issues in the IRS APA Training Materials." *Insights*, 35th Anniversary Issue, 2004.

Schioldager, Richard, and Weston Anson. "What's It Worth—Borrowing on Your Good Name." *The Licensing Journal*, June/July 2002.

Soroosh, Jalal, and Jack T. Cieselski. "When Good Assets Go Bad." *The CPA Journal*, 2002.

Wolf-Smith, Risa Lynn, and Erin L. Connor. "Bankruptcy Considerations in Technology Transactions." *ABI Journal*, April 2004.

Books and Book Chapters

"An Arm's Length View of Transfer Pricing," *The 1999 Guide to the World's Leading Transfer Pricing Advisors*. Euromoney Institutional Investor PLC, December 1999.

"Chapter 9, Section 1: Business Aspects of Licensing." *Trademark Law Basics, Basics of Trademark Law Forum Course Book,* International Trademark Association, February 2001.

Goldscheider, R. *Technology Management: Law, Tactics, Forms*. 1984, Clark Boardman Callaghan, §24.02.

Lee, W.M. "Determining Reasonable Royalty" in J. Simon and W. Friedlander, eds., *The Law and Business of Licensing*, New York, Clark Boardman Callaghan, 1996.

Licensing Economics Review. New Jersey, AUS Consultants, December 2003.

McCarthy, Thomas J. *McCarthy's Desk Encyclopedia of Intellectual Property*. Washington, DC, BNA Books, 1991.

"Monetary Relief—Quantum." *Intellectual Property Disputes: Resolutions & Remedies*, Toronto, Thomson Canada Limited, 2002.

Parr, Russell L. "Advanced Royalty Rate Determination Methods" in *Technology Licensing: Corporate Strategies for Maximizing Value*, Toronto, John Wiley & Sons, 1996.

Parr, Russell L. *Intellectual Property Infringement Damages: A Litigation Support Handbook*, Toronto, John Wiley & Sons, 1993.

Parr, Russell L. and P. Sullivan. *Technology Licensing*, Toronto, John Wiley & Sons, 1996.

Reilly, Robert F. and Robert P. Schweihs. *Valuing Intangible Assets*. New York, McGraw-Hill, 1999.

Smith, Gordon V. and Russell L. Parr, *Valuation of Intellectual Property and Intangible Assets*, 2nd ed., Toronto, John Wiley & Sons, 1994.

Smith, Gordon V. and Russell L. Parr. *Valuation of Intellectual Property and Intangible Assets*, 3rd ed., Toronto, John Wiley & Sons, 2000.

The Licensing Letter. Copyright 2003 EPM Communications, Inc.

"Transfer Pricing—Managing Intercompany Pricing in the 21st Century." *Baker & McKenzie, North American Tax Practice Group*, Baker & McKenzie, 2002.

Legal Briefs Cited

Brooktree v. Advanced Micro Devices Inc. 977 F.2d 1555 at 1578–81, 24 USPQ2d 1401 at 1417–19 (Fed. Cir. 1992).

Georgia-Pacific Corp v. United States Plywood Corp. 318 F. Supp 116 (S.D.N.Y., 1970), mod'd & aff'd 496 F.2d 295 (2d Cir., 1971).

Georgia-Pacific Corp. v. U.S. Plywood-Champion Papers, Inc. 446 F.2d 295, 170 USPQ 369 (2d Cir 1971).

Honeywell v. Minolta case (D.N.J. January 28, 1992, Civil Nos. 87-4847, 88-1624).

Mahurkar Patent Litigation 831 F.Supp 1354; 28 USPQ2d 1801 (ND Ill. 1993), aff'd 71 F.3d 1573; 37 USPQ2d1138 (Fed Cir. 1995).

Minnesota Mining and Manufacturing v. Johnson & Johnson Orthopedics 976 F.2d 1559; 24 USPQ2d 1321 (Fed Cir 1992).

Panduit supra, Tektronix Inc. v. U.S. 552 F.2d 343, 193 USPQ 385 (Ct. Cl. 1977).

Paper Converting Machinery v. Magna-Graphics 745 F.2d 11, 223 USPQ 591 (Fed. Cir 1984).

SmithKline Diagnostics Inc. v. Helena Laboratories Corp. 926 F.2d 1161 at 1168; 17 U.S.P.Q. (2d) 1922 at 1928 (Fed Cir, 1991).

The Copyright Act (17 U.S.C. Section 101).

TWG Mfg. Co. v. Dura Corp. 789 F.2d 895 at 899 (Fed. Cir. 1986).

Organizations

AIPPI: International Association for the Protection of Intellectual Property

IACC: International AntiCounterfeiting Coalition

INTA: International Trademark Association

IPO: Intellectual Property Owners Association

LES: Licensing Executives Society

LIMA: Licensing Industry Merchandisers Association. www.licensing.org.

USPTO: United States Patent Trademark Office. www.uspto.gov.

WIPO: World Intellectual Property Organization

Presentations

Anson, Weston. "Identifying and Measuring the Value of Intellectual Property Assets," Glendale, CA, March 4, 2003.

Anson, Weston. "Building and Measuring Value Via International Licensing," Hong Kong, March 14, 2003.

Anson, Weston. "Different Approaches to Valuing Intellectual Property, Leveraging Intangibles," Washington, D.C., June 10, 2003.

Anson, Weston. "Hidden Value: Identifying and Accurately Valuing Intellectual Property and Intellectual Assets," Norwalk, CT, June 12, 2003.

Anson, Weston. "Quantification of Core and Incremental Brand Value Elements to Constituent Banks," Purchase, NY, August 1, 2003.

Anson, Weston. "Intellectual Property Issues in Bankruptcy," San Diego, September 21, 2003.

Anson, Weston. "Cross-Border Transaction Issues in Electronic Commerce and Internet Licensing Transactions," San Diego, September 23, 2003.

Anson, Weston. "Hidden Value: Identifying and Accurately Valuing Intellectual Property and Intangible Assets," New York, October 1, 2003.

Anson, Weston. "Identifying, Valuing and Licensing Intellectual Property," New York, October 1, 2003.

Anson, Weston. "Accurately Valuing Trademarks and Intellectual Property in Multiple Environments," San Diego, November 14, 2003.

Anson, Weston. "Problem Areas in Trademark Licensing and Merchandising Issues and Solutions," Paris, March 31, 2004.

Anson, Weston. "Valuing Intangible Assets for Secured Lending in International Bankruptcy," London, May 25, 2004.

Anson, Weston. "Licensing in Key Global Markets," New York, June 8, 2004.

Anson, Weston. "Intellectual Property Valuation," Toronto, June 16, 2004.

Anson, Weston. "Financing and Securitization of Intellectual Property Portfolios," New York, July 21, 2004.

Press Releases

Boeing Press Release, October 15, 2001.

NTTC Press Release, April 2, 2002.

ABOUT THE AUTHOR AND CO-EDITOR

Weston Anson, Chairman of CONSOR®

Weston Anson is chairman of CONSOR®, an intellectual asset consulting firm specializing in trademark, patent, and copyright licensing; valuations; and expert testimony. The firm is headquartered in La Jolla, California, and has offices in New York and London. Mr. Anson served for six years as vice president of the Licensing Industry Merchandisers' Association and is a lifetime member of the board of advisors. He is currently co-chair of the ABA Trademark Licensing Committee. An active member of the Licensing Executives Society (LES), he is a past chairman of the Valuation Committee; the Internet Licensing E-Commerce Committee; and the Trademark Licensing Committee, a position that he resumed for the 2003–2004 term. He is currently on the International Board of LES. He is also active in INTA, the ASA, and the Euro-American Tax Institute. In addition, Mr. Anson is an International Intellectual Property Arbitrator with National Arbitration and Mediation (NAM) and a WIPO-approved arbitrator.

A seasoned consumer goods marketer, after receiving his MBA (honors) from Harvard University, Mr. Anson served a stint with the management-consulting firm of Booz Allen Hamilton. Subsequently, he was the youngest vice president and corporate officer at Playboy Enterprises, Inc., where he launched many of their licensing programs. Mr. Anson, for the last 20 years, has also led the way in developing and establishing accepted methods to value brands, technologies, and other Intellectual Property for companies. He is an expert in establishing licensing strategies for brands, as well as developing and managing licensing programs for a number of clients. He is a lecturer

and author of over 120 articles on the subjects of licensing, valuation, reorganization in bankruptcy, technology and brand values, and the impact of licensing on value.

Mr. Anson was also senior vice president of Hang Ten International, which grew to nearly 100 licensees in 30 countries under his direction. Since founding CONSOR (and its predecessor company Trademark & Licensing Associates), he has developed numerous licensing strategies for major corporations and has performed valuations of hundreds of intellectual property components including: AAA, Barneys, America's Cup, Budget Rent A Car, Caterpillar, Inc.,

Estate of Dr. Seuss, Donna Karan, Amazon.com, DuPont, Ford Motor Company, General Motors Corporation, Hard Rock Café, Harrods, Hilton, IBM, L. L. Bean, Inc., Levi Strauss & Co., L'Oreal, Louisville Slugger, Lucasfilms, Ltd., Marvel, Mattel, McDonald's Corporation, MGM/UA, NCR, The Olympics, PepsiCo, Polaroid, Polo/Ralph Lauren, Procter & Gamble, QVC, Sara Lee, Sesame Street, Sony Corporation, the Vatican Library, and Xerox Corporation.

ABOUT THE CO-EDITOR/CONTRIBUTOR

Donna Suchy, Patent attorney with Harter, Secrest & Emery LLP

Donna Suchy is an advisor in intellectual property including patent, trademark, copyright and trade secret law. She has extensive experience in patent and trademark prosecution and related litigation and transactional work. Ms. Suchy has a diversified practice including mechanical and electrical intellectual property, computer technologies, heat transfer, energy-related technologies, and new media law. Prior to moving to New York, Ms. Suchy practiced as a patent attorney in the Southwest. She is a member of the Intellectual Property prosecution and litigation group of Harter, Secrest & Emery.

Prior to practicing law, Ms. Suchy was involved in the energy and environmental fields as an engineer for an energy company, a regional bank, and an environmental company. During this time she was responsible for many projects that included project management and asset evaluation. She is a registered engineer in Texas and Oklahoma.

Ms. Suchy has written and lectured on legal topics relating primarily to patent prosecution, corporate transactions, and intellectual property value. She is a member

of the American Intellectual Property Law Association and the American Bar Association, including the ABA Section of Intellectual Property where she chairs the Special Committee on Intellectual Property Valuation. She is also a member of the Patent Law Committee, Society of Petroleum Engineers, and the ABA Section of Environment, Energy and Resources.

Ms. Suchy earned her J.D. from Oklahoma City University and her Masters in engineering from the University of Texas. Her thesis is titled "The Bioremediation of Petroleum-contaminated Soils". She graduated from University of Iowa in Physics and Math and completed her Masters Program in Mechanical Engineering at New Mexico State University. She is admitted to practice in New York and Oklahoma as well as the U.S. Federal Courts. Ms. Suchy is also registered to practice before the United States Patent and Trademark Office.

ABOUT THE CONTRIBUTORS

Chaitali Ahya, Senior Analyst at CONSOR®

Chaitali Ahya is a lead analyst for the valuation division, responsible for analyzing all types of intellectual property, including trademarks, copyrights, patents, trade secrets, domain names, mailing lists, and customer databases. She began her career in India, where she gained much of her industry and finance experience. Her background, combined with her strong financial and analytical skills, brings a global perspective to our client assignments. Ms. Ahya earned her Bachelor of Science degree from Oregon State University and went on to earn a Masters degree in business administration, with an emphasis in finance and international business, from San Diego State University.

A. Scott Davidson, Partner with Cole & Partners

Scott Davidson is a Partner with Cole & Partners, chartered business valuators and corporate financial advisors in Toronto, Canada. He has an Honor Business Administration degree from the Ivey School at the University of Western Ontario and is a Canadian chartered accountant and a chartered business valuator.

Cole & Partners is a leading Canadian firm specializing in business valuations, corporate finance, and financial litigation support for a diverse corporate client base, ranging from medium-sized private companies to some of North America's largest publicly listed companies.

Mr. Davidson has completed expert reports for use in court and other forums, including those quantifying financial damages, accountings of profits, and business values pursuant to a variety of dispute matters. He has completed financial analyses and valuations of intellectual property, intangibles, and companies in various industries for purposes that include dispute resolution, corporate reorganizations, income tax (including transfer pricing), purchase price allocations, goodwill impairment testing, and corporate finance activities. Mr. Davidson has provided expert testimony on a number of matters and has provided financial advisory services as intermediary in corporate mergers, acquisitions, divestitures, and financing transactions, as well as fairness opinions.

David C. Drews, Founder of IPMetrics LLC

David Drews is a founder of IPMetrics LLC, an intellectual property valuation firm based in San Diego, California, and currently serves as its president. Mr. Drews has extensive experience in performing valuations of intellectual property of all types, including trademarks, copyrights, patents, know-how, and trade secrets in situations such as use as collateral, potential donation activities, transactions, joint ventures, licensing, transfer pricing, and bankruptcy filings. He has frequently been called on to calculate damages related to infringement of Intellectual Property in numerous litigation and arbitration proceedings. Mr. Drews earned a Bachelor of Science degree in business administration/economics from the University of Nebraska in 1986. He has taught the Valuation of Intellectual Property course offered by the National Technology Transfer Center in Wheeling, West Virginia, is a frequent lecturer on Intellectual Property valuation issues, and has written several relevant articles for publication.

Carmen R. Eggleston, Managing Director, Intecap, Inc.

Carmen Eggleston has managed numerous litigation, valuation, corporate restructuring, and strategic consulting engagements. Her experience includes consulting to both small firms and Fortune 500 companies in a variety of manufacturing, retail, and service industries. Ms. Eggleston is a CPA, accredited in business valuation by the AICPA, and a certified fraud examiner.

Ms. Eggleston has performed valuations of specific intangible assets such as patents, trademarks, and copyrights, as well as the valuation of entire businesses. These valuations have been performed in the context of corporate restructurings, estate planning, technology transfer agreements, purchase and sale agreements, equity and debt financing, and dispute resolution.

Ms. Eggleston has participated in numerous strategic consulting assignments related to the management of intellectual property, including drafting of business plans, determining licensing strategies, and assessing intellectual property portfolios.

Ms. Eggleston has provided expert testimony regarding accounting, financial, and economic issues in Federal District Court, United States Tax Court, United States Bankruptcy Court, State District Court, and arbitration settings. She has been involved in a variety of litigation matters, including patent infringement, theft of trade secrets, breach of contract, tax disputes, breach of fiduciary duty, and others. Ms. Eggleston has determined lost profits, reasonable royalties, delay damages, and employee compensation. She has also analyzed financing arrangements and their impact on the borrower and performed asset tracing and other forensic-related reviews of a company's or individual's books and records.

Ms. Eggleston earned a Masters of Accounting and Bachelor of Arts, economics and managerial studies from Rice University. Her practice areas include business valuation, solvency analysis, corporate restructuring, general commercial litigation, Intellectual Property litigation, mergers and acquisitions, and finance and economics.

R. Mark Halligan, Esq., Welsh & Katz, Ltd.

R. Mark Halligan, Esq. is a principal in the Chicago intellectual property law firm of Welsh & Katz, Ltd. He also serves on the adjunct faculty at John Marshall Law School in Chicago, where he teaches advanced trade secrets law and trade secrets litigation. A prolific lecturer and writer on the law of trade secrets, Mr. Halligan has sponsored the world-renowned Trade Secrets Home Page on the Internet since 1994 and is recognized nationally as an expert in trade secrets law and the Economic Espionage Act of 1996. Mr. Halligan is a first-chair litigator, and his practice includes all aspects of intellectual property law, Internet law, and related licensing and antitrust matters. In recent years, Mr. Halligan has been at the forefront of several emerging legal practice areas, including intellectual asset management (IAM), competitive intelligence and counterintelligence programs, and digital evidence discovery techniques.

Richard F. Weyand, President of The Trade Secret Office, Inc.

Richard F. Weyand is the president of The Trade Secret Office, Inc., which is developing methods and software for the automated discovery, inventory, evaluation, and tracking of trade secret intellectual property assets. He has been an engineering professional in the computer software, hardware, and communications fields since 1977. Mr. Weyand has also served as a testifying technical expert in trade secrets cases involving computers, communications, and the electronic discovery of evidence.

INDEX

B